Longman Dictionary of Common Errors

Longman Dictionary of Common Errors

J. B. Heaton and N. D. Turton

Longman

Longman Group UK Limited,
Longman House, Burnt Mill, Harlow,
Essex CM20 2JE, England
and Associated Companies throughout the world.

First published 1987
Seventh impression 1991

Set in 9½ on 11pt Monophoto Helvetica 764 and 766

Produced by Longman Group (FE) Ltd
Printed in Great Britain by
Courier International, Tiptree, Essex

British Library Cataloguing in Publication Data

Heaton, J. B.
   Longman dictionary of common errors.
   1. English Language—Errors of usage
   —Dictionaries
   I. Title   II. Turton, Nigel D.
   423.1   PE1460

ISBN 0-582-96410-5

Contents

Acknowledgements
The authors would like to thank the University of
Cambridge Local Examinations Syndicate for
allowing them access to the First Certificate in
English composition scripts from which most of the
errors listed in this dictionary derive. They are also
indebted to Susan Maingay, Kelly Davis, and Diane
Sutton for their help in preparing the manuscript,
and to Mona Scheraga for acting as consultant in
American English. Finally, they wish to thank the
many students who have taken the Cambridge First
Certificate examination in recent years, without
whose contributions the book could not have been
written.

Preface

There are a number of words and phrases which regularly cause difficulty for learners of English of all nationalities. Students often spend a lot of time searching through general dictionaries and grammars for information about these difficult items. Sometimes they are unable to find the guidance they need; at other times the language in which the information is given is at a level beyond their understanding.

Intended to help solve these problems, the *Longman Dictionary of Common Errors* is a practical, easy-to-use dictionary written in simple language. It contains all the words and phrases which commonly cause errors and provides at a glance all the information needed to avoid or correct such mistakes. Since most of the errors have been taken from First Certificate in English composition scripts, the book will be particularly useful for students who are preparing for this examination. However, many of the errors still occur at higher levels of proficiency, and the *Longman Dictionary of Common Errors* is therefore also recommended as a helpful guide through the pitfalls of English for learners at the intermediate level and above. In addition, teachers of English will find the book an invaluable reference tool and marking aid.

How to use the dictionary

This book provides learners of English with a quick and easy way of avoiding or correcting their mistakes. When writing an essay or the answers to an exercise, the learner often wishes to use a particular word or phrase but feels uncertain about its correct usage. For example, which is correct: 'succeed **to do** something' or 'succeed **in doing** something'; '**do** a mistake' or '**make** a mistake'; 'He has **much** money' or 'He has **a lot of** money'? Searching for this information in dictionaries and grammar books can take a great deal of time. By referring to the *Longman Dictionary of Common Errors*, the user can find the required information within seconds, and in order to ensure quick and easy reference, great care has been taken to keep the explanatory note at the end of each entry as brief and simple as possible. It must be stressed, therefore, that the *Longman Dictionary of Common Errors* is not intended as a comprehensive grammar book. It has the very practical aim of providing all the information required to avoid or correct a particular error, and no more.

How to find an error quickly

This dictionary is arranged in alphabetical order: the entries beginning with **a** are to be found at the front of the book and the entries beginning with **z** at the back. To help you find an entry quickly, there is a word in heavy type at the top of each page. The word at the top of a left-hand page shows the first entry on that page; the word at the top of a right-hand page shows the last entry on that page.

Where to look
An entry that is made up of more than one word is
treated as if it were a single word. For example, the
entry for **go out** is placed after **goods** and before
gossip, not at **go**.

---

goods 1   ✗ The goods was not delivered in time.
     ✓ **The goods were not delivered in time.**
Goods is a plural noun and takes a plural verb.

2   ✗ He had very little money and very few goods.
     ✓ **He had very little money and very few**
       possessions.
goods = things for sale: 'leather goods'
possessions = all the things a person owns

go out   ✗ As soon as the bus stopped, he went out.
     ✓ **As soon as the bus stopped, he got off.**
get on/off a bus/train/plane etc.

gossip   ✗ She told me gossips about all her relations.
     ✓ **She told me a lot of gossip about all her**
       relations.
gossip (uncountable) = talk concerned with people's
private lives
Note also: 'bits/pieces of gossip'

As a basic guideline, you are advised to look for
information in this dictionary <u>in the same way as in
any other dictionary</u>. For example, if you are in doubt
about whether to write 'marry someone' or 'marry **with**
someone', you should look for the relevant information
at the entry for **marry**, not at **with**. Similarly, if you feel
uncertain about which is correct – '**in** guarantee' or
'**under** guarantee' – you should turn to **guarantee**, not
in or **under**.

---

guarantee 2   ✗ May I remind you that the cassette recorder is
       still in guarantee.
     ✓ **May I remind you that the cassette recorder is**
       still under guarantee.
(be) under guarantee, NOT **in**

In each of these cases, the entry is located at the keyword. This is the most important word in a group of words which regularly occur together. Therefore the entry for **in spite of** is to be found at **spite**, the entry for **of/on your own accord** at **accord**, and the entry for **do/make a mistake** at **mistake**.

mistake 2   × I rarely do more than three mistakes in an essay.
✓ **I rarely make more than three mistakes in an essay.**
make a mistake, NOT **do**

On the other hand, if you want to know what is wrong with 'I went **out** the room' or '**at** 1984', you should turn to **out** (not **go** or **house**) or **at** (not **1984**). In these cases, there is no fixed group of words and there is therefore no keyword. Again, the user should follow standard dictionary practice.

out 2   × I felt very cold when I went out the room.
✓ **I felt very cold when I went out of the room.**
Out is an adverb: 'Alan went out, leaving just the two of us in the room.'
Out of is a preposition.
Note that in informal conversation, **out** is sometimes used instead of **out of**: 'I saw someone jump out the window.'

Spelling errors
Spelling errors are treated slightly differently. In each case, the entry will be found at the correct form of the word, not at the incorrect form. For example, the entry **dinning room** is shown at **dining room**, **pronounciation** at **pronunciation**. If you are unable to find an entry involving spelling, you should refer to the checklist of common misspellings at the back of the book.

Examining an entry

An entry usually has three parts. As an example, look at the entry for **noise**. The first part is a sentence containing the error. It is printed in ordinary type and has a cross (×) next to it. Beneath this, in heavy type and marked with a tick (√), is the correct sentence. In many cases, the user will see the mistake when he or she compares the two sentences but there is also a brief explanation at the end of the entry. As already mentioned, this has been kept as short as possible and concentrates on the particular problem underlying the error.

noise × I turned on the radio but there was no noise.
√ **I turned on the radio but there was no sound.**
noise = loud unpleasant sounds: 'The noise of the traffic gave me a headache.'
sound = something noticed by the ear: 'the sound of a guitar', 'the sound of a car engine'

Sub-entries

Sometimes a single word or phrase can produce two or more types of error. In these cases, the entry will be divided into several sub-entries, each dealing with a particular error, and having its own number. Grammatical errors generally come before errors involving usage or meaning, and errors which are very common are usually placed before those which occur less frequently.

no matter 1 × No matter he tries hard, he never succeeds in passing.
√ **No matter how hard he tries, he never succeeds in passing.**
no matter how much he studies/often he goes/well he plays etc. + main clause

2 × No matter the recession, sales remained high.
√ **In spite of the recession, sales remained high.**
No matter is ALWAYS followed by a **wh-** word: 'No matter what they did, they couldn't put the fire out.'

When a sub-entry consists of a cross-reference, this always come last.

according to 1	× According to me, we should spend more money on education.
	✓ **In my opinion, we should spend more money on education.**
	According to cannot be followed by **me** or **us**.
2	See OPINION

When a cross-reference is made to a particular sub-entry, the number of the sub-entry is shown.

| **invitation** | See AGREE 5 |

However, when the cross-reference is to both or all of the sub-entries at a headword, then no number is given.

| **evening** | See AFTERNOON |

Cross-references

You will find a number of cross-references in the dictionary. The purpose of these cross-references is simply to help you find the information you are looking for. For example, in the case of **do/make a mistake**, if you turn to **do** instead of **mistake**, you will find a cross-reference to **mistake**. Similarly, if you want to know what is wrong with **reach an aim** and look under **reach**, you will be directed to the entry at **aim**.

| **reach 2** | See AIM 2 |

Cross-references also help to avoid a lot of repetition in the dictionary. For example, when a small group of words such as **dozen/hundred/thousand/million** or **spring/summer/autumn/winter** follow the same rule or pattern, this is explained just once – at **hundred** and **summer**. If you look up one of the other words in the group, you will find a cross-reference to the entry where the explanation is given.

dozen   See HUNDRED 2

Cross-references are also used in entries dealing with British English and American English usage. The way in which this is treated in the dictionary is described below.

British and American differences
Whereas speakers of British English say **aerial**, speakers of American English say **antenna**. Pairs of this type have been included in the dictionary, not because either usage is wrong or substandard but simply in order to draw attention to the differences between the two language varieties. Some students are unaware of these differences and make the stylistic mistake of switching from one variety to the other within the same piece of written work.

In these cases, the entry is placed at the American English variant, while a cross-reference is given at the British English word. Unlike the other entries in the dictionary, no mistake is involved. Both variants are simply shown one above the other with the labels *AmE* and *BrE*.

Glossary
If an explanatory note contains a technical word which you do not understand, you should refer to the glossary of technical terms at the back of the book. It should be remembered, however, that the glossary is not intended to be comprehensive. It aims to provide sufficient information for the user to understand the notes, and no more.

Use by the teacher

Although designed primarily for the needs of the learner, the *Longman Dictionary of Common Errors* can also be used by the teacher of English in a number of ways. Some of these are outlined below.

– While students are engaged in writing tasks, the teacher might walk round the classroom, briefly checking the work in progress. Instead of correcting the errors observed and explaining the reasons for their correction, the teacher could simply call students' attention to the appropriate entries in the dictionary. In this way the students become actively involved in discovering and correcting their errors themselves.

– The same technique could be used when dealing with errors after written work has been handed in. Instead of writing lengthy corrections and comments on the scripts, the teacher could simply underline the error, adding a brief reference to the appropriate dictionary entry.

– After marking a batch of written work, the teacher might wish to select certain common errors as a focus for remedial teaching. The dictionary provides easy access to clear and concise notes which can serve as a basis for such teaching.

– Familiarity with the dictionary will also enable the teacher to predict the types of error that students are likely to make when introduced to a new grammatical or lexical item. Such awareness will be of considerable help in the preparation of effective teaching materials.

a 1 × I hope you all have a enjoyable stay.
✓ **I hope you all have an enjoyable stay.**

Always use **an** (NOT **a**) before a word beginning with a vowel sound: 'an egg', 'an envelope'.

2 × My husband is doing a MSc in civil engineering.
✓ **My husband is doing an MSc in civil engineering.**

Use **an** (NOT **a**) before an abbreviation that begins with a vowel sound: 'an MSc' /em es siː/, 'an MP' /em piː/.

3 × Sometimes it is difficult to live a honest life.
✓ **Sometimes it is difficult to live an honest life.**

Use **an** (NOT **a**) before words beginning with **h** when the **h** is not pronounced: 'an honour', 'an hour'.

4 × A bottle of milk is in the fridge.
✓ **There is a bottle of milk in the fridge.**
× A party will be at the language schcol.
✓ **There will be a party at the language school.**

In many sentences, the verb **be** is used to mean 'exist' or 'take place'. If the subject has not been mentioned before, it is placed immediately after the verb and the sentence begins with **there**.

a lot of See LOTS

about × I was about leaving when the telephone rang.
✓ **I was about to leave when the telephone rang.**
be about + to-v

above × There were above a hundred people in the crowd.
✓ **There were over a hundred people in the crowd.**

Do not use **above** with numbers (unless referring to points on a scale): 'He is over eighty years of age,' 'I receive over twenty letters a day,' BUT 'Don't let the temperature get above thirty degrees.'

above-mentioned   × I would be grateful if you would send it to the address above-mentioned.
√ **I would be grateful if you would send it to the above-mentioned address.**

Above-mentioned ALWAYS comes before the noun it modifies: 'above-mentioned person', 'above-mentioned company'.

absent 1   × The sales manager was absent at the meeting.
√ **The sales manager was absent from the meeting.**
absent from, NOT **at**

2   × I went to her house at four o'clock but she was absent.
√ **I went to her house at four o'clock but she wasn't in.**
absent = not present at something that you are supposed to attend: 'absent from school'

absolutely   See TIRED

accept 1   × These people accept to take risks in order to succeed.
√ **These people accept the need to take risks in order to succeed.**
Accept is NEVER followed by to-v.

2   × The company will not accept to buy new machines.
√ **The company will not agree to buy new machines.**
We **accept** a person's advice, opinion, or suggestion BUT **agree** to do something. Compare: 'I accepted her suggestion and agreed to see the doctor that evening.'

3   × To tell you the truth, I can't accept people who think about money all the time.
√ **To tell you the truth, I can't stand/bear/abide people who think about money all the time.**
cannot stand/bear/abide = cannot tolerate

accommodation 1 × I couldn't find the right accomodation.
✓ **I couldn't find the right accommodation.**
accommodation (DOUBLE **c**, DOUBLE **m**)

2 ✓ **AmE Accommodations in London are very expensive.**
✓ **BrE Accommodation in London is very expensive.**
In British English **accommodation** (= a place to live or spend the night) is ALWAYS uncountable. In American English it can be countable.

accord × People think he resigned on his own accord.
✓ **People think he resigned of his own accord.**
of your own accord, NOT **on**

according to 1 × According to me, we should spend more money on education.
✓ **In my opinion, we should spend more money on education.**
According to cannot be followed by **me** or **us**.

2 See OPINION

accuse × Some unemployed men accuse women for taking their jobs.
✓ **Some unemployed men accuse women of taking their jobs.**
accuse someone **of** something, NOT **for**

accustomed 1 × Having lived in England for two years, I am now accustomed myself to the cold weather.
✓ **Having lived in England for two years, I am now accustomed to the cold weather.**
be/grow accustomed to something OR **accustom yourself to** something
Compare: 'He soon grew accustomed to the harsh working conditions.' 'He soon accustomed himself to the harsh working conditions.'
Note the more informal alternative: 'He soon got used to the harsh working conditions.'

2   × It took me six months to get accustomed with the climate.
✓ **It took me six months to get accustomed to the climate.**

get accustomed to something, NOT **with**

3   × Where I come from, we are not accustomed to see so many things in the shops.
✓ **Where I come from, we are not accustomed to seeing so many things in the shops.**

be accustomed to + v-ing

actual   × We'd like to know more about the actual crisis, not the economic problems of the past.
✓ **We'd like to know more about the present/ current crisis, not the economic problems of the past.**

actual = real (as opposed to 'guessed', 'supposed', etc.): 'People think he is over fifty but his actual age is forty-eight.'
present/current = happening or existing now

actually   × We need to produce and export more than we do actually.
✓ **We need to produce and export more than we do at present.**

actually = strange as it may seem; in fact (despite what is said or thought): 'People think we've got lots of money, but actually we're very poor.'
at present = now

address   × I'll give you my adress.
✓ **I'll give you my address.**
address (DOUBLE **d**)

advice 1   × I adviced him to tell the police.
✓ **I advised him to tell the police.**
Advice/əd'vaɪs/ is a noun.
Advise/əd'vaɪz/ is a verb.

2   × She gave me a good advice.
    ✓ **She gave me some good advice.**
Advice is an uncountable noun.
Note the alternative: 'She gave me a good piece of advice.'

advise   × I asked my lawyer for her advise.
    ✓ **I asked my lawyer for her advice.**
Advise is a verb.
Advice is a noun.

aerial   See ANTENNA

affair   × There is a new affair in the middle of Helsinki which sells them.
    ✓ **There is a new shop in the middle of Helsinki which sells them.**
affair = (1) a thing, matter, or happening: 'The murder of the politician was a terrible affair.'
(2) a sexual relationship between two people not married to each other: 'She accused him of having an affair with her best friend.'

affect   × It's a magazine about computers and their affects on our lives.
    ✓ **It's a magazine about computers and their effects on our lives.**
Affect (WITH **aff**) is a verb. To **affect** something is to have an **effect** on it: 'Smoking affects your health.'
(= Smoking has an effect on your health.)

afford 1   × A newspaper can be afforded by most people.
    ✓ **Most people can afford a newspaper.**
Afford is rarely used in the passive.

2   × My father couldn't afford paying for my education.
    ✓ **My father couldn't afford to pay for my education.**
afford (to do) something

3 × My father couldn't afford himself to lend me any money.

✓ **My father couldn't afford to lend me any money.**

Afford is NOT a reflexive verb.

4 × I want to get my coat back because I can't afford the money for a new one.

✓ **I want to get my coat back because I can't afford (to buy) a new one.**

Money is rarely used as an object of **afford**.

afraid × The road to the airport was very busy and we were afraid to miss the plane.

✓ **The road to the airport was very busy and we were afraid of missing the plane.**

be afraid to do something = be unwilling to do something because you are frightened: 'She was afraid to eat it in case it was poisonous.'

be afraid of doing something = be worried or anxious about something which might happen

after 1 × The flight had been very pleasant until a man sitting after me started to shout.

✓ **The flight had been very pleasant until a man sitting behind me started to shout.**

after = following in time or order: 'I'll see you after lunch.' 'Remember to put a full stop after the last word.'

behind = at the back of

2 × After a week we're going to Italy.

✓ **In a week's time we're going to Italy.**

in a week OR **in a week's time** = after or at the end of a week

3 × Most of the people on the bus were after sixty.

✓ **Most of the people on the bus were over sixty.**

The preposition **over** is used with ages (and numbers) to mean 'more than'.

4 × I promised to meet Hitomi at the exhibition a
week after.

✓ **I promised to meet Hitomi at the exhibition a
week later.**

The use of **after** as an adverb (in place of **later**) is
very colloquial and is likely to be regarded as non-
standard by careful users.

5 ✓ **AmE A police car arrived within minutes and
soon after, an ambulance came.**

✓ **BrE A police car arrived within minutes and
soon afterwards, an ambulance came**.

In British English the use of **after** as an adverb (in
place of **afterwards**) is common in informal usage but
is regarded by careful users as non-standard.

6 × After you will leave, we will write to you every
day.

✓ **After you leave/have left, we will write to you
every day.**

After is followed by the present simple tense (or
present perfect) for future reference, NOT
shall/will + verb.

after all × After all, I'd like to thank you all for coming
here today.

✓ **Finally, I'd like to thank you all for coming
here today.**

Use **after all** when (1) you want to introduce an idea
which seems to contradict something which has been
said before: 'They had planned to go by train, but they
went by car after all.'
(2) you want to remind someone of a fact which they
should consider: 'I'm not surprised you're tired. After
all, you were working all night.'
finally = to conclude

afternoon 1   × The afternoon I met them at the hotel and **we** went to the beach.

√ **In the afternoon I met them at the hotel and we went to the beach.**

in the morning/afternoon/evening
Compare: 'The next afternoon I met them again.'

2   × On the afternoon we have two hours of classes.

√ **In the afternoon we have two hours of classes.**

When talking about a particular afternoon, use **on**. When speaking generally, use **in**: **on the afternoon/morning/evening of** 3rd July BUT **in the morning/afternoon/evening**

age   × I met a group of youngsters at my age in Trafalgar Square.

√ **I met a group of youngsters (of) my own age in Trafalgar Square.**

(of) my own age, NOT **at**

agenda   × In the left-hand pocket you will find a little red agenda that I need urgently.

√ **In the left-hand pocket you will find a little red diary that I need urgently.**

agenda = a list of topics for discussion at a meeting
diary = a book in which a person writes appointments or things to be remembered

ages   × The glasses haven't been washed since ages.

√ **The glasses haven't been washed for ages.**
See SINCE 2

ago 1   × It is a month ago since I left Germany.

√ **It is a month since I left Germany.**
Do not use **ago** before **since**.

2 × I'm writing in reply to your letter that I've received two days ago.

 ✓ **I'm writing in reply to your letter that I received two days ago.**

The present perfect tense is NOT used with words showing past time such as **yesterday**, **last week**, **a year ago**.

3 × The inspector asked to see his ticket, as I had done a few minutes ago.

 ✓ **The inspector asked to see his ticket, as I had done a few minutes before.**

Ago is used of a period in the past that is measured from the present moment.
Before is used of a period that is NOT measured from the present.
a few minutes ago = before now
a few minutes before = before then

4 × The accident happened at ten years ago.

 ✓ **The accident happened ten years ago.**

Do not use **at** to introduce a time expression with **ago**.

agree 1 × Unfortunately not many people agreed helping us.

 ✓ **Unfortunately not many people agreed to help us.**

agree + to-v

2 × I don't agree the people who say women should stay at home.

 ✓ **I don't agree with the people who say women should stay at home.**

agree with someone or something = have the same opinion as

3   × In many ways I agree to his statement.
        √ **In many ways I agree with his statement.**
        agree with = have the same opinion as: 'I fully agree
        with you/your opinion.'
        agree to = be willing to accept or allow something:
        'The bank manager has agreed to our request for a
        loan.'

4   × In some ways I am agree with those who want
        stricter punishments.
        √ **In some ways I agree with those who want
        stricter punishments.**
        Agree is a verb, NOT an adjective.

5   × Although I didn't really like him, I agreed his
        invitation.
        √ **Although I didn't really like him, I accepted his
        invitation.**
        accept an invitation, NOT **agree**

agreed   × We were both agreed with him.
            √ **We both agreed with him.**
            Agreed cannot be used as an adjective when it is
            followed by **with**. Compare: 'When it comes to the
            question of finance, we are all agreed.' (= have the
            same opinion)

aid   × Many more will die unless there is an
          increase in foreign aids.
          √ **Many more will die unless there is an
          increase in foreign aid.**
          Aid (= support or help) is an uncountable noun.

aim 1   × I started to learn English with the aim to
            become a teacher.
            √ **I started to learn English with the aim of
            becoming a teacher.**
            with the aim of + v-ing
            Note however: 'My aim is to become a teacher.'

2 × Everybody should be given the chance to
reach their aims.
✓ **Everybody should be given the chance to
achieve their aims.**
achieve an aim, NOT **reach**

alive 1 × Every alive creature in the sea is affected by
pollution.
✓ **Every living creature in the sea is affected by
pollution.**
Alive is the opposite of **dead**.
Living is the opposite of **non-living**.
Alive ALWAYS follows the noun it modifies: 'Some of the
fish in the boat were still alive.'

2 × Our teacher, Mr Collins, is very alive.
✓ **Our teacher, Mr Collins, is very lively**
alive = not dead (rarely modified)
lively = full of energy and action

all 1 × I like all the kinds of music.
✓ **I like all kinds of music.**
Do not use **the** after **all** when the reference is general.
Compare: 'I like all kinds of fruit.' (general reference) 'I
like all the kinds of fruit that my wife likes.' (specific
reference)

2 × We all were delighted when we heard the
news.
✓ **We were all delighted when we heard the
news.**
× We all must try to find a solution to the
problem.
✓ **We must all try to find a solution to the
problem.**
All usually goes immediately after the (first) auxiliary
verb: 'You should all pass the exam if you work hard.'
'They have all been working hard.' When there is no
auxiliary verb, **all** is placed immediately before the
main verb: 'They all passed the exam.' However, when
the main verb is **be**, **all** is placed immediately after it:
'The letters are all on your desk.'

3   × All of us didn't want to go to bed.
✓ **None of us wanted to go to bed.**
Use **none of** with an affirmative verb, NOT **all of** with a negative verb.

4   × I was alone in the house as all my parents were at work.
✓ **I was alone in the house as both my parents were at work.**
All is used for three or more people or things.
Both is used for two people or things.

5   × If you sit down and listen, I will explain all the situation.
✓ **If you sit down and listen, I will explain the whole situation.**
× He spent all the journey talking about accidents.
✓ **He spent the whole/entire journey talking about accidents.**
All is rarely used with the singular form of a countable noun. Compare: 'All the walls have been painted green.' (plural) 'The whole wall has been painted green.' (singular)

allow   × It is not allowed to talk in the library.
✓ **People are not allowed to talk in the library.**
✓ **Talking in the library is not allowed.**
It is NOT used as a preparatory subject before **allow**.

all right   × The man was covered in blood but the woman was allright.
✓ **The man was covered in blood but the woman was all right.**
× I hope you are feeling alright now.
✓ **I hope you are feeling all right now.**
Allright (one word) does not exist. Note that, although it is widely used, **alright** (one l) is considered non-standard by careful users of British English.

almost × The suitcase almost was too heavy to lift.
√ **The suitcase was almost too heavy to lift.**

When there is no auxiliary verb, **almost** is placed immediately before the main verb: 'She almost fell over.' However, when the main verb is **be**, **almost** is placed immediately after it: 'He is almost blind.' Otherwise **almost** goes immediately after the (first) auxiliary verb: 'I had almost finished the letter when the telephone rang.'

alone 1 × I think I will buy a dog because sometimes I feel alone.
√ **I think I will buy a dog because sometimes I feel lonely.**

alone = by yourself (not with anyone): 'I've thought about getting married, but I prefer living alone.'
lonely = sad because you are alone

2 × A child learns a lot by doing things alone.
√ **A child learns a lot by doing things on his or her own.**

alone = without other people present
on your own = without anyone's help or supervision; independently: 'He built the car all on his own.'

already 1 × I think my English has improved a bit allready.
√ **I think my English has improved a bit already.**

already = by now: 'The plane has already taken off.'
all ready = all prepared: 'The suitcases are all ready to take out to the taxi.'
Allready (one word) does not exist.

2 × Most of the food is cold already when you get it.
√ **Most of the food is already cold when you get it.**

When there is no auxiliary verb, **already** is usually placed immediately before the main verb: 'They already know.' However, when the main verb is **be**, **already** is usually placed immediately after it: 'They are already aware of the problem.' Otherwise **already** goes immediately after the (first) auxiliary verb: 'They have already discussed the various solutions.'

alright   See ALL RIGHT

also 1   × Of course, there also are people who steal because they are greedy.
✓ **Of course, there are also people who steal because they are greedy.**
× We also would like to be given more fresh food.
✓ **We would also like to be given more fresh food.**
Also usually goes immediately after the (first) auxiliary verb: 'I would also like to play squash if I had the time.' When there is no auxiliary verb, **also** is placed immediately before the main verb: 'I also play tennis in the summer.' However, when the main verb is **be**, **also** is placed immediately after it: 'I am also interested in golf.'

2   × I don't like your climate and I don't like English food also.
✓ **I don't like your climate and I don't like English food either.**
In a negative clause use **either**, NOT **also**.

alternate   ✓ **AmE We decided to make alternate arrangements in case the hotel was fully booked.**
✓ **BrE We decided to make alternative arrangements in case the hotel was fully booked.**
In British English **alternate** and **alternative** have different meanings.
alternate = (1) happening in turn, first one then the other: 'alternate periods of sun and rain'
(2) every second (day, week, etc.): 'Our local football team plays at home on alternate Saturdays.'
alternative = (of two or more things) that may be used, had, done, etc., instead of another; other
Note that in American English **alternate** can also be used with the same meaning as **alternative**.

alternatively   × In Sweden many wives and husbands stay at home alternatively to look after their children.
✓ **In Sweden many wives and husbands stay at home alternately to look after their children.**
alternatively = another possibility is: 'I thought we'd stay at home. Alternatively, you might like to go for a walk.'
alternately = in turns, first one then the other

although 1   × Although I was frightened, but I couldn't
scream.
✓ **Although I was frightened, I couldn't scream.**

When the subordinate clause begins with **although**, the
main clause does not usually begin with **but** or **yet**.

2   × Although the problem with the car, we enjoyed
the journey very much.
✓ **In spite of/Despite the problem with the car,
we enjoyed the journey very much.**

In spite of/Despite are prepositions and are usually
followed by a noun or noun phrase. **Although** is a
conjunction and must therefore be followed by a
clause. Note the alternative: 'Although we had a
problem with the car, we enjoyed the journey very
much.'

3   × Even although he couldn't swim, he jumped
straight into the water.
✓ **Even though he couldn't swim, he jumped
straight into the water.**

When **even** is used like this to give emphasis, it is
followed by **though**, NOT **although**.

altogether   × He put the knives altogether in the middle of
the table.
✓ **He put the knives all together in the middle of
the table.**

altogether = completely or thoroughly: 'I'm not
altogether sure what to do.'
all together = together in a group

always 1   × I have always the feeling that she enjoys
teaching us.
✓ **I always have the feeling that she enjoys
teaching us.**

When there is no auxiliary verb, **always** is placed
immediately before the main verb: 'She always arrives
late.' However, when the main verb is **be**, **always** is
placed immediately after it: 'He is always in a bad
mood.' Otherwise **always** goes immediately after the
(first) auxiliary verb: 'You should always take care
when crossing the road.'

2   × He is the most boring man I've always known.
  √ **He is the most boring man I've ever known.**

always = all the time; at all times; every time: 'Have you always lived in London?' 'Whenever I start singing, she always laughs.'
ever = at any time: 'Have you ever been to Paris?'

3   × While he was writing the letter, he always scratched his chin.
  √ **While he was writing the letter, he kept scratching his chin.**

always = (1) at all times; all the time: 'She always has a lot of work to do.'
(2) every time: 'Why do you always ask the same questions?'
keep + v-ing = do something repeatedly

a.m.   See O'CLOCK 3

amount 1   × The amount of crime have increased.
  √ **The amount of crime has increased.**

amount of (singular) + uncountable noun + singular verb
amounts of (plural) + uncountable noun + plural verb: 'Large amounts of money are required.'

2   × The amount of accidents is steadily increasing.
  √ **The number of accidents is steadily increasing.**

an amount of money ('money' is an uncountable noun)
BUT **a number of coins** ('coins' is a countable noun)

3   See BIG 1

an   × I had never visited an hospital before.
  √ **I had never visited a hospital before.**

Use **a** (NOT **an**) before a word beginning with **h**, unless the **h** is not pronounced: 'a house', 'a half' BUT 'an hour', 'an honour'.
Note that **an** may also be used before a word beginning with **h** when the syllable it introduces is unstressed: 'an historical novel'. However, this usage is usually regarded as old-fashioned nowadays.

and 1 × The magazine has many and beautiful
photographs.
✓ **The magazine has many beautiful
photographs.**

many + adjective + noun WITHOUT **and**

2 × She was carrying a long and green umbrella.
✓ **She was carrying a long green umbrella.**

Two adjectives coming before a noun are not usually
separated by **and** unless (1) they are both colours: 'a
red and green umbrella', (2) they are both materials:
'a gold and silver bracelet', (3) they describe similar or
related qualities: 'a cold (and) windy day'.

3 × The problem was that he didn't have any
money and clothes.
✓ **The problem was that he didn't have any
money or clothes.**

Use **and** when the sentence is affirmative: 'He had a
pen and a ruler.' Use **or** when the sentence is
negative: 'He didn't have a pen or a ruler.'
Note, however, the use of **and** when the two items are
considered as a single thing: 'He didn't want any fish
and chips.'

4 × She said she couldn't remember who she was
and where she lived.
✓ **She said she couldn't remember who she was
or where she lived.**

Use **and** when the sentence is affirmative: 'She smokes
and drinks.' Use **or** when the sentence is negative:
'She never smokes or drinks.'
Note, however, the use of **and** when the two actions
are closely connected or happen at the same time:
'She never drinks and drives.'

5 × Rollo Martins was a very good writer and he
was not famous.
✓ **Rollo Martins was a very good writer but he
was not famous.**

Do not use **and** to link clauses which contain
contrasting ideas: 'He loves her and wants to marry
her.' (NOT **but**) 'He hates her but wants to marry her.'
(NOT **and**)

announcement × On almost every page there were announcements for cigarettes and tobacco.
✓ **On almost every page there were advertisements for cigarettes and tobacco.**

announcement = the act of making something known publicly, especially by means of radio, television, or newspapers: 'Following the announcement of her marriage to the Prince of Wales, Lady Diana was pursued by crowds of journalists.'
advertisement = a film, broadcast, newspaper item, poster, etc., designed to persuade the public to buy, use, or hire something

another 1 × Rio has another important sights such as the famous football stadium.
✓ **Rio has other important sights such as the famous football stadium.**

another + singular: 'another mistake'
other + plural: 'other mistakes'

2 × My mother loved her old sewing machine, but on her birthday my father bought her another new one.
✓ **My mother loved her old sewing machine, but on her birthday my father bought her a new one.**

Compare: 'another new one' (= a second new one: i.e. she now has two new sewing machines)
'a new one' (= one new sewing machine)

answer 1 × They still can't find an answer for this problem.
✓ **They still can't find an answer to this problem.**

an answer to a problem or question, NOT **for**

2 × I don't think we will ever be able to answer to these questions correctly.
✓ **I don't think we will ever be able to answer these questions correctly.**

× I'm sorry that I didn't answer to your letter
earlier but I've been very busy.

✓ **I'm sorry that I didn't answer your letter
earlier but I've been very busy.**

answer someone or something WITHOUT **to**

antenna ✓ **AmE The radio won't work if the antenna is
broken.**

✓ **BrE The radio won't work if the aerial is
broken.**

Note that in British English **antenna** usually means 'a
long, thin, sensitive organ, commonly found in pairs,
on the heads of some insects and other animals'.

anxious × We were anxious for knowing whether he had
arrived safely.

✓ **We were anxious to know whether he had
arrived safely.**

anxious + **to-v**, NOT + **for** v-ing
Compare: 'Both parents were anxious for/about the
child's safety.' (= worried about)

any × When he asked if he could use the telephone,
he was told that the family didn't have any.

✓ **When he asked if he could use the telephone,
he was told that the family didn't have one.**

Do not use **any** as a pronoun for a singular countable
noun. Compare: 'He asked for some help but nobody
gave him any.' (**help** is an uncountable noun)
'She wanted to borrow some books but nobody would
lend her any.' (**books** is a plural countable noun)
'I need a new typewriter but I can't afford one.'
(**typewriter** is a singular countable noun)

anything See SOMETHING

anywhere See SOMEWHERE

apart from × Apart of a few minor problems, the trip was a
great success.

✓ **Apart from a few minor problems, the trip was
a great success.**

apart from, NOT **of**

apartment   ✓ AmE I'm renting a small apartment in Paris.
✓ BrE I'm renting a small flat in Paris.
Apartment is chiefly American English.
Flat is more common in British English.

apologize 1   ✕ The waiter was made to apologize my father for being so rude to him.
✓ **The waiter was made to apologize to my father for being so rude to him.**
apologize to someone (**for** something)

2   ✕ She insisted on apologizing her husband's behaviour.
✓ **She insisted on apologizing for her husband's behaviour.**
apologize (to someone) **for** (doing) something

appreciate   ✕ I would really appreciate if you could let me have her address as soon as possible.
✓ **I would really appreciate it if you could let me have her address as soon as possible.**
appreciate + **it** + **if/when** clause: 'We really appreciated it when she offered to help.'

approach   ✕ He approached to my table and took a seat opposite me.
✓ **He approached my table and took a seat opposite me.**
approach someone or something WITHOUT **to**

approve   ✕ I personally do not approve to the image of women as housewives.
✓ **I personally do not approve of the image of women as housewives.**
✕ Some husbands do not approve the idea of their wives having a job.
✓ **Some husbands do not approve of the idea of their wives having a job.**
approve of something = think it is good

argument   × By the next afternoon they had completely forgotten the arguement.
✓ **By the next afternoon they had completely forgotten the argument.**
argue (WITH **e**) BUT **argument** (WITHOUT **e**)

armchair   × She was sitting on a big armchair.
✓ **She was sitting in a big armchair.**
sit on a chair BUT **sit in** an armchair

arrival   × At his arrival in Vienna, he was surprised not to find his friend.
✓ **On his arrival in Vienna, he was surprised not to find his friend.**
on/upon someone's arrival, NOT **at**

arrive 1   × She arrived the station just in time to catch the train.
✓ **She arrived at the station just in time to catch the train.**
× We arrived to the hotel in time for dinner.
✓ **We arrived at the hotel in time for dinner.**
arrive at a building, station, airport, etc.
See also HOME

2   × I arrived to London on 21st May.
✓ **I arrived in London on 21st May.**
× When he arrived at Vienna, he was told that his aunt had died.
✓ **When he arrived in Vienna, he was told that his aunt had died.**
arrive in a country, city, etc.

as 1   × It looked very fragile and so I handled it as china.
✓ **It looked very fragile and so I handled it like china.**
× He started to cry as a hungry baby.
✓ **He started to cry like a hungry baby.**
When the intended meaning is 'as if he/she/they etc. were', use **like**, NOT **as**.

(as) 2   × I prefer eating fresh things as tomatoes and lettuce.
✓ **I prefer eating fresh things like tomatoes and lettuce.**
✓ **I prefer eating fresh things such as tomatoes and lettuce.**

Examples of a class or category (e.g. 'fresh things') are introduced by **such as** or **like**.

3   × As I decided to learn English, I didn't know how difficult it would be.
✓ **When I decided to learn English, I didn't know how difficult it would be.**

If the verb in the main clause describes a state or condition ('I didn't know'), the subordinate clause describing an action or event ('I decided to learn English') begins with **when**, NOT **as**.

4   × That night he thought there was nothing better as to be home again.
✓ **That night he thought there was nothing better than to be home again.**

comparative adjective/adverb + **than**, NOT **as**

5   × As I know you are interested in ballet, that's why I decided to write to you about the performance.
✓ **As I know you are interested in ballet, I decided to write to you about the performance.**

When the subordinate clause begins with **as**, the main clause cannot begin with **that's why**. Note the alternative: 'I know you are interested in ballet, and that's why I decided to write to you about the performance.'

6   × As I can remember, I left the coat in the cupboard in my room.
✓ **As far as I can remember, I left the coat in the cupboard in my room.**

as/so far as I (can) remember

7   See THAT 4

ashamed × I always feel ashamed when I have to speak in public.
√ **I always feel embarrassed when I have to speak in public.**

ashamed = feeling guilt and disgust for yourself: 'How can you admit to stealing from your own mother without feeling ashamed?'
embarrassed = feeling socially uncomfortable or anxious

ask 1 × He asked her a glass of water.
√ **He asked her for a glass of water.**

ask (someone) **for** something = ask to be given something

2 × I asked to the man if he knew the way to the airport.
√ **I asked the man if he knew the way to the airport.**

ask someone something WITHOUT **to**

3 × He asked for watching television.
√ **He asked if he could watch television.**

Use **ask** + **if** clause when reporting a request.

4 × She asked me what was the time.
√ **She asked me what the time was.**

When the object of the sentence is a **wh-** clause, the subject and the verb in the **wh-** clause do not change places.

as long as 1 × I'll go with you as long as I won't have to sing.
√ **I'll go with you as long as I don't have to sing.**

After **as long as** (= if), use the present simple tense for future reference, NOT **shall/will** + verb.

2 × He wants me to send him all the newspapers because he doesn't want to miss anything as long as he's out of the country.

√ **He wants me to send him all the newspapers because he doesn't want to miss anything while he's out of the country.**

as long as = (1) for (NOT during) a length of time: 'You can stay here as long as you like.' 'You can stay here as long as three weeks but no longer.'
(2) provided that: 'You can stay as long as you keep quiet.'

as soon as × I'll pay you as soon as I will receive the parcel.

√ **I'll pay you as soon as I receive the parcel.**

After **as soon as**, use the present simple tense for future reference, NOT **shall/will** + verb.

as though × I felt as though if somebody had kicked me.

√ **I felt as if somebody had kicked me.**

√ **I felt as though somebody had kicked me.**

Use **as if** OR **as though**.

astonishment × The old man shook his head astonishedly.

√ **The old man shook his head in astonishment.**

Astonishedly does not exist. This meaning is expressed by the phrase **in astonishment**.

as well × When he reached her house, he noticed that there were no lights on. He couldn't see her car as well.

√ **When he reached her house, he noticed that there were no lights on. He couldn't see her car either.**

As well is rarely used in a negative clause.

as well as × Each week he wrote her three letters, as well as telephoned her.

√ **Each week he wrote her three letters, as well as telephoning her.**

clause + **as well as** + v-ing

at 1   × It was almost midnight when we landed at France.

✓ **It was almost midnight when we landed in France.**

× At last I can study English at London.

✓ **At last I can study English in London.**

Use **in** (NOT **at**) before the names of countries, regions, cities, and large towns.

2   × In Germany we have a lot of snow at wintertime.

✓ **In Germany we have a lot of snow in wintertime.**

Use **in** (NOT **at**) with seasons, months, and years: 'in the summertime', 'in February', 'in 1985'.

3   × I bought the tape recorder just a week ago, at 4th December.

✓ **I bought the tape recorder just a week ago, on 4th December.**

Use **on** (NOT **at**) before dates.

4   × At about one and a half hours later I took the cake out of the oven.

✓ **About one and a half hours later I took the cake out of the oven.**

'an hour before', 'a week later', 'two years afterwards' WITHOUT **at**

5   See AGO 4

athletic   × A lot of athletic reporters write for the magazine.

✓ **A lot of athletics reporters write for the magazine.**

athletic reporters = reporters who are good at running, jumping, etc.
athletics reporters = reporters who write about athletics

attention 1   × I told him that I wanted to read, but he didn't pay any attention at me.

✓ **I told him that I wanted to read, but he didn't pay any attention to me.**

pay attention to a person or thing, NOT **at**

2   × 'You won't know what to do if you don't give attention,' she said.

✓ **'You won't know what to do if you don't pay attention,' she said.**

pay attention (**to** someone or something) OR **give** someone **your attention**
Compare: 'I'd like you to give me your full attention.'

3   × The driver of the car was very young and I paid attention that he was drunk.

✓ **The driver of the car was very young and I noticed that he was drunk.**

pay attention (to) = watch and listen to with full concentration: 'If you don't pay attention, you won't know what to do.'
notice = see and make a mental note of: 'I noticed that someone had opened the window.'

autumn   See SUMMER

average   × In average about ten people die every day.

✓ **On average about ten people die every day.**

on average, NOT **in**

avoid 1   × Some criminals use guns to avoid to be caught.

✓ **Some criminals use guns to avoid being caught.**

avoid + v-ing

2   × He is such a nice man that you cannot avoid
     liking him.
     √ **He is such a nice man that you cannot help
     liking him.**
     cannot help + v-ing (= cannot stop yourself from doing
     something): 'Whenever he smiles at me, I just can't
     help laughing.'

3   × Some parents try to avoid their children from
     leaving home.
     √ **Some parents try to prevent their children
     from leaving home.**
     avoid + v-ing = keep or save yourself from doing
     something: 'Where possible, try to avoid drinking
     unboiled water.'
     prevent someone (**from**) + v-ing = stop someone doing
     something

4   × I told him that we would be grateful if he
     would kindly avoid ringing our doorbell after
     midnight.
     √ **I told him that we would be grateful if he
     would kindly refrain from ringing our doorbell
     after midnight.**
     avoid = keep or save yourself from (doing something):
     'Most film stars try to avoid being recognized when
     they are on holiday.'
     refrain from (formal) = stop yourself from (doing
     something) because other people do not like it
     Note the phrase: 'Would/could you kindly refrain
     from' + v-ing

awaken   × I was awakened by the ticket inspector.
     √ **I was woken up by the ticket inspector.**
     Awakened is grammatically possible but is used only
     in a very formal or literary context.

aware   × Only those aware of the subject could join in the discussion.
✓ **Only those familiar with the subject could join in the discussion.**

aware of = conscious (of): 'I became aware of someone following me.' 'Are you aware that the train leaves in five minutes?'
familiar with = acquainted with: 'The aim of the course is to make you fully familiar with the latest teaching methods.'

baby   × Sitting in the next seat was a young woman who was having a baby.
✓ **Sitting in the next seat was a young woman who was expecting a baby.**

have a baby = give birth
expect a baby = be pregnant
In informal conversation **she's having a baby** can be used to mean 'she's pregnant' but it is better to use this phrase only when there is no risk of confusion.

back 1   See SIDE 1
2   See RETURN 1

bad 1   × A country can be different without being better or badder than your own.
✓ **A country can be different without being better or worse than your own.**
× Despite the medicine, I started to feel more bad.
✓ **Despite the medicine, I started to feel worse.**
bad, worse, worst

2   × I'm afraid I speak English very bad.
✓ **I'm afraid I speak English very badly.**
Bad is an adjective.
Badly is an adverb.

baggage   × All the passengers carried their own baggages.
         ✓ **All the passengers carried their own baggage.**
         × Takashi had five baggages.
         ✓ **Takashi had five pieces of baggage.**
         Baggage is an uncountable noun.
         A piece of baggage is a single suitcase or bag.

band   × The first time I played the tape recorder it 'ate'
         the band.
         ✓ **The first time I played the tape recorder it**
         'ate' the tape.
         band = a thin flat narrow piece of material which is
         joined at the ends: 'Her dress had a green band round
         the hem.' 'A band of metal was used to strengthen the
         joint.'
         tape = (1) a cassette tape
         (2) a thin flat narrow piece of material

bank   × Finally he stopped running and sat down on a
         bank, completely exhausted.
         ✓ **Finally he stopped running and sat down on a**
         bench, completely exhausted.
         bank = the ground at the edge of a river, lake, etc.:
         'He jumped out of the boat onto the bank.'
         bench = a long seat, especially in a park or other
         public place

bath   × It is not possible to take a bath along this
         coast because the sea is badly polluted.
         ✓ **It is not possible to bathe along this coast**
         because the sea is badly polluted.
         take a bath = wash yourself (and relax) in a bath
         bathe = swim

be 1   × Nowadays is very difficult to get a job.
         ✓ **Nowadays it is very difficult to get a job.**
         In statements, **be** (like all other verbs) must ALWAYS
         have a subject. When the real subject is a to-v or v-ing
         structure, use the preparatory subject **it** and put the
         real subject later. Compare: 'To get a job is very
         difficult.' 'It is very difficult to get a job.'

2   × The grammar teacher is easily to understand.
✓ **The grammar teacher is easy to understand.**
Be is followed by an adjective, NOT an adverb.

because 1   × Because her terrible behaviour, the flight became a nightmare.
✓ **Because of her terrible behaviour, the flight became a nightmare.**

because of (preposition) + noun or noun phrase
because (conjunction) + clause: 'Because she behaved terribly, the flight became a nightmare.'

2   See REASON 1

become   See DARK, TRUE

bed 1   × His grandmother gave him some dinner and brought him to bed.
✓ **His grandmother gave him some dinner and put him to bed.**
× When he got home, his mother put him in bed.
✓ **When he got home, his mother put him to bed.**
put (a child) **to bed**

2   × Every morning I have to get up from my bed very early.
✓ **Every morning I have to get up very early.**
Bed is rarely used with **get up**. Note, however, the phrase **get out of bed**: 'I got out of bed and opened the windows.'

been   × After been sent to prison, some criminals feel hatred for society.
✓ **After being sent to prison, some criminals feel hatred for society.**
preposition (**after**) + v-ing

before 1   × On the bus he was sitting right before me.
✓ **On the bus he was sitting right in front of me.**
Before is used mainly when talking about time, NOT place. The most common exception is when people are talking about order or sequence: 'She was before me

in the queue.' 'I looked at the list to see whose name was before mine.' 'Two comes before three.'

2   ✗ 'I bought the tape recorder the week before,' he said.
    ✓ **'I bought the tape recorder last week,' he said.**
In direct speech, use **last week/month/year**.
In reported speech, use **the week/month/year before**.

3   ✗ The war ended over forty years before.
    ✓ **The war ended over forty years ago.**
Before is used of a period that is NOT measured from the present: 'The war ended two months before I was born.'
Ago is used of a period in the past that is measured from the present moment.

4   See EVER 2

begin   ✗ As she left the house, it began raining.
    ✓ **As she left the house, it began to rain.**
When the subject is inanimate, **begin** is usually followed by to-v

beginning 1   ✗ I started my course at the begining of November.
    ✓ **I started my course at the beginning of November.**
begin (ONLY ONE **n**)
beginning (DOUBLE **n**)

2   ✗ At the beginning I thought that the switch was broken but then I discovered it was all right.
    ✓ **At first I thought that the switch was broken but then I discovered it was all right.**
At the beginning usually refers to something that is mentioned in the **of** phrase that follows: 'at the beginning of the week', 'at the beginning of the book', or to something that is mentioned in or understood from the context: 'Start at the beginning and read until you get to the bottom of page three.'
At first usually refers to the first of two or more stages or steps and conveys a strong idea of sequence.

behave   × The magazine teaches parents how to behave
with their children.
✓ **The magazine teaches parents how to behave
towards their children.**
behave towards someone, NOT **with**

behaviour   × We were surprised by their peculiar
behaviours.
✓ **We were surprised by their peculiar
behaviour.**
Behaviour is an uncountable noun.

behind   × The school has a little garden behind of it.
✓ **The school has a little garden behind it.**
in front of someone or something BUT **behind** someone
or something (WITHOUT **of**)

believe   × Some people are believing that the increase in
crime is because of all the unemployment.
✓ **Some people believe that the increase in
crime is because of all the unemployment.**
Believe is NOT used in progressive tenses.

belong 1   × The coat belongs my daughter.
✓ **The coat belongs to my daughter.**
belong to someone

2   × 'Are these gloves belonging to you?' she
asked.
✓ **'Do these gloves belong to you?' she asked.**
Belong is NOT used in progressive tenses.

3   × The car is belong to my wife.
✓ **The car belongs to my wife.**
Belong is a verb, NOT an adjective.

benefit   × I think small children can only benefit to be by
the side of their parents all the time.
✓ **I think small children can only benefit from
being by the side of their parents all the time.**
benefit from/by + v-ing

besides   × My sister's old boyfriend was sitting besides me.
√ **My sister's old boyfriend was sitting beside me.**

besides = in addition to: 'There were three other people there besides me.' 'Besides tennis, what other games do you play?'
beside = next to

best 1   × I trust you will do your best in repairing the cassette recorder as quickly as possible.
√ **I trust you will do your best to repair the cassette recorder as quickly as possible.**

do your best + to-v

2   × We all made our best to see that they enjoyed themselves.
√ **We all did our best to see that they enjoyed themselves.**

do your best, NOT **make**

better 1   × German cars are more expensive but they are more better.
√ **German cars are more expensive but they are better.**

good, better, best

2   × You better stop smoking.
√ **You'd better stop smoking.**

had better (not) + infinitive WITHOUT **to**: 'If the phone rings again, you'd better answer it.' 'You'd better not tell her if it's a secret.'

3   × 'You had better to hurry up,' she shouted.
√ **'You had better hurry up,' she shouted.**

had better + infinitive WITHOUT **to**

4   × I advised him that he should better inform the police.
√ **I advised him that he had better inform the police.**

× If you don't feel well, you would better not go to work.

✓ **If you don't feel well, you had better not go to work.**

Had in **had better do something** is fixed. No other word or form may be used in its place.

5   × It would be better you sent me the coat.

✓ **It would be better if you sent me the coat.**

This follows the usual pattern of conditional sentences. Compare: 'It would be very convenient if you sent me the coat.' 'I would be delighted if you sent me the coat.'

between   × Between all the magazines on the shelf, there was one that was very interesting.

✓ **Among/Amongst all the magazines on the shelf, there was one that was very interesting.**

× He wandered silently between the passengers on the boat.

✓ **He wandered silently among/amongst the passengers on the boat.**

Between is used when two or more objects, people, or places are considered separately.

Among/amongst is used with three or more objects, etc., considered as a group or mass.

big 1   × I would like to remind you that I paid a big amount for this radio-cassette and I expect it to work properly.

✓ **I would like to remind you that I paid a large amount for this radio-cassette and I expect it to work properly.**

× Quite a big number of people believe in ghosts.

✓ **Quite a large number of people believe in ghosts.**

Amount and **number** (= quantity) are used with **small** and **large**, NOT **little** and **big**.

2   × While on holiday she caught a big disease.

✓ **While on holiday she caught a serious disease.**

× Instead of having a pleasant journey, I reached my destination with a big headache.
✓ **Instead of having a pleasant journey, I reached my destination with a bad/severe/terrible headache.**
Big is NOT used of illnesses, aches, and pains.

3 × It is a big pleasure to have you all here.
✓ **It is a great pleasure to have you all here.**
Big and **large** are not usually used to describe abstract qualities.
Great is often used instead: 'great happiness/ sorrow/difficulty'.

birthday × My husband gave me this coat as a present on our last wedding birthday.
✓ **My husband gave me this coat as a present on our last wedding anniversary.**
birthday = the date on which a person was born
anniversary = the day of the year when an important event happened and on which it is remembered or celebrated

bite × He told me he had been biten by a cobra.
✓ **He told me he had been bitten by a cobra.**
bite, biting, bit (ONLY ONE **t**)
bitten (DOUBLE **t**)

blame × I really don't think it was the driver's blame.
✓ **I really don't think it was the driver's fault.**
✓ **I really don't think the driver was to blame.**
Blame is NOT used after a possessive form. Compare: 'It's my fault.' 'I am to blame.'

board × Within a week, I found myself on board of an aeroplane.
✓ **Within a week, I found myself on board an aeroplane.**
on board an aircraft, ship, etc. WITHOUT **of**

body See NOBODY 4

book in   × We booked in a hotel in Istanbul.
✓ **We booked in at a hotel in Istanbul.**
In British English **book in at a hotel** means 'reserve a room'.

bored 1   × The book has no pictures and is very bored.
✓ **The book has no pictures and is very boring.**
See BORING

2   × She soon got bored of talking to him.
✓ **She soon got bored with talking to him.**
Bored with (doing) something is the correct form. **Of** is sometimes used in informal English but is regarded by careful users as non-standard.

boring   × We get very boring with the same dishes every day.
✓ **We get very bored with the same dishes every day.**
'They are boring' = They bore people.
'They are bored' = Someone/something bores them.
Compare: 'a boring film' and 'a bored audience'

born   × I have been born in a town just outside Paris.
✓ **I was born in a town just outside Paris.**
Always use 'I was born', NOT 'I have been born' or 'I am born'.

borrow 1   × The garage has borrowed me another car while mine is being repaired.
✓ **The garage has lent me another car while mine is being repaired.**
borrow = take or receive (something) for a certain time, intending to return it
lend = give (someone) the use of (something) for a certain time

2   × Can I borrow your bathroom, please?
✓ **Can I use your bathroom, please?**
You can only use **borrow** with movable objects.

both 1   × Both of them were not telling the truth.
       ✓ **Neither of them was/were telling the truth.**
       Use **neither** + affirmative verb, NOT **both** + negative verb.
       See also NEITHER 5

     2   × It is no good unless the both countries agree to stop fighting.
       ✓ **It is no good unless both (the) countries agree to stop fighting.**
       × I am pleased that my both children have written to me.
       ✓ **I am pleased that both my children have written to me.**
       Both comes before a determiner, NOT after it.

     3   × Two of the biggest firms are Apple and IBM, which both are in the computer business.
       ✓ **Two of the biggest firms are Apple and IBM, which are both in the computer business.**
       ✓ **Two of the biggest firms are Apple and IBM, both of which are in the computer business.**
       Both cannot be placed immediately before **be** unless it is used as a pronoun: 'Two of the biggest firms are Apple and IBM. Both are in the computer business.'

     4   × Lappish is completely different from both the two Norwegian languages.
       ✓ **Lappish is completely different from both the Norwegian languages.**
       Do not use **two** after **both**.

     5   × I'm writing this letter to tell both about my time in England.
       ✓ **I'm writing this letter to tell you both about my time in England.**
       ✓ **I'm writing this letter to tell both of you about my time in England.**
       Both cannot replace a first person pronoun ('we/us') or second person pronoun ('you').

bother   ✓ **AmE I am sorry that I have to bother you about this problem.**
✓ **BrE I am sorry that I have to bother you with this problem.**
In American English, use **bother** someone **with** OR **about** something.
In British English, use **bother** someone **with** something.

boyfriend   See FRIEND

brake   × He really didn't mean to brake the plate.
✓ **He really didn't mean to break the plate.**
brake = cause (a car, motorcycle, etc.) to slow down or stop: 'Don't brake too suddenly when there is ice on the road.'
break = damage or become damaged; separate into two or more pieces

brand   × He bought a very well-known brand of car.
✓ **He bought a very well-known make of car.**
Brand is used of soap, toothpaste, butter, etc.
Make is used of cars, washing machines, refrigerators, etc.

break   × When the driver saw the truck, he tried to break but it was too late.
✓ **When the driver saw the truck, he tried to brake but it was too late.**
break = damage or become damaged; separate into two or more pieces: 'Careful! Don't break those eggs!'
brake = cause (a vehicle) to slow or stop

breakfast   × Every morning my first job is to prepare a breakfast.
✓ **Every morning my first job is to prepare (the) breakfast.**
make/prepare (the) breakfast, NOT **a**

breath   × She had a very bad cold and couldn't breath
             properly.
         ✓ **She had a very bad cold and couldn't breathe
             properly.**
         Breath /breθ/ is a noun.
         Breathe /briːð/ is a verb.
         The verb is longer than the noun both in its spelling
         and in its vowel sound.

briefly   × They set out over an hour ago and so they
             should be here briefly.
         ✓ **They set out over an hour ago and so they
             should be here shortly.**
         briefly = for a short time
         shortly = soon

bring 1   × I am going abroad next week and would like
             to bring the cassette recorder with me.
         ✓ **I am going abroad next week and would like
             to take the cassette recorder with me.**
         × Would you like me to bring you home?
         ✓ **Would you like me to take you home?**
         Bring is used for movement towards the place where
         the speaker is, was, or intends to be, or towards the
         person being talked about: 'He asked me to bring him
         a dictionary.'
         Take is used for movement in other directions.

   2   See BED 1

British   × I am sharing a room with one of my
             classmates. She is a British.
         ✓ **I am sharing a room with one of my
             classmates. She is British.**
         British is an adjective. Note, however, that it is used
         as a noun in the phrase **the British**, when this means
         'the British people'.

broken   × The car could not stop because its brakes
             were broken.
         ✓ **The car could not stop because its brakes
             were not working.**
         broken = physically damaged: 'a broken windscreen'
         not working = not functioning properly

burst × He was so frightened that he burst in tears.
✓ **He was so frightened that he burst into tears.**
burst into tears / shrieks of laughter / flames, etc., NOT **in**

bus 1 × Mr Masui travelled to Osaka by a bus.
✓ **Mr Masui travelled to Osaka by bus.**
travel/go by bus WITHOUT **a**

2 × He ran down the road and went into a bus.
✓ **He ran down the road and got on a bus.**
get on/off a bus

business × I'm sorry for not replying sooner but I had a business to take care of.
✓ **I'm sorry for not replying sooner but I had some business to take care of.**
business (countable) = a shop, company, etc.
business (uncountable) = matters or duties

but See ALTHOUGH 1

by 1 × He managed to open the lid by a screwdriver
✓ **He managed to open the lid with a screwdriver.**
do something **with** a tool, instrument, etc., NOT **by**

2 × They watch the customers by a little window.
✓ **They watch the customers through a little window.**
watch/look/see through a window, NOT **by**

3 × I hope you feel better by this letter reaches you.
✓ **I hope you feel better by the time this letter reaches you.**
By is NEVER used as a conjunction.

cabinet   × The ship was very small, so in order to avoid
my aunt, I had to stay in my cabinet all day.
✓ **The ship was very small, so in order to avoid
my aunt, I had to stay in my cabin all day.**
cabinet = a piece of furniture used for storing or
displaying things
cabin = a small room on a ship

call   × I ran to the telephone and called to the fire
brigade.
✓ **I ran to the telephone and called the fire
brigade.**
call/ring/telephone a person or place WITHOUT **to**

can 1   × I can not see why the machine stopped
working.
✓ **I can't/cannot see why the machine stopped
working.**
Can not usually becomes **can't** (chiefly spoken,
informal) or **cannot** (more formal).

2   × As you can remember, I was always interested
in scientific subjects.
✓ **As you may remember, I was always
interested in scientific subjects.**
× I think you can remember me as I was the
only Japanese in the group.
✓ **I think you may remember me as I was the
only Japanese in the group.**
May is used to express possibility.
Can is used to express ability.

3   See COULD 2

cancel   × The meeting has been cancelled until next
Thursday.
✓ **The meeting has been postponed until next
Thursday.**
cancel = decide that something (previously arranged)
will no longer take place
postpone = move to a later time or date

capable   × I took the machine back to the shop but there
          was nobody there capable to repair it.
          √ **I took the machine back to the shop but there
          was nobody there capable of repairing it.**
          able + to-v BUT **capable of** + v-ing

car   × Are you going by taxi or by your own car?
          √ **Are you going by taxi or in your own car?**
          √ **Are you going by taxi or by car?**
          go by car BUT **go in** your (own) car

care 1   × My host family took a good care of me.
          √ **My host family took good care of me.**
          take (good/great) care of someone or something

2   × She had to stay at home to take care after her
          family.
          √ **She had to stay at home to take care of her
          family.**
          look after someone or something BUT **take care of**
          someone or something

3   × If you want to lose weight you'll have to
          take care of what you eat.
          √ **If you want to lose weight you'll have to
          be careful about what you eat.**
          take care of = look after: 'Who will take care of the
          dog while we're away?'
          be careful about = pay close attention to, especially to
          avoid doing the wrong thing

4   × Some criminals simply don't care of being
          caught.
          √ **Some criminals simply don't care about being
          caught.**
          care about (doing) something, NOT **of**

care for   × The only thing they cared for was how to
make money.
√ **The only thing they cared about was how to
make money.**

care for (formal) = (1) like: 'Would you care for
another drink?'
(2) take care of: 'The child was well cared for.' (usually
adjectival)
care about = be concerned about

careless   × How wonderful it would be to be young and
careless again!
√ **How wonderful it would be to be young and
carefree again!**

The opposite of **careless** is **careful**: 'If you weren't so
careless, you wouldn't make so many mistakes.'
The opposite of **carefree** is **worried**.

carry   × An ambulance arrived and carried her to the
hospital.
√ **An ambulance arrived and took her to the
hospital.**

A vehicle **takes** a person somewhere.

case 1   × Switzerland has very little unemployment and
in this case we are very lucky.
√ **Switzerland has very little unemployment and
in this respect we are very lucky.**

in this/that case = in these/those circumstances: 'What
shall I do if there are no trains?' 'In that case go by
bus.'
in this/that respect = with regard to this/that point or
detail: 'The film is full of violence and in this respect is
unsuitable for children.'

2   × I advise you to eat something now in case
there won't be any food when we get there.
√ **I advise you to eat something now in case
there isn't any food when we get there.**

After **in case**, use the present simple tense for future
reference, NOT **shall/will** + verb: 'Take an umbrella in
case it rains.'

3   ✓ **AmE In case you need any more information, please contact me.**
✓ **BrE If you need any more information, please contact me.**
✓ **AmE In case a woman goes out to work, she shouldn't have to do all the housework.**
✓ **BrE If a woman goes out to work, she shouldn't have to do all the housework.**

This usage of **in case** is acceptable in American English but NOT in British English. Note that **if ...** can be used in both British and American English.

catch   × We catched him stealing our luggage.
✓ **We caught him stealing our luggage.**
× She catched the first train to London.
✓ **She caught the first train to London.**
catch, catching, caught, caught

cause 1   × The police wanted to know the cause for the accident.
✓ **The police wanted to know the cause of the accident.**
cause of, NOT **for** something

2   × This causes that the children look for affection elsewhere.
✓ **This causes the children to look for affection elsewhere.**
cause somebody **to do** something, NOT **cause that**

center   ✓ **AmE The cinema was in the middle of a large shopping center.**
✓ **BrE The cinema was in the middle of a large shopping centre.**
Center is American English.
Centre is British English.

certain 1   × She was extremely certain that they would offer her the job.
   ✓ **She was absolutely/quite certain that they would offer her the job.**

Although usage varies, an adjective which contains the sense 'very', 'extremely', or '100%' as part of its meaning is NOT usually used with **very** or **extremely**. Examples are: **boiling** (= very hot), **certain** (= very sure), **convinced** (= very sure), **delighted** (= very pleased), **desperate** (= very worried), **fascinated** (= very interested (by)), **fine** (= very well, as in 'I feel fine'), **freezing** (= very cold), and **starving** (= very hungry). To intensify such adjectives, use **absolutely**, NOT **very** OR **extremely**.

2   × The present government is certain of losing the next election.
   ✓ **The present government is certain to lose the next election.**

certain of doing something = feel sure that you will do something: 'John is certain of being invited.' (= John's opinion)
certain to do something = will definitely do something: 'John is certain to be invited.' (= the speaker's opinion)

certainly   × I certainly will try harder the next time.
   ✓ **I will certainly try harder the next time.**

Certainly usually goes immediately after the (first) auxiliary verb: 'His work has certainly improved this year.' When there is no auxiliary verb, **certainly** is placed immediately before the main verb: 'She certainly likes you.' However, when the main verb is **be**, **certainly** is usually placed immediately before or immediately after it.

chair   × During the flight she sat on the chair behind me.
   ✓ **During the flight she sat in the seat behind me.**

seat = a place for sitting, as found in a cinema, train, bus, etc.
chair = a movable seat for one person

chance 1   × The higher your qualifications, the better your chances to find a job.
✓ **The higher your qualifications, the better your chances of finding a job.**
chance/s of + v-ing

2   × I spent the whole morning looking for the ring but had no chance.
✓ **I spent the whole morning looking for the ring but had no luck.**
chance = the force that seems to make something happen or not happen: 'It was by sheer chance that I discovered he had been telling lies.'
luck = good fortune

cheap   × The wages in Taiwan are very cheap.
✓ **The wages in Taiwan are very low.**
Use **cheap** with goods.
Use **low** with wages, costs, payments, etc.

check 1   ✓ **AmE I paid for the radio by check.**
✓ **BrE I paid for the radio by cheque.**

2   ✓ **AmE Although he had invited me, he asked me to pay the check.**
✓ **BrE Although he had invited me, he asked me to pay the bill.**
In American English **check** means (1) 'a form instructing a bank to pay money to someone' (BrE **cheque**)
(2) 'a list of things bought and their price' (BrE **bill**).

cheerful   × The old couple are very cheerful in their new home.
✓ **The old couple are very happy in their new home.**
happy = feeling satisfied or contented: 'We're very happy with our new car.'
cheerful = tending to smile and laugh, or be in good spirits: 'Despite all her problems, she's always cheerful.'

cheque 1 × Would you please cheque whether the coat has been found?

✓ **Would you please check whether the coat has been found?**

cheque (noun) = a form instructing a bank to pay money to someone
check (verb) = look or enquire in order to discover something

2 See CHECK 1

child × Many childs are born every day.

✓ **Many children are born every day.**

Child is singular.
Children is plural.

children × Some of the childrens wanted to phone their parents.

✓ **Some of the children wanted to phone their parents.**

Child is singular.
Children is plural.

choose 1 × They choosed to stay at home.

✓ **They chose to stay at home.**

× We are very glad that you have choosen Stockholm for your visit.

✓ **We are very glad that you have chosen Stockholm for your visit.**

choose, choosing, chose, chosen

2 × Many women choose for children at an early age.

✓ **Many women choose to have children at an early age.**

choose (to do) something, NOT **for**

church   × Not so long ago nearly everybody used to go to the church.

✓ **Not so long ago nearly everybody used to go to church.**

Use **go to church** WITHOUT **the** when referring to church as an institution and not to one church in particular. Compare: 'the church on the hill'.

circulate   × On weekdays, cars are not allowed to circulate in the centre of the city.

✓ **On weekdays, cars are not allowed to go into/ enter the centre of the city.**

circulate = move around in a steady stream: 'A one-way system has been introduced to keep the traffic circulating.'

classic   × I prefer classic music to pop.

✓ **I prefer classical music to pop.**

classic = being among the best or most typical of its class; serving as a standard or model: 'The painting is a classic example of sixteenth-century Venetian art.'
classical music = the music of Mozart, Beethoven, etc.

clothing   × The women were selling second-hand clothings.

✓ **The women were selling second-hand clothing.**

Clothing is an uncountable noun. Note the more common alternative: 'The women were selling second-hand clothes.'

cloths   × I spent the morning unpacking my cloths.

✓ **I spent the morning unpacking my clothes.**

In British English **cloth** /klɒθ/ = (a piece of) material made of cotton, wool, etc.: 'I'm afraid I've spilled some milk. Have you got a cloth?'
clothes /kləʊðz/ (plural noun) = the things a person wears, such as trousers, sweaters, etc.

coat 1   × I must have left my coat in one of the drawers in the dressing table.
   ✓ **I must have left my jumper/pullover/cardigan in one of the drawers in the dressing table.**

A **coat** is an outer garment that is worn on top of other garments when you go outside.

2   See RAINCOAT

collaboration   × The police were grateful to the public for their collaboration.
   ✓ **The police were grateful to the public for their co-operation.**

Collaboration comes from the verb **collaborate** (= work in partnership with someone on the same task): 'The two writers have decided to collaborate on the biography.'
Co-operation comes from the verb **co-operate** (= be willing to help someone to achieve something; be helpful).

college   × After a year he decided to leave his college and get a job.
   ✓ **After a year he decided to leave college and get a job.**

Use **leave/go to college** WITHOUT a determiner when referring to college as an institution and not to one college in particular.

colour 1   × The belt has the same colour as the coat.
   ✓ **The belt is the same colour as the coat.**

Use **be** (NOT **have**) when describing the colour of something.

2   × I bought a blue colour shirt and a pair of socks.
   ✓ **I bought a blue shirt and a pair of socks.**
   × The handbag is a brown colour and is made of leather.
   ✓ **The handbag is brown and is made of leather.**

The name of a colour ('red/blue/green' etc.) is not usually used with the noun **colour**. Note, however, the exception ('red/blue/green' etc. **in colour**): 'The handbag is brown in colour.'

coloured   × The cardigan is pink-coloured and is made of wool.
✓ **The cardigan is pink and is made of wool.**
pink-coloured = not quite pink
When talking about colours, it is usual to say simply 'It is red/blue/green' etc. Adjectives like **pink-coloured** are quite rare. They are sometimes used when you are not sure of the exact colour.

come 1   × The little boy was afraid of his father and didn't want to come back home.
✓ **The little boy was afraid of his father and didn't want to go back home.**

Come is used for movement towards the place where the speaker is, was, or intends to be, or towards the person being talked about: 'Why have you come here?' 'Suddenly a tall woman came into his office.'
Go is used for movement in other directions.

2   × The students who are coming from Japan are hard-working.
✓ **The students who come from Japan are hard-working.**

When **come from** means 'have as a place of origin' or 'was born in', it is NEVER used in a progressive tense. However, when **come from** means 'travel from', the progressive forms can be used. Compare: 'She comes from Germany.' (= she was born in Germany) 'She is coming from Germany.' (= she is travelling from Germany)

committee   × The comittee meets once a month.
✓ **The committee meets once a month.**
committee (DOUBLE **m**, DOUBLE **t**)

common   × Nowadays it is common that women go out to work.
✓ **Nowadays it is common for women to go out to work.**

be common for someone to do something, NOT **that**

company   × I work for a construction company which have a lot of contracts in other countries.
√ **I work for a construction company which has a lot of contracts in other countries.**

Company (= firm or business) cannot be used with a plural verb when preceded by **a/an**.

compare   × The teachers will be able to visit our schools and compare our teaching methods to their own.
√ **The teachers will be able to visit our schools and compare our teaching methods with their own.**

compare to = describe (someone or something) as being similar to (someone or something else); liken: 'She compared the child to a noisy monkey.'
compare with = examine (someone or something) in order to discover similarities with or differences from (someone or something else): 'Having compared the new dictionary with the old one, she found the new one more helpful.'

complain   × For the first time in twenty years, I have to complain on one of your products.
√ **For the first time in twenty years, I have to complain about one of your products.**
× He called the waitress and started complaining over the service.
√ **He called the waitress and started complaining about the service.**

complain about someone or something, NOT **on** or **over**

complement   × He was complemented on doing a good job.
√ **He was complimented on doing a good job.**

compliment (WITH **lim**) someone; pay someone a **compliment** = express your praise or admiration
complement (WITH **lem**) something; be a **complement** to something = make it more complete and satisfying: 'The dry white wine complemented the meal perfectly.'

completely   See TIRED

comprehension × There is not enough comprehension between our two countries.
  ✓ **There is not enough understanding between our two countries.**

  Comprehension and **understanding** are often interchangeable when they refer to mental ability but NOT when **understanding** means 'feelings of sympathy or friendship'.

comprehensive × The teachers are very kind and comprehensive.
  ✓ **The teachers are very kind and understanding.**
  comprehensive = including everything or almost everything; all-inclusive: 'The witness provided a comprehensive account of the accident.'
  understanding = sympathetic

comprise × The Soviet Union comprises of fifteen union republics.
  ✓ **The Soviet Union comprises fifteen union republics.**
  × The Soviet Union is comprised of fifteen union republics.
  ✓ **The Soviet Union comprises fifteen union republics.**

  comprise something WITHOUT **of**
  Note the alternatives: 'The Soviet Union consists of/is made up of/is composed of fifteen union republics.'

concentrate × I am concentrated on both speaking and writing.
  ✓ **I am concentrating on both speaking and writing.**
  Compare: 'The orange juice is concentrated.' (= with little or no water added)

concern × As far as I concern, the cost of the repair is not my responsibility.
  ✓ **As far as I am concerned, the cost of the repair is not my responsibility.**
  as far as I am/he is etc. **concerned**, NOT **concern**

concerned   × The magazine is concerned about
motor-cycles.
√ **The magazine is concerned with motor-cycles.**
be concerned about something (of people) = be
anxious or worried about (something)
be concerned with something (of a book, programme,
etc.) = be about (a particular subject)

conclusion   × As a conclusion, I'd like to say that everyone
should be able to work if they want to.
√ **In conclusion, I'd like to say that everyone
should be able to work if they want to.**
In conclusion is a fixed phrase.

condition   × You should try to keep the car in a good
condition.
√ **You should try to keep the car in good
condition.**
in good/excellent/terrible condition WITHOUT **a**

consider   × We are considering to visit Switzerland next
year.
√ **We are considering visiting Switzerland next
year.**
consider + v-ing

consist 1   × The house was consisting of three bedrooms,
a kitchen, and a bathroom.
√ **The house consisted of three bedrooms, a
kitchen, and a bathroom.**
Consist of is NOT used in progressive tenses.

2   × The group was consisted of ten people.
√ **The group consisted of ten people.**
Consist of is used only in the active.
See also note at COMPRISE

consult   ✓ AmE At last we persuaded him to consult with his doctor.
✓ BrE At last we persuaded him to consult his doctor.

Consult with someone and consult someone are both acceptable in American English. However, only **consult someone** is possible in British English.

continual   × The canals join to form one continual waterway.
✓ **The canals join to form one continuous waterway.**
× A line of cars stretched continually down the motorway.
✓ **A line of cars stretched continuously down the motorway.**

A **continual** action happens repeatedly over a long period of time, and often refers to unpleasant things: 'That telephone has been ringing continually.'
A **continuous** action/performance/line is uninterrupted or without a break.

continuous   × I grew tired of his continuous moaning.
✓ **I grew tired of his continual moaning.**
× The meeting was continuously interrupted.
✓ **The meeting was continually interrupted.**

continuous = uninterrupted
continual = happening repeatedly over a long period of time

contribute   × Oxfam and Save the Children have contributed a lot of money for the relief work.
✓ **Oxfam and Save the Children have contributed a lot of money to the relief work.**

contribute (money etc.) to something, NOT for

control 1   × These people want to control over our lives.
✓ **These people want to control our lives.**
✓ **These people want control over our lives.**

control something (verb) BUT **control over** something (noun)

2 × Nobody wanted to control my luggage.

✓ **Nobody wanted to inspect my luggage.**

control = guide, regulate, or restrain: 'Who will control the aircraft if the pilot falls sick?' 'The police were unable to control the crowd.'
inspect = check or examine

controller × On the train the controller wanted to see my ticket.

✓ **On the train the inspector wanted to see my ticket.**

inspector = someone who checks or examines something, e.g. tickets on trains

convinced 1 × I'm extremely convinced that there will not be another war.

✓ **I'm absolutely/totally convinced that there will not be another war.**

See note at CERTAIN 1

2 × I'm convinced to have left my leather coat at the hotel.

✓ **I'm convinced (that) I left my leather coat at the hotel.**

convinced (+ **that**) + clause

cooker × The cooker puts too much salt in the food.

✓ **The cook/chef puts too much salt in the food.**

cooker = an apparatus for cooking food
cook/chef = a person who cooks

corner × I have written my address on the top right-hand corner.

✓ **I have written my address in the top right-hand corner.**

× We sat on the right-hand corner of the room, near the window.

✓ **We sat in the right-hand corner of the room, near the window.**

in the corner, NOT **on**

cost 1   ✗ It will cost to the church a great deal to repair the roof.
             ✓ **It will cost the church a great deal to repair the roof.**

             cost someone **a certain amount** WITHOUT **to**

2   ✗ The cassette recorder costed £200.
        ✓ **The cassette recorder cost £200.**
        cost, costing, cost, cost

3   ✗ I'll send you a cheque to cover the cost for the stamps.
        ✓ **I'll send you a cheque to cover the cost of the stamps.**
        the cost of something, NOT **for**

4   ✗ I will be happy to pay for the costs of the postage.
        ✓ **I will be happy to pay for the cost of the postage.**
        costs (plural) = expenses incurred in making or producing something: 'Our costs have doubled in the last five years as a result of the increase in oil prices.'

5   ✗ That shop was always empty because the costs were too high.
        ✓ **That shop was always empty because the prices were too high.**
        cost = the expense of doing something or having something done
        price = the amount of money asked for something which is for sale

6   ✗ They agreed to repair the damage free of cost.
        ✓ **They agreed to repair the damage free of charge.**
        charge = a fee that is demanded for a service
        Free of charge is a fixed phrase which is often used when talking about services.

7   ✗ In London the cost of life is very expensive.
        ✓ **In London the cost of living is very expensive.**
        the cost of living, NOT **life**

could 1 × By reading quickly, I could finish the book before the library closed.

✓ **By reading quickly, I was able to finish the book before the library closed.**

When talking about the successful performance of a difficult task, use **be able to**, NOT **could**.

2 × Could you to tell me how long the journey will take?

✓ **Could you tell me how long the journey will take?**

can/could + infinitive WITHOUT **to**

couple 1 × She said it wouldn't take more than couple of minutes.

✓ **She said it wouldn't take more than a couple of minutes.**

A couple of is a fixed phrase in British English.

2 × The couple was sitting just behind me.

✓ **The couple were sitting just behind me.**

A **couple** (such as a husband and wife) is used with a plural verb (unless identified as one of a number of couples).

Compare: 'And tonight's winning couple is George and Dorothy Lightfoot.'

course 1 × I am taking an intermediate course of English.

✓ **I am taking an intermediate course in English.**

take a course in something, NOT **of**

2 ✓ **AmE The boys and girls in my English course come from all over the world.**

✓ **BrE The boys and girls on my English course come from all over the world.**

crash × There was a terrible noise as the car and truck crashed each other.

✓ **There was a terrible noise as the car and truck crashed into each other.**

× The motorcyclist couldn't stop and crashed
with the truck.
√ **The motorcyclist couldn't stop and crashed
into the truck.**

crash into something, NOT **(with)** something

crime   × We need to understand why people do these
crimes.
√ **We need to understand why people commit
these crimes.**
× Somehow we must stop people from making
these crimes.
√ **Somehow we must stop people from committing
these crimes.**

commit a crime, NOT **do** or **make**

criticism   × The government can hardly do anything
without raising criticism.
√ **The government can hardly do anything
without attracting criticism.**

attract criticism, NOT **raise**

cry   × Mrs Sarto cryed the whole trip and I had to
keep holding her hand until we arrived in Rio.
√ **Mrs Sarto cried the whole trip and I had to
keep holding her hand until we arrived in Rio.**

cry, crying, cried, cried

cup   × We enjoyed a cup of wine with our meal.
√ **We enjoyed a glass of wine with our meal.**

a cup of tea/coffee BUT **a glass of** wine/beer/whisky

curiosity   × Several passers-by stopped to look at the
strange bicycle from curiosity.
√ **Several passers-by stopped to look at the
strange bicycle out of curiosity.**

do something **out of curiosity**, NOT **from**

custom   × He has a custom of coughing before he speaks.
√ **He has a habit of coughing before he speaks.**
Custom is used of the established practices of a society or very large group: 'In Hong Kong I learned a lot about Chinese customs.'
Habit is used of an individual.

damage   × The fire caused a lot of damages.
√ **The fire caused a lot of damage.**
× The car crashed into a tree and suffered a severe damage.
√ **The car crashed into a tree and suffered severe damage.**
Damage is an uncountable noun.

dare 1   × 'How dare you to come in without knocking!' he shouted.
√ **'How dare you come in without knocking!' he shouted.**
how dare you/they, etc. + infinitive WITHOUT **to**

2   × His mother thinks that somebody must have dared him steal the bicycle.
√ **His mother thinks that somebody must have dared him to steal the bicycle.**
dare someone **to** do something = to challenge

daren't   × I daren't to ask her for any more money.
√ **I daren't ask her for any more money.**
daren't/wouldn't dare + infinitive WITHOUT **to**

dark   × Soon it began to become dark and it was time to go back home.
√ **Soon it began to get dark and it was time to go back home.**
get dark, NOT **become**

day 1   × The bus arrived in Luxor the following day
          morning.
          ✓ **The bus arrived in Luxor (on) the following
          morning.**
          Compare: 'the following day', 'the following morning'
          WITHOUT **day**

2   × We were all very tired at the last day of our
          journey.
          ✓ **We were all very tired on the last day of our
          journey.**
          × I made an appointment for the following
          Friday. In that day I got up early so as to have
          plenty of time.
          ✓ **I made an appointment for the following
          Friday. On that day I got up early so as to
          have plenty of time.**
          on + a day or date (NOT **at** or **in**): 'on Tuesday', 'on the
          following day', 'on the third day', 'on 19th March', etc.

3   See MONTH

4   See IN

5   See OF 2

days   × Unemployment is a major problem in these
          days.
          ✓ **Unemployment is a major problem these days.**
          'These days' is used WITHOUT **in** or any other
          preposition. Note however: 'In those days cigarettes
          were much cheaper.'

dead 1   × One of the passengers was dead in the
          accident.
          ✓ **One of the passengers died in the accident.**
          Dead is an adjective: 'dead soldiers', 'Is the plant
          dead?'
          Died is the past tense and past participle of **die**.

2 × Although it was dead cold, she went out without a coat.

✓ **Although it was extremely cold, she went out without a coat.**

Dead is used to intensify an adjective only in informal speech.

deal × We have been receiving a great deal of complaints.

✓ **We have been receiving a great number of complaints.**

A great deal of is ALWAYS followed by an uncountable noun: 'a great deal of money/time/meat' etc.

deal in × The play deals in the struggle of a married couple to live their own lives.

✓ **The play deals with the struggle of a married couple to live their own lives.**

deal in = buy and sell: 'The company deals in textiles.'
deal with = be about

defect × He told me that any goods that were defect could be returned for a refund.

✓ **He told me that any goods that were defective could be returned for a refund.**

Defect is a noun.
Defective is an adjective.

definitely See SURELY 1

delay × Because of the bad weather, the match was delayed for a week.

✓ **Because of the bad weather, the match was postponed for a week.**

delay = cause to arrive, leave, or happen, at a time that is later than the one arranged: 'The departure of the flight was briefly delayed.'
postpone = move to a later time or date

delighted   × When they knew that they had won, they were very delighted.
✓ **When they knew that they had won, they were absolutely delighted.**
See note at CERTAIN 1

delightful   × Her parents were delightful that she had won and ran over to kiss her.
✓ **Her parents were delighted that she had won and ran over to kiss her.**
delightful = causing delight: 'a delightful party'
delighted = feeling delight

demand   × The union demanded for more money.
✓ **The union demanded more money.**
demand something WITHOUT **for**

demonstration   × Many demonstrations have been made in recent years in protest against the level of pollution.
✓ **Many demonstrations have been held in recent years in protest against the level of pollution.**
hold/stage a demonstration NOT **make**

deny 1   × She asked him if he had seen a little boy but he denied.
✓ **She asked him if he had seen a little boy but he said he hadn't.**
deny an accusation or claim, NOT a question

2   × Mary wanted Arthur to help her but he denied.
✓ **Mary wanted Arthur to help her but he refused.**
deny (an accusation etc.) = declare something to be untrue
refuse (to do something) = not agree to do something
Compare: 'He denied that he had refused to help her.'

3   × She accused him of cheating but he denied.
✓ **She accused him of cheating but he denied it.**
Deny is a transitive verb: 'He denied it.' 'He denied that he had.'

depend 1 × Whether or not she passes is depending upon how hard she works.
√ **Whether or not she passes depends upon how hard she works.**

Depend (on/upon) (= may or may not happen according to) is rarely used in progressive tenses.

2 × The number of hours he worked was depend on the number of absentees.
√ **The number of hours he worked depended on the number of absentees.**

Depend (on) is a verb, NOT an adjective.

dependant × Most wives don't like being dependant on their husbands.
√ **Most wives don't like being dependent on their husbands.**

In British English **dependant** (WITH **ant**) is a noun: 'Do you have any other dependants, apart from your widowed mother?'
Dependent (WITH **ent**) is an adjective.

describe × I want to describe you some of the difficulties.
√ **I want to describe to you some of the difficulties.**

With **describe**, the preposition **to** must ALWAYS be used before an indirect object.

description × I'll send you some English food and a description on how to prepare it.
√ **I'll send you some English food and a description of how to prepare it.**

a description of someone or something, NOT **on**

desire × They came to Hong Kong because they desired for a higher standard of living.
√ **They came to Hong Kong because they desired a higher standard of living.**

desire something (verb) BUT **a desire for** something (noun)
Compare: 'They came to Hong Kong because of their desire for a higher standard of living.'

desperate × It was almost midnight and his parents were getting very desperate.
✓ **It was almost midnight and his parents were getting desperate.**
See note at CERTAIN 1

despite 1 × Despite the train was empty, he came and sat in front of me.
✓ **Despite the train being empty, he came and sat in front of me.**

Despite is a preposition (NOT a conjunction) and cannot introduce a clause which contains a finite verb. Note the alternative: 'Although the train was empty, he came and sat In front of me.'

2 × Despite of my qualifications, I couldn't get a job.
✓ **Despite my qualifications, I couldn't get a job.**

despite something WITHOUT **of**
Note the alternative: '**In spite of** my qualifications, I couldn't get a job.'

destroy × This unpleasant man with his endless complaints destroyed my journey.
✓ **This unpleasant man with his endless complaints ruined/spoilt my journey.**

To express the meaning 'remove the pleasure or enjoyment from', use **ruin** or **spoil**, NOT **destroy**.

detail × Please contact Mrs Oda for further detail.
✓ **Please contact Mrs Oda for further details.**

further information (uncountable) BUT **further details** (countable)
Note, however, the fixed phrase **in detail**: 'Will you explain in detail what happened?'

deter × How can we deter our leaders to use the atomic bomb?
✓ **How can we deter our leaders from using the atomic bomb?**

deter someone **from** + v-ing

dialled   ✓ AmE I hurried to the telephone and dialed the police.
✓ BrE I hurried to the telephone and dialled the police.

Note the spelling of **dialed** (ONLY ONE l) in American English and **dialled** (DOUBLE l) in British English.

die   × People say she died with pneumonia.
✓ **People say she died of pneumonia.**

die of a disease, NOT **with**

differ   × My own beliefs differ to those of the church in several ways.
✓ **My own beliefs differ from those of the church in several ways.**

differ from, NOT **to**

difference   × You have to make a difference between women who have to work and women who choose to work.
✓ **You have to make a distinction between women who have to work and women who choose to work.**

make **a distinction** between A and B = not regard or treat A and B in the same way

different 1   × My new school was very different than the old one.
✓ **My new school was very different from/to the old one.**

Different than is much less common in British English than **different from/to**. It is not usually used except to avoid awkwardness or repetition.

2   × In Argentina, Christmas celebrations are completely different as the ones in England.
✓ **In Argentina, Christmas celebrations are completely different from/to the ones in England.**

A is **different from/to** B, NOT **as**.
Note that careful speakers prefer **from**.

3 × Opinions are more different than ever.
✓ **Opinions differ more than ever.**

We say that people or things **differ** when we are talking about differences within a group. Compare: 'I asked the class and opinions differed.' (= there were many different opinions)
'I asked the class again and opinions were different this time.' (= different from the first time)

difficulty × Initially I had a difficulty to understand people.
✓ **Initially I had difficulty in understanding people.**

have difficulty/difficulties in + v-ing, NOT **a difficulty**

dining room × She thinks she left her key in the dinning room.
✓ **She thinks she left her key in the dining room.**

dining room (ONLY ONE **n**)

dinner × They decided to take dinner in a café.
✓ **They decided to have dinner in a café.**

have dinner, NOT **take**

dirty × She had fallen over in the rain and her clothes were completely dirty.
✓ **She had fallen over in the rain and her clothes were very dirty.**

See note at TIRED

disagree 1 × Nowadays most people disagree to work very long hours.
✓ **Nowadays most people refuse to work very long hours.**

disagree (with) ≠ not have the same opinion/s; quarrel: 'I tend to disagree with what you say.' 'She disagreed with him about how much they should spend.'
refuse = not do something because you are unwilling to do it

2 × She disagreed totally to what I said.
✓ **She disagreed totally with what I said.**

disagree with someone or something, NOT **to**

disappear × My money was missing and the man had disapeared.
✓ **My money was missing and the man had disappeared.**

disappear (ONLY ONE **s**, DOUBLE **p**)

disappeared × When I got home I realized that one of my suitcases was disappeared.
✓ **When I got home I realized that one of my suitcases had disappeared.**

Disappeared is NOT used as an adjective. Note the alternative: 'When I got home I realized that one of my suitcases was missing.'

disappointed × I felt very disapointed when the tape recorder wouldn't work.
✓ **I felt very disappointed when the tape recorder wouldn't work.**

disappointed (ONLY ONE **s**, DOUBLE **p**)

discourage × Of course we have to discourage people to commit crimes.
✓ **Of course we have to discourage people from committing crimes.**

encourage someone **to do** something BUT **discourage** someone **from doing** something

discuss 1 × Some people were discussing; some listening to the radio.
✓ **Some people were talking; some listening to the radio.**
× We're pleased that you have agreed to discuss with us.
✓ **We're pleased that you have agreed to discuss the matter with us.**

Discuss is a transitive verb.

2 × We spent almost two hours discussing about the course.
✓ **We spent almost two hours discussing the course.**

discuss something BUT **(have) a discussion about** something

discussion   × He ran away from home after a discussion
with his father.
√ **He ran away from home after an argument
with his father.**

discussion = a talk about something, especially one
which allows different points of view to be expressed:
'After further discussion, the government has decided
to reject the American offer.'
argument = a quarrel or disagreement

disease   See BIG 2

dispose   × Jumble sales provide people with a good
opportunity to dispose all their unwanted
goods.
√ **Jumble sales provide people with a good
opportunity to dispose of all their unwanted
goods.**

dispose of something = get rid of

distance   × From the distance we could hear a fire engine.
√ **In the distance we could hear a fire engine.**

in the distance, NOT **from**

distinctive   × The audience showed a distinctive lack of
enthusiasm.
√ **The audience showed a distinct lack of
enthusiasm.**

distinctive = clearly marking a person or thing as
different from others; characteristic: 'It was easy to
identify the German wine because of its distinctive
taste.'
distinct = clearly seen, heard, or sensed; noticeable

divide   × For lunch and dinner we were divided in
groups of ten.
√ **For lunch and dinner we were divided into
groups of ten.**

divide something **into** (sections), NOT **in**

do 1 × 'Do you know who did write the poem?' she
asked.
√ **'Do you know who wrote the poem?' she
asked.**

Do not use the auxiliary verb **do** in a dependent **wh**-
clause unless the clause is negative or the intention is
to provide emphasis: 'We know it wasn't Monet or
Manet but do you know who did paint that picture?'

2 × What can we do against the problem?
√ **What can we do about the problem?**
do something **about** something, NOT **against**

3 See CRIME, EFFORT 2, FLIGHT, JOURNEY, MISTAKE 2,
PROGRESS, VISIT

doubt 1 × There is no doubt whether the government has
made the right decision.
√ **There is no doubt that the government has
made the right decision.**
no doubt that, NOT **if** or **whether**
Compare: 'There is no doubt that she will pass.' 'There
is some doubt as to whether she will pass.'

2 × Without doubt you're tired after your journey.
√ **No doubt you're tired after your journey.**
Without doubt is used to express certainty.
No doubt is used to mean 'I think' or 'I suppose'.

downstairs × I was in a hurry and I forgot to bring the coat
to downstairs with me.
√ **I was in a hurry and I forgot to bring the coat
downstairs with me.**
Do not use **to** or any other preposition before
downstairs/upstairs.

dozen See HUNDRED 2

dream 1 × I have always dreamed to visit America.
√ **I have always dreamed of visiting America.**
dream of + v-ing

2   × He has got everything he ever dreamed for.
       √ **He has got everything he ever dreamed of.**
       dream of something, NOT **for**

3   × I saw a strange dream last night.
       √ **I had a strange dream last night.**
       √ **I dreamed/dreamt a strange dream last night.**
       have a dream OR **dream a dream**
       In the case of **dream a dream**, the noun **dream** is
       usually modified: 'I dreamt the most
       unusual/peculiar/fascinating dream last night.'

dress   × Everybody arrived dressed with their smartest
            clothes.
          √ **Everybody arrived dressed in their smartest
            clothes.**
          (be) dressed in, NOT **with**

dress up   × Even though they don't have much money,
              their children are always dressed up very
              nicely.
            √ **Even though they don't have much money,
              their children are always dressed very nicely.**
            dress up = (1) put on fancy dress: 'Henry and Alice
            went to the party dressed up as a prince and
            princess.'
            (2) put on formal or smart clothes: 'Helen has invited
            us to dinner but says we shouldn't bother to dress up.'

drink   × He drunk too much and had lots of accidents.
           √ **He drank too much and had lots of accidents.**
           drink, drinking, drank, drunk

drunken   × That man who kept falling over was obviously
             drunken.
           √ **That man who kept falling over was obviously
             drunk.**
           drunken (attributive only) = caused by drinking too
           much alcohol: 'drunken driving', 'a drunken brawl'
           drunk = having drunk too much alcohol

dull   × This knife is too dull to cut the bread.
✓ **This knife is too blunt to cut the bread.**
dull = not bright: 'If you think it's too dull in here, I'll change the light bulb for a more powerful one.'
blunt = not sharp

during 1   × It is difficult to concentrate during such a long time.
✓ **It is difficult to concentrate for such a long time.**
× The little boy walked through the forest during hours without seeing anybody.
✓ **The little boy walked through the forest for hours without seeing anybody.**
During answers the question 'when?'
For answers the question 'how long?'

2   × During waiting for the ship to leave, I met an old friend of mine.
✓ **While waiting for the ship to leave, I met an old friend of mine.**
During must be followed by a noun, noun phrase, or pronoun. Compare: 'during the holiday' and 'while I was on holiday'

each   × Each of us did not have an umbrella.
✓ **None/Neither of us had an umbrella.**
Use **none/neither** + affirmative verb, NOT **each** + negative verb.

each other   × I hope that you will both write to each others.
✓ **I hope that you will both write to each other.**
Each other has no plural form.

easily   See BE

East   See NORTH

easy × Life is more easier than it used to be.
✓ **Life is easier than it used to be.**

Two-syllable adjectives ending in **-y** form their comparatives and superlatives with **-er** and **-est** (NOT with **more** and **most**): 'easy, easier, easiest', 'pretty, prettier, prettiest'.

economical × First we need to improve our economical situation.
✓ **First we need to improve our economic situation.**

economic = concerned with trade, industry, economics; economical
economical = not wasteful; money-saving: 'A large packet is more economical.'

economics × The Brazilian economics seem to be improving.
✓ **The Brazilian economy seems to be improving.**

economics = (1) the science of the production, distribution, and use of goods and services: 'students of economics'
(2) the financial aspects of something: 'the economics of dairy farming'
economy = the system by which a country produces or tries to produce wealth

economies × In his bag he packed his favourite toys and his piggy bank with all his economies.
✓ **In his bag he packed his favourite toys and his piggy bank with all his savings.**

economy = a way of saving money: 'The first economy introduced by the government involved the reduction of fuel consumption.'
savings = money which has been saved, usually by a person or family

edit × I have never seen the magazine before; I think it's only just been edited.
√ **I have never seen the magazine before; I think it's only just been published.**

publish = produce and distribute (a book, newspaper, etc.) for sale to the public
edit = correct or revise a manuscript in preparation for printing

effect 1 × I thought that the long illness would effect my chances of passing the exam.
√ **I thought that the long illness would affect my chances of passing the exam.**

effect = bring about; accomplish: 'The new president effected several major changes.'
affect = have an effect (on something)

2 × They think that stricter punishments will have the effect to reduce the amount of crime.
√ **They think that stricter punishments will have the effect of reducing the amount of crime.**

have/produce the effect + **of** + v-ing

efficient × The medicine proved very efficient.
√ **The medicine proved very effective.**

efficient = working quickly and without waste: 'The more efficient the engine, the less petrol it uses.'
effective = having the desired effect

effort 1 × The authorities have put a lot of efforts into making the streets cleaner.
√ **The authorities have put a lot of effort into making the streets cleaner.**

effort (countable) = a determined attempt: 'Despite all his efforts, the prisoner failed to escape.'
effort (uncountable) = the use of strength over a period of time; hard work: 'Digging the tunnel demanded a great deal of effort.'

2   × Little effort has been done to solve the
       problem.
       ✓ **Little effort has been made to solve the
       problem.**
       make an effort, NOT **do**

either   × I shall either go home to Brazil or my family
            will come to England.
            ✓ **Either I shall go home to Brazil or my family
            will come to England.**

The position of **either** should be the same as the
position of **or** (i.e. immediately before a subject,
immediately before a main verb, immediately after a
verb, etc.): 'Either stay or go.' 'You should either stay
or go.' 'You should stay either here or at home.' 'You
should stay with either me or your uncle.'

elder 1   × My sister is just two years elder than me.
             ✓ **My sister is just two years older than me.**

Elder cannot be followed by **than.** Nor can it come
after 'two years/six months' etc. It is mainly used
either as an attributive adjective ('my elder sister') or
as a pronoun ('Which of the two sisters is the elder?')

2   × The young man was unhurt but the elder one
       was taken to hospital in an ambulance.
       ✓ **The young man was unhurt but the older one
       was taken to hospital in an ambulance.**

Elder is used only of family relations: 'her elder
brother'.

elderly   × Every Saturday he went to the cinema with his
             elderly brother.
             ✓ **Every Saturday he went to the cinema with his
             elder brother.**

elderly = approaching old age: 'an elderly man with
white hair and a stick'
elder (of brothers, daughters, etc.) = older

elect   × Some people elect marriage partners who are
totally unsuitable.
✓ **Some people choose/select/pick marriage
partners who are totally unsuitable.**
elect = choose (someone) by voting for them: 'The
committee has elected a new chairman.'

electric 1 × My father's company imports electric goods.
✓ **My father's company imports electrical goods.**
Use **electric** when talking about specific things
powered by electricity ('an electric fire') and **electrical**
when talking about the general class of things
('electrical equipment').

2   × My brother is an electric engineer.
✓ **My brother is an electrical engineer.**
electric = produced by, worked by, or charged with
electricity: 'an electric shock', 'an electric light', 'an
electric fence'
electrical = related to (the subject of) electricity

else   × Parents who go out to work have to think
about something else than just children.
✓ **Parents who go out to work have to think
about something other than just children.**
Something else cannot be followed by **than**. Compare:
'I'm tired of this conversation; let's talk about
something else.'

embark   × My friend and I had just embarked the plane
and were looking for our seats.
✓ **My friend and I had just boarded the plane
and were looking for our seats.**
embark (intransitive) = board a ship: 'An hour after
embarking, we set sail.'
board a plane/train/ship

embarrass × The question obviously embarassed him.
✓ **The question obviously embarrassed him.**
embarrass (DOUBLE **r**, DOUBLE **s**)

embarrassed   × He was a bit embarrassed of what he had
                       said.
                    √ **He was a bit embarrassed by what he had
                       said.**
                    (be) embarrassed by something, NOT **of**

end 1   × In the end, I should like to wish you all a very
                interesting and enjoyable stay.
             √ **Finally, I should like to wish you all a very
                interesting and enjoyable stay.**
             in the end = the final outcome was that: 'We tried lots
             of different medicines but they didn't do any good. In
             the end we had to take her to hospital.'
             finally = to conclude

2   × Since nobody would lend me the money, I
            ended asking my father for it.
         √ **Since nobody would lend me the money, I
            ended up asking my father for it.**
         × Nowadays very few criminals end in jail.
         √ **Nowadays very few criminals end up in jail.**
         end = finish or cause (something) to finish: 'The
         lessons usually end at five o'clock but some teachers
         end their lessons early.'
         end up = (1) be forced to do something (when
         everything else has failed): 'For months she refused to
         pay us any rent, so we ended up taking her to court.'
         (2) eventually find yourself in a particular place or
         condition: 'If you don't stop smoking, you'll end up in
         hospital.'

energetic   × Our main energetic source is nuclear power.
                 √ **Our main energy source is nuclear power.**
                 energetic = having energy; active: 'Does anyone feel
                 energetic enough to go for another swim?'
                 energy = power

engage   × My husband gave me the coat when we
                 engaged (to be married).
              √ **My husband gave me the coat when we
                 got engaged (to be married).**
              get/become engaged
              With this meaning **engage** is NOT used as a verb.

engaged × Why did you get engaged with him if you don't want to marry him?
✓ **Why did you get engaged to him if you don't want to marry him?**
get/become **engaged to** someone, NOT **with**

English × Our teacher is a typical English.
✓ **Our teacher is a typical Englishwoman.**
the English (= English people) but NEVER **an English**

enjoy 1 × I enjoy to speak foreign languages.
✓ **I enjoy speaking foreign languages.**
enjoy + v-ing

2 × We were working very hard but we were enjoying.
✓ **We were working very hard but we were enjoying ourselves.**
enjoy something; **enjoy** yourself
Enjoy is transitive

3 × I really enjoy my stay in London.
✓ **I am really enjoying my stay in London.**
The present progressive tense is used because the emphasis is on the present moment. Compare: 'I enjoy a book at bedtime and I'm really enjoying this one.'

enough 1 × The time isn't enough for us to catch the next train.
✓ **There isn't enough time for us to catch the next train.**
Enough is not usually used predicatively except when the subject is **there**, **it**, or a specific number or amount. Compare: 'There is enough for everyone.' 'Two pints isn't enough for all of us.'

2 × As they were busy, they did not have time enough to talk to her.
✓ **As they were busy, they did not have enough time to talk to her.**
enough + noun + to-v

3   × Olga was not enough old to drive a car at that time.
✓ **Olga was not old enough to drive a car at that time.**
adjective/adverb + **enough** + to-v

4   × We forgot to take enough of food with us.
✓ **We forgot to take enough food with us.**
enough (determiner) + noun WITHOUT **of**

5   × Another advantage is that flying is cheap enough.
✓ **Another advantage is that flying is fairly/quite cheap.**
Enough is not used to mean 'fairly' or 'quite' except in very informal speech. '

enquire   × I'm writing to you to enquire for a jacket that I left at your hotel last week.
✓ **I'm writing to you to enquire about a jacket that I left at your hotel last week.**
enquire about something, NOT **for**
Note that **enquire** may also be spelt **inquire**.

enter 1   × A strange woman entered into the room and closed the window.
✓ **A strange woman entered the room and closed the window.**
enter a room, building, etc. WITHOUT **into**

2   × I entered the train in Oslo.
✓ **I boarded the train in Oslo.**
✓ **I got on the train in Oslo.**
board/get on a train/plane/ship

entertainment   × We spend our holidays there because there is always a lot of entertainments for the children.
✓ **We spend our holidays there because there is always a lot of entertainment for the children.**
Entertainment (= all the various things that provide amusement) is an uncountable noun.

equally   × In my opinion the old wooden rackets are equally as good as the new steel ones.
√ **In my opinion the old wooden rackets are (just) as good as the new steel ones.**
Equally cannot be placed before **as ... as**.

equipment 1   × They were not satisfied with the new equipments.
√ **They were not satisfied with the new equipment.**
Equipment is an uncountable noun.

2   × It's a useful equipment and I intend to have it repaired.
√ **It's a useful piece of equipment and I intend to have it repaired.**
a piece of equipment

error   × I dialled the wrong number by error.
√ **I dialled the wrong number by mistake.**
by mistake BUT **in error**
Note that **by mistake** is the more common expression.

especially   × In the south of Germany there is a different mentality. Especially the Bavarians are very lively and cheerful.
√ **In the south of Germany there is a different mentality. The Bavarians especially are very lively and cheerful.**
× Looking after children can be very tiring. Especially young children need a lot of attention.
√ **Looking after children can be very tiring. Young children especially need a lot of attention.**
When the focus of **especially** is the subject of a sentence, **especially** is usually placed immediately after the subject.

European   × His grandfather built the first european dam in Siberia.
✓ **His grandfather built the first European dam in Siberia.**

An adjective derived directly from a proper noun also starts with a capital letter: 'Europe—European', 'Sweden—Swedish', etc.

even 1   × Some people think a mother should stay at home during the first year, even she has someone who could look after the child.
✓ **Some people think a mother should stay at home during the first year, even if she has someone who could look after the child.**

Even is an adverb, NOT a conjunction.
even + **if/though/when** + clause

2   × Even though I paid her for the room, but I knew she would prefer to live alone.
✓ **Even though I paid her for the room, I knew she would prefer to live alone.**

When the subordinate clause begins with **even though**, the main clause cannot begin with **but** or **yet**.

3   × Many people think that it even snows in Norway in the summer.
✓ **Many people think that it snows in Norway even in the summer.**

When there is a danger of confusion, put **even** immediately before the word or phrase that it qualifies.

4   × In the future it even might be possible to work only thirty-five hours a week.
✓ **In the future it might even be possible to work only thirty-five hours a week.**

When the verb has more than one part, **even** is usually placed immediately after the (first) auxiliary.

5   See ALTHOUGH 3

evening   See AFTERNOON

ever 1 × He has ever been my hero.
      √ **He has always been my hero.**

      ever = at any time: 'Have you ever been to Paris?' 'If you ever do that again, I'll be very annoyed.'
      always = from the very beginning until now; continuously/at all times

    2 × She was the most unpleasant person that I had ever met before.
      √ **She was the most unpleasant person that I had ever met.**

      ever (used with a verb in the past perfect tense) = at any time before then

    3 × While a child is very young, one of the parents should stay at home if ever possible.
      √ **While a child is very young, one of the parents should stay at home if at all possible.**

      ever = at any time
      at all = (1) at any time: 'Have you been to Germany at all?'
      (2) in any way; to any degree: 'If at all unsure, you should ask for advice.'

every 1 × I go to the library everyday.
      √ **I go to the library every day.**
      Everyday (one word) is an adjective: 'an everyday event'.

    2 × The shop sells every thing, from toothbrushes to radios.
      √ **The shop sells everything, from toothbrushes to radios.**
      × Every thing went according to plan.
      √ **Everything went according to plan.**
      Every thing (two words) may be used only when the things are considered as separate items. Compare: 'Everything looked new but every (single) thing I bought turned out to be second-hand.'

    3 × Every one was tired of listening to her voice.
      √ **Everyone was tired of listening to her voice.**
      See note at EVERYONE 1

4   × There is a park nearby where the sun shines
    every time.
    ✓ **There is a park nearby where the sun shines
    all the time.**

every = each
all = the whole of
Compare: 'On holiday it rained every day and it was
cold all the time.'

5   × I have to visit the hospital every six week.
    ✓ **I have to visit the hospital every six weeks.**
    'every day', 'every week' BUT 'every two days', 'every
    six weeks'

6   × I think every job have its good points.
    ✓ **I think every job has its good points.**
    Every is followed by the singular form of a countable
    noun and a singular verb. Compare: 'All jobs have
    their good points.'

everybody   × Everybody have to work.
    ✓ **Everybody has to work.**
    Everybody and **everyone** are used with a singular
    verb.

everyday   See EVERY 1

everyone 1   × There are amusements and places of interest
    for everyone of you.
    ✓ **There are amusements and places of interest
    for every one of you.**

everyone = everybody
every one = each single one (of a group or number)
Compare: 'Everyone liked her children because every
one of them was well-behaved.'

2   × There are no other restaurants so everyone
    have to go to the canteen.
    ✓ **There are no other restaurants so everyone
    has to go to the canteen.**
    Everyone and **everybody** are used with a singular
    verb.

everything	× In London everything are more expensive than in Rio.
	√ **In London everything is more expensive than in Rio.**
	Everything is used with a singular verb.
everywhere	× It's a really beautiful park; there are flowers in everywhere.
	√ **It's a really beautiful park; there are flowers everywhere.**
	Prepositions are NOT used before **everywhere** if there is no idea of movement. Compare: 'Congratulations poured in from everywhere.'
evidence	× Is there any evidences that ghosts exist?
	√ **Is there any evidence that ghosts exist?**
	Evidence is an uncountable noun. Note also: 'a piece/pieces of evidence'
examination	See PASS 4
example	× Each situation is different. By example, a man with a rich wife doesn't have to work.
	√ **Each situation is different. For example, a man with a rich wife doesn't have to work.**
	for example, NOT **by**
except 1	× The old lady never spoke to anyone except someone came to visit her.
	√ **The old lady never spoke to anyone unless someone came to visit her.**
	√ **The old lady never spoke to anyone except when someone came to visit her.**
	Except is a preposition (NOT a conjunction) and cannot introduce a clause containing a finite verb.
2	× She was willing to do anything except to tell me her name.
	√ **She was willing to do anything except tell me her name.**
	except + infinitive WITHOUT **to**

3   × Except smoke and traffic fumes, there are several other types of pollution.
✓ **Besides/In addition to smoke and traffic fumes, there are several other types of pollution.**
except (preposition) = not including; but not: 'She eats everything except fish.'

4   × Some people are unable to except criticism.
✓ **Some people are unable to accept criticism.**
accept (= take or receive willingly), NOT **except**

exception   × Every major city keeps changing and Lisbon is not an exception.
✓ **Every major city keeps changing and Lisbon is no exception.**
Note the phrase: **be no exception** (to something).

exchange   × Would it be possible to exchange this cassette recorder with a new one?
✓ **Would it be possible to exchange this cassette recorder for a new one?**
exchange something **for** something, NOT **with**

excited 1   × Although he was scared, he was excited to sit in a police car for the first time in his life.
✓ **Although he was scared, he was excited about sitting in a police car for the first time in his life.**
excited about + v-ing

2   × I felt very excited with the idea of having my own car.
✓ **I felt very excited about the idea of having my own car.**
excited about something, NOT **with**

excitement   × After all the excitements the children were tired.
✓ **After all the excitement the children were tired.**
Excitement is an uncountable noun.

exciting × It is wonderful to be in London at last. I feel
so exciting.
✓ **It is wonderful to be in London at last. I feel
so excited.**

'They are exciting.' = They excite people.
'They are excited.' = Someone/something excites
them.
Compare: 'an exciting film' and 'an excited audience'.

excuse 1 × When he got back home he excused himself
and promised that he would never run away
again.
✓ **When he got back home he apologized and
promised that he would never run away again.**

excuse yourself = give a reason for having to leave or
be absent: 'She excused herself from the meeting,
saying that she was not feeling well.'
apologize = say you are sorry for (doing) something

2 × He was sorry that he had lied to her and
asked her to excuse him.
✓ **He was sorry that he had lied to her and
asked her to forgive him.**

Excuse is used only for minor faults and offences: 'I
hope you'll excuse my untidy handwriting. I am trying
to write this letter on a train.'
Forgive is used for all faults and offences, both minor
and major.

exhausting × I had been working hard all day and felt really
exhausting.
✓ **I had been working hard all day and felt really
exhausted.**

'The journey was exhausting.' = The journey made
them feel very tired.
'They were exhausted.' = They felt very tired.

exhaustive × An exhausting investigation finally revealed
the cause of the accident.
✓ **An exhaustive investigation finally revealed
the cause of the accident.**

exhausting = causing tiredness: 'Pushing the car uphill
was exhausting.'
exhaustive = thorough; very careful

exist × The problem of hunger has been existing for centuries.

√ **The problem of hunger has existed for centuries.**

When its meaning is 'be real or be in existence', **exist** is NOT used in progressive tenses.

expect 1 × After a few minutes he stopped speaking and expected their reaction.

√ **After a few minutes he stopped speaking and waited for their reaction.**

× She was standing by the reception desk, expecting a taxi.

√ **She was standing by the reception desk, waiting for a taxi.**

expect = consider (something) likely: 'I expect they'll arrive late as usual.'

wait for = stay in a place or remain inactive until something (that you have been expecting) happens

2 × In London there were more foreigners than I was expecting for.

√ **In London there were more foreigners than I was expecting.**

expect something WITHOUT **for**

experience 1 × I made my first teaching experience in Scotland.

√ **I had my first teaching experience in Scotland.**

have an experience, NOT **make**

2 × A lot of people think it is cruel to do experiences on animals.

√ **A lot of people think it is cruel to do experiments on animals.**

experience = any event that affects or makes an impression on a person: 'He found flying a wonderful experience.'

experiment = a test done in order to discover something, especially by a scientist

explain   × Your teachers will explain you where you are
            going to stay.
            √ **Your teachers will explain to you where you
            are going to stay.**
            explain something **to** someone

explode   × The hijackers threatened to explode the plane.
            √ **The hijackers threatened to blow up the plane.**
            People **blow up** buildings or objects; bombs **explode**.
            Compare: 'They had planned to blow up the bridge but
            their bombs failed to explode.'

extinguish   × By that time the flames had extinguished.
            √ **By that time the flames had been extinguished.**
            Extinguish is a transitive verb. Compare: 'By that time
            the firemen had extinguished the flames.'

extreme   × Since he stopped smoking, there has been an
            extreme improvement in his health.
            √ **Since he stopped smoking, there has been a
            great/major/considerable/dramatic
            improvement in his health.**
            × Doctors have to know about all the extreme
            new medical developments.
            √ **Doctors have to know about all the important/
            major new medical developments.**
            Extreme is NOT used with nouns which describe a
            change in state or condition.

extremely   See CERTAIN 1

fabric   × The new fabric will provide hundreds of jobs.
            √ **The new factory will provide hundreds of jobs.**
            fabric = cloth or material
            factory = a large building or group of buildings where
            things are manufactured

fact   × Despite the fact he felt guilty, he ate all his
            brother's sweets.
            √ **Despite the fact that he felt guilty, he ate all
            his brother's sweets.**
            In formal writing, use **the fact that** + clause.

fairly × Japanese cars are fairly cheaper than
European ones.
✓ **Japanese cars are rather cheaper than
European ones.**
Fairly cannot be used with comparatives.

faithfully See SINCERELY

fall 1 × He was very tired and immediately falled
asleep.
✓ **He was very tired and immediately fell asleep.**
fall, falling, fell, fallen

2 × He hates to see anybody falling rubbish in the
street.
✓ **He hates to see anybody dropping rubbish in
the street.**
drop = let (something) fall
Compare: 'If the man on the roof dropped a brick, it
might fall on your head.'

fall down × A car hit the woman and fell her down.
✓ **A car hit the woman and knocked her down.**
fall down (intransitive) = (of people) fall to the ground
from an upright position: 'He was so weak from hunger
that he kept falling down.'
knock down (transitive) = (of a moving vehicle or its
driver) strike someone to the ground

familiarize × I would like to familiarize with the latest
teaching methods.
✓ **I would like to familiarize myself with the
latest teaching methods.**
familiarize someone/yourself **with** something

fantasy × Were the voices real or just products of his
fantasy?
✓ **Were the voices real or just products of his
imagination?**
fantasy = a picture in the mind produced by the
imagination, especially one which is very different from
reality: 'He lived in a world of fantasy.'
imagination = (the part of the mind with) the ability to
produce mental pictures

far 1 × 'It's far to the nearest garage,' she said.
✓ **'It's a long way to the nearest garage,' she said.**
In affirmative sentences, use **a long way**, NOT **far**, unless **far** is part of a phrase such as 'very far', 'awfully far', 'too far', etc. Compare 'It's quite far to the station.'

2 × When the bomb exploded, everyone tried to get as far as possible.
✓ **When the bomb exploded, everyone tried to get as far away as possible.**
Use **away** when you want to emphasize the distance from a place.

3 × The house is two kilometres far from the school I attend.
✓ **The house is two kilometres (away) from the school I attend.**
Far cannot be used after a unit of distance. Compare: 'The house is rather far from the school.' (WITHOUT unit of distance)
'The house is about two kilometres (away) from the school.' (WITH unit of distance)

fare × He went straight to a travel agency to buy a fare.
✓ **He went straight to a travel agency to buy a ticket.**
fare = the price of a journey on a bus, train, etc.: 'She offered to pay my fare.'
ticket = a printed piece of paper which shows that a person has paid for a journey

farther × If you need farther information, I suggest you go to the library.
✓ **If you need further information, I suggest you go to the library.**
Farther is used only of distance: 'We had to travel farther/further than I had expected.'

fascinated   × I was very fascinated by the speed with which
                 they worked.
                 √ **I was (absolutely) fascinated by the speed with
                 which they worked.**
                 See note at CERTAIN 1

fault   × In my opinion both of the drivers were in fault.
            √ **In my opinion both of the drivers were at fault.**
            be at fault, NOT in

favourable   × Our government is favourable to nuclear
                 missiles.
                 √ **Our government is in favour of nuclear
                 missiles.**

                 favourable = (1) approving, encouraging, or saying
                 what someone wants to hear: 'a favourable report', 'a
                 favourable reply'
                 (2) (of conditions) advantageous: 'a favourable wind'
                 be in favour of = approve of

favourite   × My most favourite drink is lemonade.
                √ **My favourite drink is lemonade.**
                An adjective which contains the sense **most** as part of
                its meaning cannot be used with **most**. **Favourite**
                means 'most preferred'.

fear   × He suddenly felt fear.
           √ **He suddenly felt afraid.**
           feel afraid, NOT feel fear

fed up   × I soon became fed up of his bad temper.
             √ **I soon became fed up with his bad temper.**
             tired of BUT fed up with

feel 1   × As the plane took off, I felt myself very happy
             because I was finally going to London.
             √ **As the plane took off, I felt very happy
             because I was finally going to London.**
             When **feel** is followed by an adjective or adjectival
             phrase, it is NOT used with a reflexive pronoun.
             Compare: 'I suddenly felt myself go cold.'

2   × I suddenly felt someone to touch my arm.
✓ **I suddenly felt someone touch my arm.**
feel someone/something + infinitive WITHOUT **to**

3   × He is feeling that they have made a mistake.
✓ **He feels that they have made a mistake.**
Feel (= think; have an opinion) is NOT used in progressive tenses.

feel like   × I often feel like to change my job.
✓ **I often feel like changing my job.**
feel like + v-ing

feeling   × The meeting provided a good opportunity for her to express her feeling.
✓ **The meeting provided a good opportunity for her to express her feelings.**
express your feelings (plural) = express your views or opinions

feet   × In front of them was a six-feet wall.
✓ **In front of them was a six-foot wall.**
See note at MONTH

female   × The way he dresses is rather female.
✓ **The way he dresses is rather feminine.**
female = (1) of the sex that produces eggs or gives birth to young: 'a female elephant'
(2) for or made up of women or girls: 'a female choir'
feminine = having qualities or features considered to be suitable for a woman

few 1   × With the few money he had been given, he bought an apple and some cheese.
✓ **With the little money he had been given, he bought an apple and some cheese.**
Few is used with plural countable nouns: 'There are very few apples left.'
Little is used with uncountable nouns.

2 × Few weeks ago I ordered a cassette recorder from your firm.
√ **A few weeks ago I ordered a cassette recorder from your firm.**

a few = not many: 'a few (minutes/days/weeks etc.) ago'
few = hardly any: 'Few people die of smallpox nowadays.'

fight 1 × They spent the whole night fighting against the fire.
√ **They spent the whole night fighting the fire.**
fight a fire/flood etc. WITHOUT **against**

2 × Some tribes have always fighted to preserve their own culture.
√ **Some tribes have always fought to preserve their own culture.**
fight, fighting, fought, fought

film See PLAY 2

find 1 × Nurses find very difficult to start a family while they are working.
√ **Nurses find it very difficult to start a family while they are working.**

find + **it** + adjective + to-v
When the real object of **find** is a to-v structure, use the preparatory object **it** and put the real object later.

2 × I am returning the machine so you can find what is wrong with it.
√ **I am returning the machine so you can find out what is wrong with it.**

find = discover by searching or by chance: 'I've looked for the cat everywhere but I can't find it.' 'I found the purse lying in a telephone box.'
find out = learn or discover (something that was previously unknown)

find out   × Looking through the magazine, I found out
several interesting articles.
√ **Looking through the magazine, I found several
interesting articles.**
See note at FIND 2

fine   × 'Hello, John. How are you?' 'Very fine, thank
you.'
√ **'Hello, John. How are you?' 'Fine, thank you.'**
Fine cannot be modified by **very** when it describes
how a person feels.
See note at CERTAIN 1

finish   × When we had finished to eat, the waiter
brought the bill.
√ **When we had finished eating, the waiter
brought the bill.**
finish + v-ing

first   × At first, may I thank you for your wonderful
hospitality.
√ **First (of all), may I thank you for your
wonderful hospitality.**
Use **at first** when you are talking about initial actions
or feelings which are in contrast with something which
comes later: 'At first I didn't want to go, but I soon
changed my mind.' Use **first** and **first of all** to refer
either to time (like **at first**) or to a series of actions,
with the suggested contrast **next, then,** etc.: 'First of
all, open the windows. Then turn off the gas and, if
necessary, call an ambulance.'

firstly   × I went and sat next to him. Firstly, I didn't
speak. I just sat there thinking what I could
say. Then I said, 'Nice day, isn't it?'
√ **I went and sat next to him. At first, I didn't
speak. I just sat there thinking what I could
say. Then I said, 'Nice day, isn't it?'**

× Firstly, I couldn't understand the local people at all.

✓ **At first, I couldn't understand the local people at all.**

Firstly conveys a strong sense that 'secondly', 'thirdly', etc. will follow: 'There are several reasons why I don't want to buy the car. Firstly, it is too expensive. Secondly ... '

At first refers to time and suggests a contrast with something which comes later: 'At first I liked the climate, but after two years I hated it.'

fish × I had never seen such brightly coloured fishes.
✓ **I had never seen such brightly coloured fish.**
The form **fishes** has almost disappeared.

flat See APARTMENT

flight × It was the worst flight I'd ever done.
✓ **It was the worst flight I'd ever been on.**
be on a flight, NOT **do**

floor 1 × My room, 229, was in the second floor.
✓ **My room, 229, was on the second floor.**
(be) **on** the ground/first floor etc. NOT **in**

2 × I was just about to enter the station when someone grabbed me by the shoulders and threw me to the floor.
✓ **I was just about to enter the station when someone grabbed me by the shoulders and threw me to the ground.**
Use **floor** when talking about the inside of a building. Use **ground** when talking about a place outside.

food × They steal because they don't have enough money to buy foods.
✓ **They steal because they don't have enough money to buy food.**
× It is a disgrace to serve such a poor food.
✓ **It is a disgrace to serve such poor food.**
Food is always uncountable except when talking about a particular kind of food: 'baby foods'.

foot   × Whenever there is a strike, we have to go to work by foot.
✓ **Whenever there is a strike, we have to go to work on foot.**

go **by car/bus/train/air** etc. BUT go **on foot**

for 1   × I have come to London for learning English.
✓ **I have come to London to learn English.**

do A **(in order) to** do B: 'They all worked hard to pass the exams.' 'She opened the door to let the cat out.'

2   × I am writing you this letter for to explain my problem.
✓ **I am writing you this letter to explain my problem.**

To express purpose, use to-v WITHOUT **for**.

3   × Unemployment has become a serious problem for the last few years.
✓ **Unemployment has become a serious problem over/during the last few years.**

Use **for** to introduce the length of time taken by an action: 'Unemployment has been rising for the last five years.'
Use **over/during** to introduce the period of time within which an action happens.

4   × I am waiting here now for an hour.
✓ **I have been waiting here now for an hour.**

An action which began in the past and which is still continuing requires a present perfect tense. When the length of time taken by the action is emphasized, the progressive form is used. Note that in this sentence **now** means 'from a time in the past up to the present moment'.

forbid   × His father has forbidden him from going out on his own at night.
✓ **His father has forbidden him to go out on his own at night.**

forbid someone **to** do something, NOT **from**

forbidden × In most cinemas nowadays it is forbidden to smoke.

✓ **In most cinemas nowadays smoking is forbidden.**

v-ing + **is/was forbidden**
'It is forbidden to smoke' is grammatically correct but sounds unnatural.

force × She had lost her car keys, so we had to open the door with force.

✓ **She had lost her car keys, so we had to open the door by force.**

do something **by force** = use force as a means of doing or accomplishing something
Compare: 'He kicked the ball with tremendous force.' (= very hard)

forever × They are for ever arguing about money.

✓ **They are forever arguing about money.**

for ever = for always: 'Nobody lives for ever.'
forever = (1) for always (2) continually; again and again: 'He is forever asking me for more pocket money.'

forget × She asked me not to forget telephoning her the next day.

✓ **She asked me not to forget to telephone her the next day.**

Compare: 'I forgot to post the letter.' (= I did not post the letter because I forgot to post it)
'I forgot posting the letter.' (= I posted the letter but forgot that I had posted it)

fortunately × Fortunatly the dog didn't bark.

✓ **Fortunately the dog didn't bark.**

fortunately (WITH **ely**)

fortune × It was a good fortune that the driver was able to stop in time.

✓ **It was fortunate/lucky that the driver was able to stop in time.**

Good fortune is quite rare. It occurs mainly in the phrase 'have the good fortune to (do something)': 'He had the good fortune to marry a woman who was both kind and understanding.'

forty
× I received over fourty birthday cards.
✓ **I received over forty birthday cards.**

four (WITH **u**) BUT **forty** (WITHOUT **u**)

found
× At first I founded driving very difficult because I forgot to stay on the left-hand side.
✓ **At first I found driving very difficult because I forgot to stay on the left-hand side.**
× Eventually both of them were founded alive and well.
✓ **Eventually both of them were found alive and well.**

Founded is the past tense of **found** (= establish; start building): 'The company was founded in 1826.'
Found is the past tense and past participle of **find**.

free
See COST 6

friend
× I spent the afternoon listening to records with my girl friend.
✓ **I spent the afternoon listening to records with my girlfriend.**

girlfriend, boyfriend, NOT **girl friend, boy friend**

friendly
× All the teachers are very friendly with me.
✓ **All the teachers are very friendly to me.**

be/become friendly with = have/enter the relationship that friends have: 'I've become very friendly with the couple who live opposite.'
be friendly to = treat in a kind way

frightened 1
× When I heard the thunder I frightened for a moment.
✓ **When I heard the thunder I was frightened for a moment.**

frighten (transitive) = make (someone) afraid: 'A strange noise under the bed frightened me.'
be frightened = be afraid

2   × I was very frightened from his appearance.
√ **I was very frightened by his appearance.**

be frightened by someone/something (on one
occasion)
Compare: **be frightened of** someone/something
(habitually): 'Why are so many people frightened of the
dark?'

frightening   × By this time it had grown dark and he felt very
frightening.
√ **By this time it had grown dark and he felt very
frightened.**

'It is frightening.' = It frightens people.
'They are frightened.' = Someone/something frightens
them.

from 1   × I have been studying at London University
from 1984.
√ **I have been studying at London University
since 1984.**

Use **from ... to ...** when you mean 'from one time in the
past to another': 'I studied at Leeds University from
1980 to 1983.'
Use **since** when you mean 'from a time in the past
until now'.

2   × She asked if I'd seen any plays from
Shakespeare.
√ **She asked if I'd seen any plays by
Shakespeare.**

a play, novel, painting, etc. **by** a writer or artist, NOT
from

3   × It's a short, knee-length coat from white rabbit
fur.
√ **It's a short, knee-length coat made of white
rabbit fur.**

made of fur/wool etc., NOT **from**

front 1 × The bus stop is in front of the library, outside the post office.
✓ **The bus stop is opposite the library, outside the post office.**

in front of = in a position directly before: 'There was a bus in front of the car and a truck behind it.'
opposite = on the other side of the street, room, etc.; facing

2 × He was standing right in the front of the television.
✓ **He was standing right in front of the television.**
in front of (preposition) WITHOUT **the**
Compare: 'Would you like to sit in the front of the train?' (= the part nearest the front)

3 See SIDE 1

fruit × The shop sells fruits and vegetables.
✓ **The shop sells fruit and vegetables.**
Fruit (= fruit in general) is an uncountable noun.
Fruits (= particular types of fruit) is rarely used in British English.

full 1 × Hospitals today are full with people with heart complaints.
✓ **Hospitals today are full of people with heart complaints.**
(be) **full of**, NOT **with**

2 × The person sitting next to the driver was full of mud.
✓ **The person sitting next to the driver was covered in mud.**
Compare: 'The glass was full of wine.' 'The tablecloth was covered in wine.'

fun × On my birthday I had a good fun with my friends.
✓ **On my birthday I had some good fun with my friends.**
Fun is an uncountable noun.

furniture × The room was so full of furnitures it was
difficult to move.
✓ **The room was so full of furniture it was
difficult to move.**
× At home he felt as if he were a furniture.
✓ **At home he felt as if he were a piece of
furniture.**
Furniture is an uncountable noun.

gain × Without a job it is impossible to gain any
money.
✓ **Without a job it is impossible to earn any
money.**
earn (a sum of) money by working, NOT **gain**

game ✓ **AmE I enjoy watching football games.**
✓ **BrE I enjoy watching football matches.**
In British English, use **a game of football** or **a football
match**.

generally × The coat is generally green.
✓ **The coat is mainly green.**
generally = (1) usually: 'It's generally very hot at this
time of year.'
(2) in most cases; widely: 'His paintings are generally
admired.'
mainly = mostly; largely

gentle × The shop assistant asked me gently what I
wanted.
✓ **The shop assistant asked me politely what I
wanted.**
gently (opposite **roughly**) = in a soft and careful way:
'She held the little bird very gently.'
politely (opposite **rudely**) = in a way that shows good
manners; courteously

get up See BED 2

girl See FRIEND

give × She gave to him some cheese sandwiches.
√ **She gave him some cheese sandwiches.**
give something **to** someone BUT **give** someone
something

glad 1 × She was a very glad person, and very
intelligent.
√ **She was a very happy person, and very
intelligent.**
glad (predicative only) = pleased and happy about
something in particular: 'I'm so glad your wife is
feeling better.' 'I'm glad it wasn't our turn to pay.'
happy = enjoying life

2 × The child's parents were glad having him back
safely.
√ **The child's parents were glad to have him
back safely.**
glad + to-v

glance × She made a quick glance over her shoulder to
see if he was following her.
√ **She gave a quick glance over her shoulder to
see if he was following her.**
Note the more usual alternative: 'She glanced quickly
over her shoulder to see if he was following her.'

glasses × He wore an old-fashioned glasses and couldn't
see very well.
√ **He wore old-fashioned glasses and couldn't
see very well.**
Glasses (= spectacles) is a plural noun. Note also: 'a
pair of glasses'.

go 1 × We go to swim every day on holiday.
√ **We go swimming every day on holiday.**
go + v-ing = perform an activity: 'go swimming', 'go
cycling', 'go fishing'

2   × The next morning she went to the hotel to visit
us.
✓ **The next morning she came to the hotel to
visit us.**

Come is used for movement towards the place where
the speaker is, was, or intends to be.
Go is used for movement in other directions.

3   See NEAR 2, TO 4

4   See CAR

5   See GO OUT

golden 1   × It's a navy blue coat with golden buttons.
✓ **It's a navy blue coat with gold buttons.**

Golden is rarely used to mean 'having the colour of
gold' except in the phrase 'golden hair'.

2   × It was a very valuable golden ring.
✓ **It was a very valuable gold ring.**

In modern use, things which are made of gold are
described as **gold** rather than **golden**.

gone   ✓ AmE **'Have you ever gone to France?' she
asked.**
✓ BrE **'Have you ever been to France?' she
asked.**

In British English, **been** is used when someone has
visited a place in the past. **Gone** is used when the
person is still in the place they are visiting. Compare:
'Peter has gone to Paris.' (= he has not yet returned)
'Peter has been to Paris.' (= he has visited Paris and
returned)

good 1   × I don't speak English very good.
✓ **I don't speak English very well.**
× His clothes were freshly ironed and his shoes
were good polished.
✓ **His clothes were freshly ironed and his shoes
were well polished.**

Good is an adjective.
Well is an adverb.

2 ✗ My mother thinks there's no good putting a very young child in a kindergarten.

✓ **My mother thinks it's no good putting a very young child in a kindergarten.**

it is no good (+ v-ing)

3 ✗ It's no good to want to help the poor if you don't do anything about it.

✓ **It's no good wanting to help the poor if you don't do anything about it.**

no good + v-ing

goods 1 ✗ The goods was not delivered in time.

✓ **The goods were not delivered in time.**

Goods is a plural noun and takes a plural verb.

2 ✗ He had very little money and very few goods.

✓ **He had very little money and very few possessions.**

Goods is most often used to refer to things for sale: 'The supermarket has a wide variety of frozen goods.' It can also have the meaning of 'personal property' but this is usually in a formal or legal context.

Possessions is a more general word meaning 'all the things a person owns.'

go out ✗ As soon as the bus stopped, he went out.

✓ **As soon as the bus stopped, he got off.**

get on/off a bus/train/plane etc.

gossip ✗ She told me gossips about all her relations.

✓ **She told me a lot of gossip about all her relations.**

gossip (uncountable) = talk concerned with people's private lives

Note also: 'bits/pieces of gossip'.

got ✗ I got several friends who don't want children.

✓ **I have (got) several friends who don't want children.**

Got is NOT used to replace **have**: 'I have several friends.' 'I've got several friends.' (NOT 'I got several friends.')

government   × Goverments all over the world are looking for a solution to the problem.
✓ **Governments all over the world are looking for a solution to the problem.**

government (WITH **rn**)
Note, however, that the **rn** is NOT pronounced.

gracious   × Even as a child, he had admired the dancer's slow, gracious movements.
✓ **Even as a child, he had admired the dancer's slow, graceful movements.**

gracious = showing courtesy and kindness: 'The duchess was gracious enough to accept the invitation.'
graceful = having beauty (of movement, form, etc.)

grade   × By the end of the war he had been promoted to the grade of captain.
✓ **By the end of the war he had been promoted to the rank of captain.**

Soldiers, policemen, etc. have different **ranks**, NOT **grades**.

grateful   See SHALL 2

ground   × On what ground do you think that the money was stolen?
✓ **On what grounds do you think that the money was stolen?**

grounds (plural) = a reason or reasons: 'She left him on the grounds of cruelty.' 'They have no grounds for complaint.' 'We rejected the proposal on the grounds that it involved further unemployment.'

grow   × Many of these children grow in an atmosphere of violence.
✓ **Many of these children grow up in an atmosphere of violence.**

grow = increase in size: 'Mary's little boy grew four centimetres last year.'
grow up = pass from childhood into maturity

grow up 1   × Some people think it is the duty of all mothers to stay at home growing up children.

✓ **Some people think it is the duty of all mothers to stay at home bringing up children.**

× My father was grown up in Kyoto.

✓ **My father grew up in Kyoto.**

✓ **My father was brought up in Kyoto.**

Grow up is an intransitive verb.
Bring up is transitive.

2   × Our production of honey grows up every year.

✓ **Our production of honey increases every year.**

grow up (of a child) = become an adult: 'Tom wants to be a scientist when he grows up.'

guarantee 1   × The machine is only two years old so it is still under garantee.

✓ **The machine is only two years old so it is still under guarantee.**

guarantee (WITH **u**)

2   × May I remind you that the cassette recorder is still in guarantee.

✓ **May I remind you that the cassette recorder is still under guarantee.**

(be) under guarantee, NOT **in**

3   ✓ **AmE I bought the machine just two weeks ago, so it is still under the guarantee.**

✓ **BrE I bought the machine just two weeks ago, so it is still under guarantee.**

In British English, use **be under guarantee** WITHOUT **the**.

guardian   × At the railway station a guardian told him that the last train had just gone.

✓ **At the railway station a guard told him that the last train had just gone.**

guardian = a person who is legally responsible for looking after a child, especially one whose parents have died: 'My wife and I became Vincent's guardians after his parents died in an earthquake.'
guard = a railway official in charge of a train

guilty   × A lot of women feel guilty to leave their children alone or with another person.
√ **A lot of women feel guilty about leaving their children alone or with another person.**
feel guilty about (doing) something

guitar   See PLAY 3

habit   × It is a habit in Japan to take off your shoes before entering a house.
√ **It is a custom in Japan to take off your shoes before entering a house.**
Custom is used of the established practices of a society or very large group.
Habit is used of an individual: 'Nail-biting is one of her bad habits.'

hair 1   × He had a black hair and very clear eyes.
√ **He had black hair and very clear eyes.**
When **hair** means 'all the hair on a person's head', it is uncountable. However, when it means 'a single hair' or 'several individual hairs', it is countable. Compare: 'There was a long black hair in my soup.' 'She has long black hair.'

2   × His sister is a beautiful dark-hair girl.
√ **His sister is a beautiful dark-haired girl.**
dark-haired, **fair-haired**, etc.

half 1   × He agreed to give her the half of the money.
√ **He agreed to give her half of the money.**
Do not use **the** before **half** except when talking about a particular half.

2   × We have a break of one and a half hour for lunch.
√ **We have a break of one and a half hours for lunch.**
number greater than one + plural form

3   × The belt is about one metre and a half long.
√ **The belt is about one and a half metres long.**
number greater than one + plural form + adjective

hand 1 × In the hands he was holding a small bird.
✓ **In his hands he was holding a small bird.**

With parts of the body, use **my, your, his,** etc., NOT **the**: 'He scratched his head.' 'She took him in her arms.' 'They held out their hands.'

2 × In the other hand, many women choose to go out to work.
✓ **On the other hand, many women choose to go out to work.**

on the one hand ... **on** the other hand ... , NOT **in**

handful × As we came around the corner, we could see a handful people gathered in front of the house.
✓ **As we came around the corner, we could see a handful of people gathered in front of the house.**

a handful of + noun

happen × Something must have happened with George to make him behave in such a way.
✓ **Something must have happened to George to make him behave in such a way.**

something **happens to** someone/something, NOT **with**

hardly 1 × It was so dark that we hardly could see.
✓ **It was so dark that we could hardly see.**

When there is no auxiliary verb, **hardly** is placed immediately before the main verb: 'I hardly know her.' However, when the main verb is **be**, **hardly** is placed immediately after it: 'Such a small amount of money is hardly worth worrying about.' Otherwise **hardly** goes immediately after the (first) auxiliary verb: 'I was so thirsty that I could hardly talk.'

2 × Hardly he had begun to speak when someone interrupted him.

✓ **Hardly had he begun to speak when someone interrupted him.**

When negative adverbs like **hardly/seldom/never** are used at the beginning of a sentence, the subject and auxiliary verb change places. Note the more common alternative: 'He had hardly begun to speak when someone interrupted him.'

3 × The other teacher speaks in a way I can't hardly understand.

✓ **The other teacher speaks in a way I can hardly understand.**

× The dog looked terrible and couldn't hardly move.

✓ **The dog looked terrible and could hardly move.**

Hardly (= almost not) is NOT used with **never**, **not**, etc.

4 × Society shouldn't punish these people too hardly.

✓ **Society shouldn't punish these people too hard.**

hardly = scarcely; almost not: 'I could hardly hear him.' 'I hardly know the woman.'
hard = severe AND severely

harmful × Traffic fumes are very harmful for our health.

✓ **Traffic fumes are very harmful to our health.**

(be) harmful to something, NOT **for**

have 1 × After buying the food, he had not very much money left.

✓ **After buying the food, he didn't have very much money left.**

When **have** is used as a main verb, the negative and question forms are made with **do**.

2 × I stayed at home yesterday because I was having a bad cold.
   ✓ **I stayed at home yesterday because I had a bad cold.**

When talking about a state or condition, use the simple (NOT progressive) forms of **have**: 'He has only one arm.' (NOT 'is having')
'I have just one sister.' (NOT 'am having')
'We have two dogs and a cat.' (NOT 'are having')

3 × I don't think that I have to say anything more, so I'll stop now and take this letter to the post office.
   ✓ **I don't think that I have anything more to say, so I'll stop now and take this letter to the post office.**

have to do something = must do something: 'My train leaves in ten minutes so I'll have to go now.'
have something **to do** = have something that you need or intend to do

4 × He was very hungry but he had no money about him.
   ✓ **He was very hungry but he had no money on him.**

have (got) something **on** you = have (got) something in your pocket, handbag, etc.: 'Have you (got) a comb on you?'

5 See COLOUR 1

have to × Some wives earn a lot of money and so their husbands haven't to work.
   ✓ **Some wives earn a lot of money and so their husbands don't have to work.**

The negative and question forms of **have to** are formed with **do**: 'I don't have to leave just yet.' 'Do you have to leave already?'

he See THEY 1

headache 1 × If I drink coffee I get headache.
                √ **If I drink coffee I get a headache.**
                Headache is a countable noun.

2 See BIG 2

health × I hope this letter finds you in a good health.
            √ **I hope this letter finds you in good health.**
            Health is an uncountable noun.

hear 1 × Suddenly I heared a loud bang.
            √ **Suddenly I heard a loud bang.**
            hear, hearing, heard, heard

2 × They all sat down and heard my story.
       √ **They all sat down and listened to my story.**
       listen (to) = hear and pay attention (to)

help 1 × The girl's parents couldn't help to worry about
              her.
            √ **The girl's parents couldn't help worrying about
              her.**
            can't/couldn't help + v-ing

2 × 'Can I help you looking after the animals?' he
         asked her.
       √ **'Can I help you (to) look after the animals?' he
         asked her.**
       help someone **(to) do** something

her See ME 1

here 1 × I can't here you.
            √ **I can't hear you.**
            here (adverb) = in, at, or to this place: 'Come over
            here!'
            hear (verb) = receive (sound) by using the ears

2 × She comes to here every afternoon to feed the birds.

✓ **She comes here every afternoon to feed the birds.**

There and **here** cannot follow **to** unless the speaker is indicating or pointing to something: 'When the tide comes in, the water reaches right up to **here**.'

3 × Here the taxi comes at last!

✓ **Here comes the taxi at last!**

Note that the subject and the verb change places after **here/there**: 'Here comes John!' 'There goes the woman I was telling you about.' However, there is no change if the subject is a pronoun: 'Here he comes!' 'There she goes!'

high × Beauvais is very proud of having the highest cathedral in Europe.

✓ **Beauvais is very proud of having the tallest cathedral in Europe.**

Use **high** to indicate (a great) distance above the ground: 'a high ceiling', 'a high shelf'.

Tall (NOT **high**) is used of people, trees, and other things which are narrow as well as above average height: 'a tall man', 'a tall chimney', 'a tall house'.

him See ME 1

hire × I am hiring a small house near the university.

✓ **I am renting a small house near the university.**

In British English, **hire** means 'obtain the use of something for a short time by paying a sum of money': 'Let's hire a car for the day.'

Rent usually refers to a series of payments made over a long period of time.

his × Yesterday I bought a new magazine. His name is 'Four Wheels'.

✓ **Yesterday I bought a new magazine. Its name is 'Four Wheels'.**

his = of/belonging to **him** (i.e. a person)

its = of/belonging to **it** (i.e. an animal or thing)

historic 1   ×   She likes reading historic novels.
              ✓   **She likes reading historical novels.**

historic = (1) very important in history: 'a historic voyage', 'a historic decision'
(2) having a long history: 'a historic tradition', 'a historic building'
historical novels = novels set in a certain time in the past

2   ×   If you have nothing to do, why don't you visit the historic museum?
        ✓   **If you have nothing to do, why don't you visit the history museum?**

a history museum = a museum dealing with the subject of history
Compare: 'a history book', 'a history lesson', 'a history teacher'

historical   ×   We shall be taking you to see several interesting historical places.
              ✓   **We shall be taking you to see several interesting historic places.**

historical = (1) about or based upon people who actually lived or events that actually happened: 'historical novels', 'historical characters'
(2) connected with or found in history: 'a historical fact', 'a historical document'
See note at HISTORIC 1

holiday   ×   She said she was going on holidays to France.
            ✓   **She said she was going on holiday to France.**
            ×   Some people always seem to be on holidays.
            ✓   **Some people always seem to be on holiday.**
go/be on holiday
Compare: 'He's gone on holiday to Spain.' 'He's spending his summer holiday(s) in Spain.'

holidays   See PASS 2

home   ×   As soon as I arrived at home, I knew that something was wrong.
          ✓   **As soon as I arrived home, I knew that something was wrong.**

× I read the magazine when I returned to my home.

√ **I read the magazine when I returned home.**

arrive at/return to/go to someone's house BUT arrive/return/go home

homework 1 × Our grammar teacher gives us a lot of homeworks.

√ **Our grammar teacher gives us a lot of homework.**

Homework is an uncountable noun.

2 × In my opinion, women who go out to work don't have enough time to do the homework.

√ **In my opinion, women who go out to work don't have enough time to do the housework.**

homework = work that a teacher gives a pupil to do at home

housework = all the jobs that have to be done regularly to keep a house or flat clean and tidy

honour 1 √ **AmE As the mayor of this town, it is my great honor to welcome you.**

√ **BrE As the mayor of this town, it is my great honour to welcome you.**

honor (WITHOUT **u**) in American English

honour (WITH **u**) in British English

2 × It is an honour to me to welcome you all to Norway.

√ **It is an honour for me to welcome you all to Norway.**

an honour for someone, NOT **to**

hope 1 × I left the bag on a bus and I have no hope for getting it back.

√ **I left the bag on a bus and I have no hope of getting it back.**

little/no hope of + v-ing NOT **for**

2   × I hope you all to have an interesting afternoon.
✓ **I hope you all have an interesting afternoon.**
When there is a change of person before and after
hope, it cannot be followed by to-v. Instead, the verb is
usually in the present simple tense.

hospital   ✓ **AmE I've been in the hospital for the last five
weeks.**
✓ **BrE I've been in hospital for the last five
weeks.**
Note the expressions: 'be taken to hospital', 'leave
hospital', 'be in hospital' WITHOUT **the**
In British English **the** is used only when talking about
a particular hospital.

hour   × It was a twelve hours trip.
✓ **It was a twelve-hour trip.**
See note at MONTH

house 1   × The policeman said he had no more questions
and told me to go to my house.
✓ **The policeman said he had no more questions
and told me to go home.**
go home = return to the place where you live

2   × It is believed that the castle was once the
house of evil monsters.
✓ **It is believed that the castle was once the
home of evil monsters.**
house = a particular type of building, usually lived in
by a family: 'Do you live in a house or a flat?'
home = any building or place in which a person lives
(and feels a sense of belonging)

household   × At the weekend they have to do all the
household.
✓ **At the weekend they have to do all the
housework.**
household = all the people living together in a house
or flat: 'Be quiet or you'll wake the whole household.'
housework = all the jobs that have to be done
regularly to keep a house or flat clean and tidy

housework   × Brian often helps Elisa to do the houseworks.
✓ **Brian often helps Elisa to do the housework.**
Housework is an uncountable noun.

how 1   × Could you describe how the driver looks like?
✓ **Could you describe what the driver looks like?**
× How is Christmas in France?
✓ **What is Christmas like in France?**
Use **what ... like** (NOT **how**) when asking for a
description of someone or something.

2   × Their decision will depend on how good is
your offer.
✓ **Their decision will depend on how good your
offer is.**
When the object of the sentence is a **wh**-clause, the
subject and verb in the **wh**-clause do NOT change
places.

3   × I must tell you how I was pleased to receive a
letter from you.
✓ **I must tell you how pleased I was to receive a
letter from you.**
how + adjective/adverb + subject + verb: 'I wonder how
far it is.' 'I can't describe how beautifully she played.'
'How clumsy you are!'

hundred 1   ✓ **AmE The magazine has a hundred fifty pages.**
✓ **BrE The magazine has a hundred and fifty
pages.**
In British English, use 'a hundred and one', 'five
hundred and sixty', etc.

2   × Five hundreds of children are born in the city
every day.
✓ **Five hundred children are born in the city
every day.**
'hundreds of children' BUT 'two hundred children', 'five
hundred children', etc.
Dozen, thousand, million, etc. behave in the same way:
'dozens of eggs' BUT 'two dozen eggs', 'thousands of
dollars' BUT 'five thousand dollars', 'millions of tourists'
BUT 'several million tourists'

3 See THOUSAND 1

hurry   × Tim was in hurry and couldn't stop to talk.
       √ **Tim was in a hurry and couldn't stop to talk.**
       (be) in a hurry

hurt   × The driver didn't hurt a lot but his passenger
       was taken to hospital.
       √ **The driver wasn't badly/seriously hurt but his**
       passenger was taken to hospital.

       hurt = cause (someone) to feel pain: 'These new
       shoes hurt my feet.' 'My feet hurt.'
       be hurt = be injured: 'Several people were hurt when
       the wall collapsed.'

I   × I and some of my classmates publish a
       monthly magazine.
       √ **Some of my classmates and I publish a**
       monthly magazine.

       It is usual to mention yourself last: 'My husband and
       I ... ', NOT 'I and my husband ... '

if 1   × If it will rain, I shall come and meet you in the
       car.
       √ **If it rains, I shall come and meet you in the**
       car.

       When talking about possible or open situations, put the
       if clause in the present tense and use **shall/will** + verb
       in the main clause.

2   × If there were no unemployment, we will not
       have the amount of crime we have today.
       √ **If there were no unemployment, we would not**
       have the amount of crime we have today.

       When talking about unreal or imaginary situations, put
       the **if** clause in the past tense and the main clause in
       the conditional tense.

3 × If you would have caught the earlier train, we could have travelled together.

✓ **If you had caught the earlier train, we could have travelled together.**

When talking about unfulfilled or impossible situations, put the **if** clause in the past perfect tense and the main clause in the perfect conditional tense.

4 See WOULD 2

ill × Most of the ill people were very old.

✓ **Most of the sick people were very old.**

Ill (= sick) cannot be placed immediately before a noun. Compare: 'Many of the old people looked ill.'

imaginary × People tend to become less imaginary as they grow older.

✓ **People tend to become less imaginative as they grow older.**

imaginary = existing in or produced by the imagination: 'The characters in the story are entirely imaginary.'

imaginative = having or showing imagination

imagine × What about all his friends? He couldn't imagine to leave them all.

✓ **What about all his friends? He couldn't imagine leaving them all.**

imagine + v-ing

immediately 1 × His fear immediatly turned to relief.

✓ **His fear immediately turned to relief.**

immediately (WITH **ely**)

2 × 'Let me know immediately she will arrive,' he shouted.

✓ **'Let me know immediately she arrives,' he shouted.**

After **immediately** use the present simple tense for future reference, NOT **shall/will** + verb.

immigrate × Some of those who can't find a job decide to immigrate.
✓ **Some of those who can't find a job decide to emigrate.**

immigrate = enter a foreign country and make your home there
This verb is seldom used. Instead people tend to use **immigrant** and **immigration** (nouns): 'When jobs became scarce, the number of new immigrants suddenly decreased.' 'Immigration has decreased in recent years.'
emigrate = leave your own country and make your home in another one

impolite × The way he shouted at me was very unpolite
✓ **The way he shouted at me was very impolite.**

Compare: **impossible** (= not possible) and **implausible** (= not plausible)

important × He said that money was not important for him.
✓ **He said that money was not important to him.**
× The pen is very important for me because it was a present from my father.
✓ **The pen is very important to me because it was a present from my father.**

When talking about how strongly a person feels about something, use **important to**, NOT **for**.

improve See PERFECT 1

impulse × I hope your trip will provide impulse for the essay you will have to write when you get back.
✓ **I hope your trip will provide inspiration for the essay you will have to write when you get back.**

impulse = a sudden desire to do something: 'I had a sudden impulse to walk out of the classroom and never return.' 'It's unwise to act on impulse.'
inspiration = (a source of) creative energy

in **1** ✗ In 1st July we went to Italy by car.
✓ **On 1st July we went to Italy by car.**
on + a day or date, NOT **in**

2 ✗ In the following morning she called me at the office.
✓ **The following morning she called me at the office.**
'in the morning/afternoon/evening' BUT 'the following morning', 'the next afternoon', 'the previous evening', etc.

3 ✗ In the first few days the radio worked very well.
✓ **For the first few days the radio worked very well.**
When talking about how long something lasts or continues, use **for**, NOT **in**.

4 ✗ In arriving at the airport we discovered that the plane would be late.
✓ **On arriving at the airport we discovered that the plane would be late.**
on/upon doing something, NOT **in**

5 ✗ It's a dark brown coat in wool.
✓ **It's a dark brown coat made of wool.**
made of wool/wood etc., NOT **in**

6 ✗ I work eight hours in a day.
✓ **I work eight hours a day.**
In is NOT used in expressions such as: 'The shop is open six days a week.' 'He visits his father three times a year.' 'Bananas cost fifty pence a pound.' 'I drove to the hospital at ninety miles an hour.'

incapable ✗ Most small children are incapable to sit still for more than five minutes.
✓ **Most small children are incapable of sitting still for more than five minutes.**
incapable of + v-ing

include × The poem includes just two short verses.
✓ **The poem consists of just two short verses.**
include = contain (in addition to something else): 'The price of the radio includes a free carrying case.'
consist of = be made up of

increase × The increase of crime is accelerating.
✓ **The increase in crime is accelerating.**
an increase in something, NOT **of**

indeed × I was having a good time indeed when suddenly the plane started to shake.
✓ **I was having a very good time indeed when suddenly the plane started to shake.**
very + adjective + noun + **indeed**: 'I thought it was a very clever answer indeed.'
very + adjective/adverb + **indeed**: 'The results are very good indeed.' 'She sang very well indeed.'

independence × Even a part-time job gives a person a certain amount of independance.
✓ **Even a part-time job gives a person a certain amount of independence.**
independence (WITH **ence**)

independent 1 × Many people would like to lead a more independant life.
✓ **Many people would like to lead a more independent life.**
independent (WITH **ent**)

2 × Nowadays young people want to be independent from their parents.
✓ **Nowadays young people want to be independent of their parents.**
independent of someone/something, NOT **from**

indoor × As it was raining we decided to stay indoor.
✓ **As it was raining we decided to stay indoors.**
Indoor is an adjective: 'an indoor swimming pool', 'indoor games'.
Indoors is an adverb.

industrious × The South has fewer industrious areas.
√ **The South has fewer industrial areas.**

industrious = hard-working: 'She's a very industrious student.'
industrial = having or concerning industries

industry × The biggest industries in Jakobsberg are Philips and IBM.
√ **The biggest companies in Jakobsberg are Philips and IBM.**

industry = all the people, factories, companies, etc. involved in a major area of production: 'the steel industry', 'the clothing industry'
Compare: 'IBM is one of the biggest companies in the electronics industry.'

in fact × The record button isn't working properly. Infact it doesn't record at all.
√ **The record button isn't working properly. In fact it doesn't record at all.**

In fact is ALWAYS two words.

inferior × Some people think that the new system is inferior than the old one.
√ **Some people think that the new system is inferior to the old one.**

inferior to, NOT **than**

influence 1 × Finally I asked him not to keep disturbing me, but it had no influence.
√ **Finally I asked him not to keep disturbing me, but it had no effect.**

When talking about the particular result of an action or event, use **effect**, NOT **influence**.
effect = result
influence = shaping force or power

2 × I don't think that longer prison sentences would influence on criminals.
√ **I don't think that longer prison sentences would influence criminals.**

have an influence on someone (noun) BUT **influence** someone (verb) WITHOUT **on**

information 1   × On Friday we'll be able to give you further information of the trip.
   ✓ **On Friday we'll be able to give you further information about the trip.**
   information about something, NOT **of**

2   × A journalist often has to travel to get the informations he requires.
   ✓ **A journalist often has to travel to get the information he requires.**
   Information is an uncountable noun. Note also: 'a piece/an item of information'

3   × I asked the salesman to tell me some information about it.
   ✓ **I asked the salesman to give me some information about it.**
   give someone **information**, NOT **tell, say,** etc.

inhabitant   × Cameroon has about twelve million habitants.
   ✓ **Cameroon has about twelve million inhabitants.**
   Habitant is not an English word.

injure 1   × He fell and was injured in the leg.
   ✓ **He fell and injured his leg.**
   be shot/wounded in the leg/arm BUT **be injured** (WITHOUT in the leg/arm) OR **injure** your leg/arm

2   × Fortunately the driver was wearing his seat belt and so he did not injure.
   ✓ **Fortunately the driver was wearing his seat belt and so he wasn't injured.**
   injure someone; injure yourself
   Injure is NOT intransitive.

inquire   See ENQUIRE

inquiry × After making several inquiries, I finally
discovered his address.
√ **After making several enquiries, I finally
discovered his address.**
Enquiry is more often used for a simple request for
information, and **inquiry** for a long serious study.
Compare: 'a court of inquiry', 'an inquiry into the
cause of the unrest'

insecure × I felt rather insecure of taking the examination.
√ **I felt rather insecure about taking the
examination.**
insecure about + v-ing, NOT **of**

inside 1 × It's a dark blue coat with a black inside.
√ **It's a dark blue coat with a black lining.**
lining = the material covering the inside of a coat,
jacket, etc.

2 × I remember leaving a blue handkerchief inside of
the right-hand pocket.
√ **I remember leaving a blue handkerchief inside
the right-hand pocket.**
inside something WITHOUT **of**

insist 1 × The porter insisted to help us with our
baggage.
√ **The porter insisted on helping us with our
baggage.**
insist on + v-ing

2 × She insisted me on carrying her enormous
suitcase.
√ **She insisted on me/my carrying her enormous
suitcase.**
insist on (someone('s) doing) something

in spite of See SPITE

instead   × I advised her to go out more instead to stay at home all the time.
                 √ **I advised her to go out more instead of staying at home all the time.**

                 instead of (doing) something

institute   × In my opinion, the monarchy is an old-fashioned institute.
                 √ **In my opinion, the monarchy is an old-fashioned institution.**

                 institute = a society or organization set up for a special purpose: 'He is a member of the Royal Institute of Architects.'
                 institution = a custom or tradition: 'Marriage is an institution.'

instruction 1   × I read the instructions book very carefully.
                     √ **I read the instruction book very carefully.**

                 Many nouns that are usually plural drop their **-s** when used to modify another noun. Compare: 'a book of instructions' and 'an instruction book', 'a shelf for books' and 'a book shelf', 'a holiday lasting ten days' and 'a ten-day holiday'

            2   × The machine is supplied with instructions how to use it.
                 √ **The machine is supplied with instructions on how to use it.**

                 instructions on how to do something
                 Note that a number of other prepositions can also be used, including **about**, **as to**, **regarding**, and **concerning**.

insure   √ **AmE People need a job to insure their independence.**
                 √ **BrE People need a job to ensure their independence.**

                 In both British and American English **ensure** means 'to make certain'. In British English **insure** is only used to mean 'to protect against loss or damage by means of insurance': 'She insured her camera for five hundred dollars.' However, in American English **insure** is used with both these meanings.

intend   × I am intending to stay in England until
         Christmas.
         √ **I intend to stay in England until Christmas.**
         Intend is rarely used in the present progressive tense.

intention   × She said that she hadn't the slightest intention
           to accept the invitation.
           √ **She said that she hadn't the slightest intention
           of accepting the invitation.**
           have not the slightest **intention of** + v-ing

interested 1   × It was a very interested idea.
            √ **It was a very interesting idea.**
            'It is interesting.' = It interests people.
            'They are interested.' = Someone/something interests
            them.

         2   × I am not interested about your opinion.
            √ **I am not interested in your opinion.**
            be interested in (doing) something, NOT **about**

         3   × If you are interested to know more about the
            town's history, you should visit the museum.
            √ **If you are interested in knowing more about
            the town's history, you should visit the
            museum.**
            interested in + v-ing

interesting   × I was interesting to hear she had got married.
            √ **I was interested to hear she had got married.**
            × I think you will be very interesting in the
            magazine.
            √ **I think you will be very interested in the
            magazine.**
            See note at INTERESTED 1

interview   × The magazine contains several interviews from
           famous racing drivers.
           √ **The magazine contains several interviews with
           famous racing drivers.**
           an interview with someone, NOT **from**

into × Into the right-hand pocket you will find a pair
of gloves.
√ **In the right-hand pocket you will find a pair of
gloves.**

Into is used with movement: 'He put his hand into his
pocket.'
In can be used with or without movement.
Compare: 'He put his hand in his pocket.' 'His hand
was in his pocket.'

intrude × I hope I'm not intruding your privacy.
√ **I hope I'm not intruding upon your privacy.**
Note that it is more natural simply to say: 'I hope I'm
not intruding.'

invent 1 × It will not be long before scientists invent a
cure for this terrible disease.
√ **It will not be long before scientists discover a
cure for this terrible disease.**

invent = create (something which has never existed
before) for the first time: 'Who invented the bicycle?'
discover = find or reveal by research: 'Penicillin was
discovered almost by accident.'

2 × I'm sure that your host families will invent lots
of interesting things for you to do.
√ **I'm sure that your host families will think of
lots of interesting things for you to do.**

invent = create (something which has never existed
before) for the first time
think of = produce (something) as an idea or
suggestion

invest × Businessmen invest vast amounts on these
industries.
√ **Businessmen invest vast amounts in these
industries.**

invest (money etc.) **in** something, NOT **on**

invitation See AGREE 5

invite 1   × I don't know why she has invited me her sister's wedding.
✓ **I don't know why she has invited me to her sister's wedding.**

invite someone **to** something

2   × She invited him for having some ice-cream.
✓ **She invited him to have some ice-cream.**

invite someone + to-v

island   × I was on holiday with my parents on the island Capri.
✓ **I was on holiday with my parents on the island of Capri.**

the island of + name

it 1   × At the end of the course, it will be a party at the language school.
✓ **At the end of the course, there will be a party at the language school.**

In sentences or clauses which express a state or fact, the subject often comes after the verb **be**. Such statements are introduced by **there** (NOT **it**).
Compare: (1) 'It was once a little boy called John.' 'There was once a little boy called John.' (2) 'I think it is something wrong.' 'I think there is something wrong.' (3) 'Something is wrong.' 'There is something wrong.'
See also NEED 1, POINT 1

2   × When I turned on the light, it happened the same thing again.
✓ **When I turned on the light, the same thing happened again.**

It is not used as a preparatory subject unless the subject is an infinitive or **that** clause: 'It was wonderful to see them again.' 'It is surprising that the letter arrived so quickly.' 'It happened that we arrived just as they were leaving.'

3   See THEY

4   See APPRECIATE, FIND 1, LIKE 4

5   See BE 1

it's   × The cat sat in front of the fire, cleaning it's whiskers.
    ✓ **The cat sat in front of the fire, cleaning its whiskers.**

its (WITHOUT an apostrophe) is the possessive form: 'The dog has hurt its nose again.'
it's (WITH an apostrophe) = (1) it is: 'it's raining'
(2) it has: 'it's been raining'

jewellery 1   × Women should keep expensive jewelleries in a bank or safe.
    ✓ **Women should keep expensive jewellery in a bank or safe.**

Jewellery is an uncountable noun.

2   × She and her husband had bought the ring at a jewellery.
    ✓ **She and her husband had bought the ring at a jeweller's.**

jeweller's = a shop which sells **jewellery** (gold rings, bracelets, etc.)

joke   × He kept saying the same joke again and again.
    ✓ **He kept telling the same joke again and again.**
tell a joke, NOT **say**

journey   × It wasn't the first journey he had done to Paris.
    ✓ **It wasn't the first journey he had made to Paris.**
make a journey, NOT **do**

just 1   × I'd like just to thank you once again for your hospitality.
    ✓ **I'd just like to thank you once again for your hospitality.**

Just usually goes immediately after the (first) auxiliary verb: 'I'd just like to ask you one more question.' When there is no auxiliary verb, **just** is placed directly before

the main verb: 'She just arrived in time.' However,
when the main verb is **be**, **just** is placed immediately
after it: 'The milk is just outside the door.'

2   × Some people think that mothers should stay at
home. I just partly agree with this opinion.
✓ **Some people think that mothers should stay at
home. I only partly agree with this opinion.**
In expressions which mean 'not completely', use **only**,
NOT **just**: 'He's only half awake.' 'I only partly believe
that.'

kid   × On the front of the box was the warning: 'Not
suitable for very young kids.'
✓ **On the front of the box was the warning: 'Not
suitable for very young children.'**
Kid is very informal.

kidnap   × We heard on the radio that the plane had been
kidnapped by terrorists.
✓ **We heard on the radio that the plane had
been hijacked by terrorists.**
Kidnap is used only for people.

kind 1   × Would you be so kind to arrange for the book
to be sent back to me?
✓ **Would you be so kind as to arrange for the
book to be sent back to me?**
× If you should find it, would you be so kind as
sending it to the following address?
✓ **If you should find it, would you be so kind as
to send it to the following address?**
be kind enough to do something: 'Would you be kind
enough to open the door for me?' BUT **be so kind as to**
do something

2   × All the people he met were very kind with him.
✓ **All the people he met were very kind to him.**
be kind to someone, NOT **with**

3   × There are many kind of job for people with
    qualifications.
    √ **There are many kinds of job for people with
    quaiifications.**
    × I enjoy all kind of sport.
    √ **I enjoy all kinds of sport.**

Kind (= type) is a countable noun. Compare: 'A
pineapple is a kind of fruit.' 'Pineapples and oranges
are kinds of fruit.'

4   × Imprisonment is not a good way of reducing
    this kind of crimes.
    √ **Imprisonment is not a good way of reducing
    this kind of crime/these kinds of crimes.**

Note the alternative: 'crimes of this kind'

know 1   × We had only just met, but it was as if we had
    been knowing each other for years.
    √ **We had only just met, but it was as if we had
    known each other for years.**

Know is NOT used in progressive tenses.

2   × The best way to know the city is to visit it on
    foot.
    √ **The best way to get to know the city is to visit
    it on foot.**
    × When a woman goes out to work, she knows
    other people.
    √ **When a woman goes out to work, she gets to
    know other people.**

know = be familiar with: 'I don't know Frankfurt at all.'
get to know = become familiar with

knowledge 1   × I have very little knowledge in electricity.
    √ **I have very little knowledge of electricity.**

knowledge of a subject, NOT **in**

2   × I am attending a course to improve my
    knowledges of English.
    √ **I am attending a course to improve my
    knowledge of English.**

Knowledge is an uncountable noun.

lack 1   × Doctors can do little when they are lacking proper medical supplies.
✓ **Doctors can do little when they lack proper medical supplies.**
Lack is not usually used in progressive tenses.

2   × At school I used to lack in confidence.
✓ **At school I used to lack confidence.**
× In those days we lacked of the money to go on holiday.
✓ **In those days we lacked the money to go on holiday.**
be lacking in something ('At school he was found to be lacking in confidence.') BUT **lack** something (WITHOUT a preposition)

3   × Singapore is in lack of natural resources.
✓ **Singapore lacks natural resources.**
Note the alternative: 'Singapore suffers from a lack of natural resources.'

landscape   × Lots of kings chose to live here because of the beautiful landscape.
✓ **Lots of kings chose to live here because of the beautiful scenery.**
landscape = (a view of) a wide stretch of land, especially in the countryside
scenery = the natural features of the countryside (hills, valleys, fields, etc.) considered in terms of their beauty

lane   × It was so dark in the park that she kept wandering from the lane.
✓ **It was so dark in the park that she kept wandering from the path.**
lane = a narrow road or street
path = a narrow strip of ground in a garden or park that is made for people to walk along

last 1 × He looks thinner than when I saw him in the last summer.

√ **He looks thinner than when I saw him last summer.**

Do not use a preposition or **the** with 'last week', 'last Tuesday', 'last winter', etc., unless **last** means 'final'. Compare: 'Last week we went to Scotland for a few days.' 'In the last week of her holiday she went to Wales.'

2 × Last evening I went to the cinema with a friend of mine.

√ **Yesterday evening I went to the cinema with a friend of mine**

last night BUT **yesterday evening**

3 × Last year we have stayed in the hotel for two weeks.

√ **Last year we stayed in the hotel for two weeks.**

Last night/week/month/year cannot usually be used with a present perfect tense.

4 × First we listened to the tape, then we answered some questions, and at last we wrote the story.

√ **First we listened to the tape, then we answered some questions, and finally we wrote the story.**

At last (= after a long delay; eventually) refers only to time: 'At last the tickets have arrived!'
Finally refers either to time: 'The train finally arrived.' or to sequence: 'Finally, I'd like to thank you all for coming and wish you a safe journey home.'

5 × As a dress designer, I am very interested in the last fashions.

√ **As a dress designer, I am very interested in the latest fashions.**

last = most recent (of a series); previous: 'Our last meeting was in Rome.'
latest = most recent (with an emphasis on newness)

late   × My late husband now works for a television company.
✓ **My former husband now works for a television company.**
✓ **My ex-husband now works for a television company.**

Late is used (attributively) when talking about someone who has died: 'his late wife', 'the late Mr Flowers'.

lately   × Lately someone told me that the fire was caused by a cigarette.
✓ **Recently someone told me that the fire was caused by a cigarette.**

Lately is usually used with the present perfect progressive to refer to a period of time.
Recently can be used in the same way to refer to a period of time. However, it can also refer to a point in time. Compare: 'Just lately/recently I have been wondering whether to look for a new job.' 'Just recently I decided to look for a new job.'

latest   × The latest election was won by the socialists.
✓ **The last election was won by the socialists.**
See note at LAST 5

laugh   × I laughed with myself and then explained to him that parents sometimes argue just like children.
✓ **I laughed to myself and then explained to him that parents sometimes argue just like children.**

laugh/talk to yourself, NOT **with**

lay   × We broke down the door and found Mrs Brown laying on the carpet.
✓ **We broke down the door and found Mrs Brown lying on the carpet.**

Do not confuse **lie (lying, lay, lain)** with **lay (laying, laid, laid)**.
Lie is ALWAYS intransitive: 'He lay on the floor asleep.'
Lay is nearly always transitive: 'She laid her books on the chair.'

lay down   × I just wanted to lay down and have a rest.
              ✓ **I just wanted to lie down and have a rest.**
              lay down = put something down: 'Lay the books down on the floor.'
              lie down = put your body into a horizontal position, especially on a bed

lead   × Ali asked us if we would lead him to the theatre one night.
          ✓ **Ali asked us if we would take him to the theatre one night.**
          lead = show (someone) the way by walking in front, holding by the arm, etc.: 'Some blind people like to be led across the road.'

learn 1   × Most of the stories are true and we can learn a lot of them.
             ✓ **Most of the stories are true and we can learn a lot from them.**
             learn something **from** a person or thing (NOT **of**) = be taught something: 'A child can learn a lot from television.'

2   × In prison they meet other criminals who learn them a lot of bad things.
       ✓ **In prison they meet other criminals who teach them a lot of bad things.**
       teach = give instruction
       learn = receive instruction

leave 1   × I left from the shop without buying anything.
             ✓ **I left the shop without buying anything.**
             leave somewhere WITHOUT **from**

2   × Ken's aunt left to New York on 17th April.
       ✓ **Ken's aunt left for New York on 17th April.**
       leave (somewhere) **for** somewhere else (NOT **to**): 'She left (Leeds) for London on the nine o'clock train.'

lend × Can I lend your pen a minute?
✓ **Can I borrow your pen a minute?**

lend = give (someone) the use of (something) for a certain time
borrow = take or receive (something) for a certain time, intending to return it

less 1 × Despite the increase in crime, punishments are still less stricter than they should be.
✓ **Despite the increase in crime, punishments are still less strict than they should be.**

The comparative ending (**-er**) is NEVER used with **less** or **more**.

2 × If there were less cars on the roads, there would be less accidents.
✓ **If there were fewer cars on the roads, there would be fewer accidents.**

Use **less** with an uncountable noun.
Use **fewer** with the plural form of a countable noun.
Compare: 'Less traffic would mean fewer accidents.'
Note that although **less** is widely used in place of **fewer** in conversational English, careful users regard it as non-standard.

let 1 × His mother didn't let him watching television for a whole month.
✓ **His mother didn't let him watch television for a whole month.**

let someone + infinitive WITHOUT **to**

2 × I refused to let him to help me.
✓ **I refused to let him help me.**

let someone + infinitive WITHOUT **to**

level × Pollution today is in a very high level.
✓ **Pollution today is at a very high level.**

be/stay/remain etc. **at a particular level,** NOT **in**

license   √ **AmE She lost her driving license.**
              √ **BrE She lost her driving licence.**
              In American English **license** (**se**) is the most usual
              form for both noun and verb. However, **licence** (**ce**)
              may also be used for both.
              In British English **licence** (**ce**) is the noun and **license**
              (**se**) is the verb.

lie   × I was sure the old woman was saying lies.
          √ **I was sure the old woman was telling lies.**
          × You should not speak lies.
          √ **You should not tell lies.**
          tell a lie, NOT **say** or **speak**

lied   × After a while he stopped running and lied
           down on the ground.
           √ **After a while he stopped running and lay down
           on the ground.**
           Lied is the past tense and past participle of **lie** (= to
           say something which is not true in an attempt to
           deceive). Compare: **lie (lying, lay, lain) down** (= be in
           or get into a resting position)

life 1   × The money has saved about four million lifes.
             √ **The money has saved about four million lives.**
             Life is singular.
             Lives is plural.

2   See COST 7

light up   × Suddenly a wonderful smile lighted up her
               face.
               √ **Suddenly a wonderful smile lit up her face.**
               Lit is the usual past participle of **light** BUT **lighted** is
               used before a noun: 'a lighted match'.

like 1   × 'Would you like going for a walk with me?' she
             asked the little boy.
             √ **'Would you like to go for a walk with me?' she
             asked the little boy.**
             would like + to-v

2   × 'Do you like me to show you where to go?' he
     asked.
     ✓ **'Would you like me to show you where to go?'**
     he asked.
     Compare: 'Do you like Russian music?' (an enquiry)
     'Would you like to play the piano?' (an invitation)

3   × Not many parents like that their children **leave**
     school without any qualifications.
     ✓ **Not many parents like their children to leave**
     school without any qualifications.
     like + someone/something + to-v

4   × She doesn't like when you use her books.
     ✓ **She doesn't like it when you use her books.**
     like + **it** + **when/if** clause: 'She won't like it if you arrive
     late.'

5   × Everyone arrived late like they often do when
     you don't want them to.
     ✓ **Everyone arrived late as they often do when**
     you don't want them to.
     Although the use of **like** as a conjunction is becoming
     fairly common and appears even in formal English, it
     has not yet been fully accepted by careful users.

6   × She spoke very loudly like I was deaf.
     ✓ **She spoke very loudly as if I was deaf.**
     The use of **like** to mean 'as if' is very informal and is
     usually regarded as non-standard.

7   See SAME 1

8   See SHALL 3

listen   × My mother never listens what I say.
         ✓ **My mother never listens to what I say.**
         listen to someone/something

lit × All I could see in the darkness was the end of his lit cigarette.
✓ **All I could see in the darkness was the end of his lighted cigarette.**

In British English **lit** (the past participle of **light**) is NOT used as an attributive adjective. Before a noun, use **lighted**. Compare: 'the cigarette was lit' BUT 'a lighted cigarette'

litter 1 × In the cities the streets are full of litters.
✓ **In the cities the streets are full of litter.**

Litter is an uncountable noun.

2 ✓ **AmE There would be less litter in the streets if there were more litter baskets.**
✓ **BrE There would be less litter in the streets if there were more litter bins.**

In British English, it is usual to talk about **a wastepaper basket** (usually inside) BUT **a litter bin** (usually outside, in the street).

little 1 × I had never seen a road accident and I was frightened a little.
✓ **I had never seen a road accident and I was a little frightened.**

When used as an adverb, **a little** ALWAYS comes before the adjective it modifies.

2 × Today there are too many people for too little jobs.
✓ **Today there are too many people for too few jobs.**

Little is used with uncountable nouns: 'There is too little cake for everyone to have a piece.'
Few is used with plural countable nouns: 'There are too few sandwiches for all the children to have one.'

live 1 × He told his family before living that he would never come back again.
✓ **He told his family before leaving that he would never come back again.**

Do not confuse the verbs **live** /lɪv/ and **leave** /liːv/.
Compare: 'I have been living in London for the last six weeks, but next Monday I am leaving for Rome.'

2   × I love my country and the people who are living
in it.
✓ **I love my country and the people who live
in it.**
Use the present simple tense for a permanent state.

3   × Whenever we go to the seaside, we live in a
hotel.
✓ **Whenever we go to the seaside, we stay at a
hotel.**
× At the hotel, we lived in room 101.
✓ **At the hotel, we stayed in room 101.**
stay at a hotel/in a hotel room, NOT **live**

lonely   ✓ **AmE Before long he began to feel hungry,
lonesome, and helpless.**
✓ **BrE Before long he began to feel hungry,
lonely, and helpless.**
Lonely is used in both American and British English.
Lonesome is not usually used in British English.

long 1   × He walked along the street as long as the bus
stop.
✓ **He walked along the street as far as the bus
stop.**
To refer to the furthest point of a distance, use **as far
as**, NOT **as long as**.

2   × I am afraid it will take long to improve my
English.
✓ **I am afraid it will take a long time to improve
my English.**
It won't take long. (negative)
Will it take long? (question)
It will take a long time. (affirmative)

look 1   × I stood in front of the window, looking the
trees.
✓ **I stood in front of the window, looking at the
trees.**
look at someone/something

2   × Someone should inspect the kitchen twice a week to look whether everything is nice and clean.

✓ **Someone should inspect the kitchen twice a week to see whether everything is nice and clean.**

see = find out (by checking)
Compare: 'I looked to see whether it was still raining.'

3   × It looked like hours before the ambulance arrived.

✓ **It seemed like hours before the ambulance arrived.**

look like = show (visible) signs of: 'It looks like it's going to rain.'
seem (like) = give the feeling or impression of: 'It seems like years since I had a holiday.'

4   See SOUND 4

look after   × Having received news of his death, they stopped looking after him.

✓ **Having received news of his death, they stopped looking for him.**

look after = take care of: 'Who will look after you if you are ill?'
look for = try to find: 'I spent a whole hour looking for my keys.'

look at   × I stayed in and looked at a film on television.
✓ **I stayed in and watched a film on television.**

look at = turn your eyes to see something (usually briefly): 'I looked at the address on the envelope, but didn't recognize it.'
watch = observe closely, often as a spectator or member of an audience (usually for a fairly long period of time)

look for   × Many women have a family to look for and
therefore cannot go out to work.
✓ **Many women have a family to look after and
therefore cannot go out to work.**

look for = search for: 'I spent a whole hour looking for
my keys.'
look after = take care of: 'Who will look after the dog
while you are on holiday?'

look forward to 1   × I'm looking forwards to seeing you.
✓ **I'm looking forward to seeing you.**
look forward to, NOT **forwards**

2   × I'm looking forward the day I can go home.
✓ **I'm looking forward to the day I can go home.**
× He said he was looking forward for his
holidays.
✓ **He said he was looking forward to his
holidays.**
look forward to something

3   × I'm looking forward to hear from you.
✓ **I'm looking forward to hearing from you.**
look forward to + v-ing

look like   See HOW 1

loose   × A lot of people are afraid of loosing their jobs.
✓ **A lot of people are afraid of losing their jobs.**
loosen (verb) = make less tight
loose (adjective) = not tight
lose (verb) = no longer have

lots   × She makes us do a lots of homework.
✓ **She makes us do a lot of homework.**
✓ **She makes us do lots of homework.**
a lot of, OR **lots of** WITHOUT **a**

love   × It was a very unusual gift and I loved it very
            much.
            ✓ **It was a very unusual gift and I liked it very
            much.**

            love someone very much BUT **like something** very
            much

luck 1 × What a rotten luck! There he was again, sitting
            right beside me.
            ✓ **What rotten luck! There he was again, sitting
            right beside me.**
            Luck is an uncountable noun.

2   × That afternoon she had luck: she found the
            keys at the bottom of a drawer.
            ✓ **That afternoon she had some luck: she found
            the keys at the bottom of a drawer.**
            Note the alternatives: 'That afternoon she had a
            piece/stroke of luck ... ' 'That afternoon she was lucky
            ... '

lucky   × It's better to have a lucky family than a lot of
            money.
            ✓ **It's better to have a happy family than a lot of
            money.**

            lucky (opposite **unlucky**) = having good luck or good
            fortune: 'You have to be lucky to win a prize.' 'You're
            lucky the car didn't hit you!'
            happy (opposite **sad**) = feeling or showing pleasure or
            contentment

luggage 1 × There was no room in the car for all our
            luggages.
            ✓ **There was no room in the car for all our
            luggage.**
            Luggage is an uncountable noun.

2   × I spent the morning packing my luggage.
            ✓ **I spent the morning packing my bags/suitcases.**
            pack your bags/suitcases, NOT **luggage**

lunch   × My plan was to visit the library and then have a lunch at a restaurant.
              √ **My plan was to visit the library and then have lunch at a restaurant.**
              have lunch/breakfast/dinner etc. WITHOUT **a/the**

luxury   × They don't have any money to spend on luxury things.
              √ **They don't have any money to spend on luxuries.**
              luxuries (plural of **luxury**) OR **luxury goods, luxury items**, but NOT **luxury things**

machine   × Over eighty per cent of these cars are old, and so are their machines.
              √ **Over eighty per cent of these cars are old, and so are their engines.**
              machine = a device which performs useful work, such as a sewing machine or lawn mower
              engine = a device which provides the power for a motor vehicle, aircraft, etc.

made   × She claimed that the jumper was made from wool.
              √ **She claimed that the jumper was made of wool.**
              Use **made from** when the original materials have been completely changed: 'Bread is made from flour and water.'
              Use **made of** when the materials in an object can still be recognized as the original materials: 'The table is made of wood and metal.'

magazine   × The magazine is on one of the busiest streets in the town.
              √ **The shop is on one of the busiest streets in the town.**
              magazine = a weekly or monthly publication; a periodical: 'I've bought a newspaper and a magazine to read on the train.'

magical   × It was a magical stick, and everything it
              touched turned to gold.
              √ **It was a magic stick, and everything it touched
              turned to gold.**

              magical = produced by or as if by magic; fascinating
              or enchanting: 'Her first sight of the Taj Mahal was a
              magical experience.'
              magic = able to perform magic; used in magic

mail   √ **AmE It would be quicker to return the book by
              mail.**
              √ **BrE It would be quicker to return the book by
              post.**

              In American English, use **send/return** something **by
              mail**.
              In British English, use **send/return** something **by post**.

majority × The majority of the sky was covered in cloud.
              √ **Most of the sky was covered in cloud.**
              Do not use **majority** with the singular form of a
              countable noun, unless it is a noun like 'committee',
              'government', or 'team' (i.e. it refers to a group).

make 1   × They made him eating his lunch in silence.
              √ **They made him eat his lunch in silence.**
              × They made her to work hard.
              √ **They made her work hard.**

              make a person or thing + infinitive WITHOUT **to**

      2   × The government has already made a lot of
              things in order to solve the problem.
              √ **The government has already done a lot of
              things in order to solve the problem.**
              × In Italy we have made a great deal to prevent
              pollution.
              √ **In Italy we have done a great deal to prevent
              pollution.**

              do a great deal/lot/lot of things, NOT **make**

      3   See BEST 2, DEMONSTRATION, EXPERIENCE 1, GLANCE, PARTY,
              TEST

male   × She has a deep male voice.
√ **She has a deep masculine voice.**

male = (1) of the sex that does not produce eggs or give birth to young: 'a male rabbit', 'a male nurse' (2) for or composed of men or boys: 'a male choir'
masculine = having qualities or features considered to be suitable for a man

man 1   × My man and I have been married since last Christmas.
√ **My husband and I have been married since last Christmas.**

husband = the man to whom a woman is married

2   × Every day the man is inventing new machines.
√ **Every day man is inventing new machines.**

When using **man** to mean 'the human race', do not use an article.

manage 1   × Unfortunately I couldn't manage to pass the exam.
√ **Unfortunately I didn't manage to pass the exam.**

Do not place **can** or **could** before **manage** when **manage** means 'succeed'.

2   × I was told that you might manage repairing it.
√ **I was told that you might manage to repair it.**

manage + to-v

3   × I will manage that the magazine is sent to you every month.
√ **I will arrange for the magazine to be sent to you every month.**

manage = control or be in charge of (a business etc.): 'I let my accountant manage all my financial affairs.'
arrange = make plans or preparations

manifestation × Several manifestations were made, causing the police a lot of problems.
✓ **Several demonstrations were held, causing the police a lot of problems.**

manifestation = a display, sign, or act of showing: 'The flowers he sent were a clear manifestation of his feelings for her.'
demonstration = a public expression of opinion, usually by a large group of people who feel that something is wrong or unjust: 'a demonstration against nuclear war'

manufacture 1 × I bought the tape recorder while visiting your manufacture in Japan.
✓ **I bought the tape recorder while visiting your factory in Japan.**

manufacture (noun) = the production of goods in large quantities by means of machines
factory = a large building or group of buildings where things are manufactured

2 × I have always been impressed by the quality of your company's manufactures.
✓ **I have always been impressed by the quality of your company's products.**

manufacture (noun) = the production of goods in large quantities by means of machines: 'Our company specializes in the manufacture of paper clips.'
product = something that a company produces for people to buy

many 1 × It's important to understand why there is so many violence in our world.
✓ **It's important to understand why there is so much violence in our world.**

Many is used only with countable nouns: 'too much traffic' but 'too many cars'.

2 × One of the policemen started asking me many questions.

✓ **One of the policemen started asking me a lot of questions.**

Many is used before a noun (or as a pronoun) mainly in questions and negative sentences: 'Does he have many friends?' 'He doesn't have many friends.' In affirmative sentences, phrases such as **a lot of** and **plenty of** are used. Note, however, that **many** is used in affirmative sentences after **too**, **so**, and **as** ('You ask too many questions.') and sometimes in formal contexts ('Many accidents arise as a result of negligence').

mark 1 × Before buying a cassette recorder, I asked my friend if he could recommend a good mark.

✓ **Before buying a cassette recorder, I asked my friend if he could recommend a good make.**

mark (also Mk) = model, type, or version (used chiefly in trade names): 'a Mk II Jaguar'
make = brand (of cars, washing machines, refrigerators, etc.)

2 × Inside the coat there is a mark which says that it is made in Italy.

✓ **Inside the coat there is a label which says that it is made in Italy.**

label = a small piece of card or material fixed to a garment which gives details about size, manufacture, and cleaning: 'The label says "Dry clean only".'

market × The magazine gives a list of all the computers in the market.

✓ **The magazine gives a list of all the computers on the market.**

on the market (= available in shops; for sale), NOT **in**

marriage × Why didn't you invite me to your marriage?

✓ **Why didn't you invite me to your wedding?**

marriage = the ceremony of becoming husband and wife considered from a purely religious or legal point of view: 'Her parents are against the marriage.'
wedding = the occasion when this ceremony takes place and the celebrations that follow it

marry 1   × When she met my father, she was about to marry to another man.
✓ **When she met my father, she was about to marry another man.**
be married to someone BUT **marry** someone WITHOUT **to**

2   × He is going to ask her to marry with him.
✓ **He is going to ask her to marry him.**
marry someone, NOT **marry with**

marvellous   ✓ **AmE There are two marvelous museums to visit.**
✓ **BrE There are two marvellous museums to visit.**
In American English, use **marvelous** (ONLY ONE **l**).
In British English, use **marvellous** (DOUBLE **l**).

match   × The colour of the jacket matches to the trousers.
✓ **The colour of the jacket matches the trousers.**
match something WITHOUT **to**

mathematics   × Mathematics are my favourite subject.
✓ **Mathematics is my favourite subject.**
Mathematics is ALWAYS singular.

matter 1   × The matter is that we won't have enough room in the car to take your mother with us.
✓ **The problem is that we won't have enough room in the car to take your mother with us.**
Matter is used to mean 'problem' or 'trouble' only in questions and negative sentences: 'What's the matter?' 'Is anything the matter?' 'There's nothing the matter.'

2   × The flight attendant told us that there wasn't any matter; it was just a storm.
✓ **The flight attendant told us that nothing was the matter; it was just a storm.**
Note the alternatives: 'She told us that there was nothing the matter.' 'She told us that there wasn't anything the matter.'

3   See NO MATTER

matters   ✗ To make the matters worse, the roof leaked and there was no heater in the room.
✓ **To make matters worse, the roof leaked and there was no heater in the room.**
to make matters worse WITHOUT **the**

may be   ✗ May be they have lost our address.
✓ **Maybe they have lost our address.**
When you mean 'perhaps', use **maybe**, NOT **may be**.
Compare: 'It may be that they have lost our address.'

me 1   ✗ I found me a seat and sat down.
✓ **I found myself a seat and sat down.**
✗ I stayed by the fire to warm me up.
✓ **I stayed by the fire to warm myself up.**
When the object or indirect object is the same as the subject, a reflexive pronoun is used: 'She got herself a drink.' 'They bought themselves some new clothes.'

2   ✗ I still remember the day me and my sister went to Buenos Aires by bus.
✓ **I still remember the day my sister and I went to Buenos Aires by bus.**
It is usual to mention yourself last.

meal   ✓ **AmE We always take our meals in the canteen.**
✓ **BrE We always have our meals in the canteen.**
In British English, use **have a meal**, NOT **take**.
In American English, you can use **take** OR **have**.

mean 1   ✗ Being a good flight attendant means to make your passengers feel relaxed.
✓ **Being a good flight attendant means making your passengers feel relaxed.**
mean + to-v = intend to do something: 'She means to find out who is to blame.'
mean + v-ing = involves doing something

2   × Some people mean that stricter punishments
will reduce the amount of crime.
✓ **Some people think/believe that stricter
punishments will reduce the amount of crime.**

mean (used of people) = intend to say: 'I'm not sure
what he's saying but I think he means that he can't
afford to wait any longer.'

meaning 1   × His meaning was to use the pin to open the
lock.
✓ **His intention was to use the pin to open the
lock.**

meaning = what a word, sign, etc. communicates: 'If
you don't know the meaning of a word, look it up in
your dictionary.'
intention = what someone plans or intends to do

2   × I asked him to explain what his meaning was.
✓ **I asked him to explain what he meant.**

Meaning (noun) is not usually used of people.
Compare: 'A word can have several meanings.'

means   × He was determined to get the money by all
means.
✓ **He was determined to get the money by whatever
means.**

by all means = certainly; please do (mainly used when
giving someone permission to do something): 'May I
smoke?' 'By all means.'
Use **by any/whatever means** when you mean 'using
whatever methods are necessary'.

measurement   × In my opinion, the authorities have to take
even stricter measurements to save our
archaeological treasures.
✓ **In my opinion, the authorities have to take
even stricter measures to save our
archaeological treasures.**

measurement = the length, width, etc. of something:
'You can't buy new curtains without knowing the
measurements of the window.'
measure = an action intended to have a particular
effect; a law or ruling: 'New measures are to be
introduced in the fight against crime.'

media   × The medias, such as radio and television, tell us what is happening in the world.
  ✓ **The media, such as radio and television, tell us what is happening in the world.**
  × Television is a very powerful media.
  ✓ **Television is a very powerful medium.**
  Medium is singular.
  Media is plural.

medicine   × The doctor gave me some medecine and told me to stay in bed.
  ✓ **The doctor gave me some medicine and told me to stay in bed.**
  medicine (WITH **ic**, NOT **ec**)

meet   ✓ **AmE I've arranged to meet with Sarah tomorrow.**
  ✓ **BrE I've arranged to meet Sarah tomorrow.**
  meet with someone (mainly American usage) = have a (previously arranged) meeting with: 'We met with their representatives to discuss the problem.'
  meet someone (British and American English) = come together (with) by chance or arrangement

melted   × The melted steel is then poured into a large tank.
  ✓ **The molten steel is then poured into a large tank.**
  'melted ice', 'melted butter' BUT 'molten steel', 'molten lava'

memories   × Casanova recorded his adventures in his memories.
  ✓ **Casanova recorded his adventures in his memoirs.**
  memories = things remembered; pictures (of past events) in a person's mind: 'I have many vivid memories of my childhood.'
  memoirs = a person's written account of (a period in) his or her life

memory   × Each visitor received a small gift as a memory.
        ✓ **Each visitor received a small gift as a souvenir.**
        × I bought six postcards and a few small memories.
        ✓ **I bought six postcards and a few small souvenirs.**

memory = something remembered: 'I have very few memories of my childhood.'
souvenir = something that is bought or received in a particular place (especially while on holiday) and is kept to remind you of it

menace   × Nowadays world peace is menaced.
        ✓ **Nowadays world peace is threatened.**

Menace (verb) is not usually used unless additional information is given about the nature of the danger. Compare: 'The whole world is threatened/menaced by the risk of nuclear war.'

Middle Age   × The history of the town dates back to the Middle Age.
        ✓ **The history of the town dates back to the Middle Ages.**

middle age = the period in a person's life between youth and old age
Middle Ages = the period in European history from about 1100 to 1500 AD

middle age   × Sitting next to me was a middle age man, probably about forty.
        ✓ **Sitting next to me was a middle-aged man, probably about forty.**

middle-aged (adjective) = in **middle age** (noun)

migrate × A lot of new doctors migrate to America where they can earn more money.
√ **A lot of new doctors emigrate to America where they can earn more money.**

migrate (of certain birds and animals) = travel (annually) from one place to spend a length of time in another
emigrate (of people) = leave your own country and make your home in another one

million 1 × Belgium has ten millions inhabitants.
√ **Belgium has ten million inhabitants.**
× Brazil has a hundred and twenty millions of inhabitants.
√ **Brazil has a hundred and twenty million inhabitants.**

See note at HUNDRED 2

2 See THOUSAND 1

mind 1 × Our teacher is very patient and doesn't mind to explain again if we don't understand.
√ **Our teacher is very patient and doesn't mind explaining again if we don't understand.**

(not) mind + v-ing

2 × It was raining but we didn't mind it.
√ **It was raining but we didn't mind.**

When the object of **mind** can be understood from the context, **mind** is not followed by a pronoun: 'Do you mind waiting a few minutes?' 'No, we don't mind.'

3 × I made up my mind going for a swim.
√ **I made up my mind to go for a swim.**

make up your mind + to-v

4 × The first thing that comes to my mind when I think about France is wine.
√ **The first thing that comes to mind when I think about France is wine.**

come to mind WITHOUT **my, his, their,** etc.

minute 1 × The train arrived at exactly twelve past three.
      ✓ **The train arrived at exactly twelve minutes past three.**
      When telling the time, **minutes** must be used after all numbers except **five**, **ten**, **twenty**, and **twenty-five**.
      Compare: 'It's twenty (minutes) past ten.' (**minutes** can be used)
      'It's twenty-three minutes past ten.' (**minutes** must be used)

   2 × The college is a twenty minutes bus ride from my flat.
      ✓ **The college is a twenty-minute bus ride from my flat.**
      See note at MONTH

   3 × All I wanted was a few minutes of sleep.
      ✓ **All I wanted was a few minutes' sleep.**
      See note at OF 2

mistake 1 × The man next to me picked up my case in mistake.
      ✓ **The man next to me picked up my case by mistake.**
      in error BUT **by mistake**
      See note at ERROR

   2 × I rarely do more than three mistakes in an essay.
      ✓ **I rarely make more than three mistakes in an essay.**
      make a mistake, NOT **do**

   3 × When I got home with the cassette recorder, it wouldn't work. I tried to find the mistake myself.
      ✓ **When I got home with the cassette recorder, it wouldn't work. I tried to find the fault myself.**
      A spelling, essay, calculation, decision, etc. may contain a **mistake** (= an error).
      A machine or electrical device may have or develop a **fault** (= a weakness or defect).

4 × The policeman said that she had made a mistake–she had stolen a ring from a jeweller's.

✓ **The policeman said that she had committed a crime-she had stolen a ring from a jeweller's.**

Mistakes are usually made unintentionally.

Mister 1 × Dear Mister Southcroft ...

✓ **Dear Mr Southcroft ...**

Mister is ALWAYS written **Mr**.

2 × Dear Mister,

✓ **Dear Sir,**

In formal letters, write **Dear Mr Smith**, **Dear Ms Jones**, etc. when the surname is known.

When the surname is not known, use **Dear Sir/Madam**.

moment 1 × In that moment the door opened.

✓ **At that moment the door opened.**

at this/that moment = at this/that particular time

Compare: **in a moment** = very soon: 'I'll have to go in a moment.'

2 × I'd like to see him in my office the moment he will arrive.

✓ **I'd like to see him in my office the moment he arrives.**

After **the moment**, use the present simple tense for future reference, NOT **shall/will** + verb.

momentary × The Pope's visit was a momentary occasion.

✓ **The Pope's visit was a momentous occasion.**

momentary = lasting for only a moment: 'a momentary glance', 'momentary hesitation'

momentous (of events) = very important

money 1 × I wonder where all their money come from.

✓ **I wonder where all their money comes from.**

Money is an uncountable noun.

2 See AFFORD 4

month   × The company provides a three months training course.
✓ **The company provides a three-month training course.**

Nouns of measurement ('week', 'gram', 'mile', etc.) are always singular when used in compound adjectives: 'a ten-second silence', 'a six-minute wait', 'a five-mile race'.

mood   × I was really not in the mood to listening to the nonsense.
✓ **I was really not in the mood to listen to the nonsense.**

in the mood + to-v

more 1   × I had never seen a more happier child.
✓ **I had never seen a happier child.**

Never use **more** with the **-er** form of an adjective.

2   × More of Japanese cars were sold in Europe this year than last year.
✓ **More Japanese cars were sold in Europe this year than last year.**

Use **more** WITHOUT **of** when the noun that follows is used in a general, unrestricted sense: 'The school should buy more books.'
When talking about a particular group of people or things, use **more of** followed by **the** + noun: 'The school should buy more of the books that are written especially for children.'

3   See MUCH 5

4   See NO MORE

more or less   × Some women more or less are forced to work nowadays.
✓ **Some women are more or less forced to work nowadays.**

When there is no auxiliary verb, **more or less** may be placed immediately before the main verb: 'She more or less forced me to invite her.' However, when the main verb is **be**, then the phrase **more or less** is

placed immediately after it: 'Don't stop now! We're more or less there!'
Otherwise **more or less** goes immediately after the (first) auxiliary verb: 'If you've more or less finished, I'll start clearing up.' Note, however, that in many cases **more or less** may be placed at the end of the clause: 'She forced me to invite her, more or less.' 'We're there, more or less!' 'They've finished the job, more or less.'

morning   See AFTERNOON, DAY 1

most 1   × Where I come from, the most teachers have to teach at two schools in order to earn enough.
√ **Where I come from, most teachers have to teach at two schools in order to earn enough.**
Do not use **the** before **most** when **most** means 'nearly all'.

2   × I think that pollution is a serious problem in most of the countries nowadays.
√ **I think that pollution is a serious problem in most countries nowadays.**
× Most of the people like to spend Christmas at home.
√ **Most people like to spend Christmas at home.**
Use **most** WITHOUT **of** + determiner when the noun that follows is used in a general, unrestricted sense.
Compare: 'Most of the people I know like to spend Christmas at home.'

3   × Most of major firms in Japan use word processors.
√ **Most of the major firms in Japan use word processors.**
√ **Most major firms in Japan use word processors.**
most of + determiner (+ adjective) + noun OR **most** (+ adjective) + noun

4 × My country is very big and occupies
the most part of the continent.
✓ **My country is very big and occupies
most of the continent.**
✓ **My country is very big and occupies
the main part of the continent.**

Most cannot be used as an adjective. The only
exception is the fixed phrase **for the most part**,
meaning 'almost completely; mainly': 'The machines
have for the most part been replaced.'

5 × Both girls are clever but Edna is the most
intelligent.
✓ **Both girls are clever but Edna is the more
intelligent.**

Use **more** when comparing two people or things.
Use **most** when comparing three or more.

motivate × She found it hard to motivate her absence.
✓ **She found it hard to justify her absence.**

motivate = provide someone with a strong reason for
doing something: 'The dream of owning their own
house motivated them to work harder.'
justify = give a good reason or excuse for

mouse × There were mouses in the canteen.
✓ **There were mice in the canteen.**

Mouse is singular.
Mice is plural.

much 1 × I should like to become an engineer because I
know much about it.
✓ **I should like to become an engineer because I
know a lot about it.**

As a noun or pronoun **much** is usually used only in ·
negative sentences and questions: 'He doesn't know
much about it.' 'Does he know much about it?' In
affirmative sentences, phrases such as **a lot** and **a
great deal** are used.

2   × As a doctor he earns much money.
   ✓ **As a doctor he earns a lot of money.**

Much is used before a noun (or as a pronoun) mainly
in questions and negative sentences: 'Does he earn
much money?' 'He doesn't earn much money.' In
affirmative sentences, phrases such as **a lot of** and
plenty of are used. Note, however, that **much** is used
in affirmative sentences after **too, so,** and **as**: 'He
spends too much money on beer.' and sometimes in
formal contexts: 'The country's economy has enjoyed
much support from foreign investment.'

3   × British culture is much different from ours.
   ✓ **British culture is very different from ours.**
   × We were much afraid that we would miss the
      flight.
   ✓ **We were very afraid that we would miss the
      flight.**

Much is used before an adjective (1) in questions and
negative sentences which involve comparison: 'Is
British culture much different from ours?' 'No, it isn't
much different.'
(2) before comparative forms: 'His last novel was much
longer and much more interesting.'
(3) before certain past participles acting as adjectives:
'Her drawings are much admired.'

4   × There are as much disadvantages as
      advantages.
   ✓ **There are as many disadvantages as
      advantages.**

as much + uncountable noun: 'You can eat as much
food as you like.'
as many + plural form of a countable noun: 'You
haven't seen as many films as Helen has.'

5   × Nowadays, there are much more criminals
      than policemen.
   ✓ **Nowadays, there are many/far more criminals
      than policemen.**

much more + uncountable noun: 'much more traffic'
many/far more + plural countable noun: 'far more cars'

6   × He was driving too much fast when the
          accident happened.
      ✓ **He was driving much too fast when the
          accident happened.**
      much/far + **too** + adjective/adverb

7   × I make much too many mistakes.
      ✓ **I make far too many mistakes.**
      With **too many, too few,** and **fewer,** use **far,** NOT **much.**

music   × I turned on the radio to listen to some musics.
          ✓ **I turned on the radio to listen to some music.**
          × We tried to listen to a music, but the sound
            was very bad.
          ✓ **We tried to listen to a piece of music, but the
            sound was very bad.**
          Music is an uncountable noun.

must 1   × In my opinion, the government must to do
             something about the problem.
           ✓ **In my opinion, the government must do
             something about the problem.**
           must do/be something WITHOUT **to**

2   × People are not as careful as they must be and
          drop their litter in the streets.
      ✓ **People are not as careful as they should be
          and drop their litter in the streets.**
      Use **must** to talk about something you are obliged to
      do, without freedom to choose or decide.
      Use **should** to talk about something you ought to do,
      but where you have freedom to choose or decide.

3   × The pupils mustn't go to the meeting if they
          don't want to.
      ✓ **The pupils needn't go to the meeting if they
          don't want to.**
      Use **must/mustn't** when you mean 'have to', without
      freedom to choose or decide.
      Use **needn't** or **don't have to** when there is freedom to
      choose or decide.

4   × If you can't find her, she must hide
        somewhere.
        √ **If you can't find her, she must be hiding
        somewhere.**
        'She must be hiding somewhere.' (= I conclude that
        she is hiding)
        Compare: 'If you don't want them to find you, you must
        hide somewhere.' (= you have to hide)

myself   × Two weeks ago my friend and myself decided
        to have a picnic.
        √ **Two weeks ago my friend and I decided to
        have a picnic.**
        Pronouns ending **-self** or **-selves** cannot be placed in
        the subject position unless they are used for emphasis:
        'I myself have never seen a ghost.' 'They themselves
        have never been to Italy.'

name   × The magazine is named 'Four Wheels'; it's
        about cars.
        √ **The magazine is called 'Four Wheels'; it's
        about cars.**
        name = (1) give a name to: 'They've named the baby
        Louise.'
        (2) identify by saying or writing the name(s) of: 'The
        students were asked to name the five largest oceans
        in the world.'
        call = (1) give a name to: 'They've called the baby
        Louise.'
        (2) be known by a particular name: 'Her mother is also
        called Louise.'

narrow   × When immersed in water, the cloth narrows.
        √ **When immersed in water, the cloth shrinks.**
        narrow (of roads, rivers, etc.) = become less wide:
        'Just beyond the bend, the river begins to narrow.'
        shrink (especially of cloth) = become smaller as a
        result of being wet or placed in water

nation × I couldn't tell what nation he came from.
√ **I couldn't tell what country he came from.**

nation = a large group of people, usually living in one area and having an independent government
country = the area occupied by or associated with a nation
Note the alternative: 'I couldn't tell his nationality.'

national × He is so national that he refuses to buy foreign goods.
√ **He is so patriotic that he refuses to buy foreign goods.**

national = of, belonging to, or concerning a country: 'a national holiday', 'a national railway'
patriotic = having or showing love for your country

nationality 1 × The harbour was full of ships of different nationalities.
√ **The harbour was full of ships from different countries.**

Nationality is used only of people.

2 × The students are from various nationalities.
√ **The students are of various nationalities.**

be of a particular nationality, NOT **from**

nationalized × Mabel Wong was born in Hong Kong but she has now become a nationalized British citizen.
√ **Mabel Wong was born in Hong Kong but she has now become a naturalized British citizen.**

nationalized = owned or controlled by a government: 'Many industries have been nationalized over the last few years.'
naturalized = made a citizen of a country (that is not the country of your birth)

nature × I have always found the nature fascinating.
√ **I have always found nature fascinating.**

Nature (= the natural world of birds, trees, rivers, etc.) is NEVER used with **the**.

near 1   × He decided to visit a friend who lived very
near from where he was at that moment.
√ **He decided to visit a friend who lived very
near (to) where he was at that moment.**
near (to), NOT **from**

2   × I went near to the girl and told her my name.
√ **I went up to the girl and told her my name.**
go up to someone = approach someone

3   × I sometimes meet friends in a near restaurant.
√ **I sometimes meet friends in a nearby
restaurant.**
× I ran to the telephone box which was near to
call an ambulance.
√ **I ran to the nearby telephone box to call an
ambulance.**
Near is not used as an attributive adjective except in
phrases such as 'a near miss' or 'the near future'.
Compare: 'The restaurant is near the town hall.'
(preposition)
'The restaurant is quite near.' (predicative adjective)
'We went to a nearby restaurant.' (attributive adjective)

nearby   × Their house is nearby the new airport.
√ **Their house is near the new airport.**
Nearby is used either as an adverb: 'There is an
airport nearby.' or an adjective: 'We flew from a
nearby airport.' but NOT as a preposition.

necessary 1   × It is necessary to some people to get more
than eight hours' sleep.
√ **It is necessary for some people to get more
than eight hours' sleep.**
necessary for someone to do something, NOT **to**

2   × Many people were necessary to leave their
homes during the earthquake.
√ **It was necessary for many people to leave
their homes during the earthquake.**
√ **Many people had to leave their homes during
the earthquake.**
Compare: 'A passport is necessary if you want to
travel overseas.'

need 1   × It is no need to tell the police about the accident.

   √ **There is no need to tell the police about the accident.**

   it is not necessary ... BUT **there is no need ...**

2   × There is a great need of international understanding.

   √ **There is a great need for international understanding.**

   a need for something, NOT **of**
   Compare: **(be) in need of** something (= require): 'The car is in need of a good clean.' 'Are you in need of any assistance?'

3   × Tina needs leave her house at seven o'clock every morning.

   √ **Tina needs to leave her house at seven o'clock every morning.**

   Compare: (1) negative form: 'She doesn't need to stay if she doesn't want to.' 'She needn't stay if she doesn't want.' (WITHOUT **to**)
   (2) question form: 'Does she need to stay any longer?' 'Need she stay any longer?' (WITHOUT **to**)

4   × Today's society needs that women work.

   √ **Today's society needs women to work.**

   need someone **to** do something, NOT **that**

needn't   × Catherine told her husband he needn't to worry.

   √ **Catherine told her husband he needn't worry.**

   needn't + infinitive WITHOUT **to**
   Note the alternative: 'Catherine told her husband that he didn't need to worry.'

negligent   × There was a negligent amount of liquid in the
                   test tube.
               ✓ **There was a negligible amount of liquid in the
                   test tube.**

               negligent = failing to take proper care or precautions;
               neglecting your duties: 'The court decided that the pilot
               of the crashed aircraft had been negligent.'
               negligible = very small

neither 1 × Inside the examination room we could neither
                   smoke or talk.
               ✓ **Inside the examination room we could neither
                   smoke nor talk.**
               × His parents neither shouted at him or smacked
                   him.
               ✓ **His parents neither shouted at him nor
                   smacked him.**

               neither ... nor ... , NOT **neither ... or ...**
               Compare: 'either ... or ... '

2   × Neither John's father nor mine couldn't
                   understand the problem.
               ✓ **Neither John's father nor mine could
                   understand the problem.**

               not/never/rarely etc. are NOT used after **neither** OR
               neither ... nor ...

3   × Henry neither told Maria nor her sister that he
                   had lost his job.
               ✓ **Henry told neither Maria nor her sister that he
                   had lost his job.**

               Neither should be placed immediately before the first
               of the connected items and **nor** immediately before the
               second. Compare: 'I've seen neither Anne nor Tina.'
               'I've neither seen Anne nor written to her.'

4   × In the library I found neither the books I was
                   looking for.
               ✓ **In the library I found neither of the books I
                   was looking for.**

               neither + singular noun form: 'Neither camera is suitable.'
               neither of + plural noun form: 'Neither of the cameras is
               suitable.'

5   × Neither teachers are coming.
        ✓ **Neither teacher is coming.**
        ✓ **Neither of the teachers is/are coming.**
        When **neither** is used with a singular noun it is
        followed by a singular verb.
        Note that in informal English **neither of . . .** and **neither
        . . . nor** are often followed by a plural verb, although
        this would be considered incorrect in formal writing:
        'Neither Paul nor John is/are coming.'

nervous 1   × The child kept pulling my sleeve, which
                  made me nervous.
                ✓ **The child kept pulling my sleeve, which
                  irritated me.**

        nervous (adjective) = rather afraid
        irritate (verb) = annoy

2   × Thinking she might be hurt, I felt very nervous.
        ✓ **Thinking she might be hurt, I felt very anxious.**
        nervous = rather afraid: 'Wouldn't you feel nervous if
        you had to make a speech to an audience of three
        hundred people?'
        anxious = worried about something which may happen
        or may have happened

never 1   × I asked him to never arrive late.
              ✓ **I asked him never to arrive late.**
              Do not split a **to** infinitive with **never/not**.

2   × You never can get really good beef in our
          local supermarket.
        ✓ **You can never get really good beef in our
          local supermarket.**
        Never goes immediately after the (first) auxiliary verb:
        'You should never cross the road without looking.'
        However, when there is no auxiliary verb, **never** is
        placed immediately before the main verb: 'She never
        lies.' When the main verb is **be**, **never** is placed
        immediately after it: 'She is never punctual.'

3 × I did never have time to read the book.

✓ **I never had time to read the book.**

Do is often used with **not** to make negative statements: 'I didn't answer the letter.' 'She doesn't invite strangers.' However, **do** is NOT used in this way with **never**: 'I never answered the letter.' 'She never invites strangers.'

The exception to this rule is when **do** is used for emphasis: 'In thirty years I never *did* have time to read the book.'

4 × She said some of the rudest things I have never heard in all my life.

✓ **She said some of the rudest things I have ever heard in all my life.**

never = at no time
ever = at any time

5 × Nobody never tells you the truth.

✓ **Nobody ever tells you the truth.**

× 'Nobody will never find me,' he thought.

✓ **'Nobody will ever find me,' he thought.**

After **nobody/nothing/rarely** and other words with a negative meaning, use **ever** (NOT **never**) to avoid a double negative.

6 × Never I had seen such an ugly face.

✓ **Never had I seen such an ugly face.**

When negative adverbs such as **never/seldom/ hardly/scarcely** are used at the beginning of a sentence, the subject and auxiliary verb change places: 'Never have I known him to lose.' 'Rarely do you find such intelligence in a child.'

nevertheless × Richard is very forgetful and unreliable. Never the less, I like him a lot because he makes me laugh.

✓ **Richard is very forgetful and unreliable. Nevertheless, I like him a lot because he makes me laugh.**

Nevertheless is ALWAYS one word.

news × The news are never very good nowadays.

√ **The news is never very good nowadays.**

× I'm looking forward to hearing a good news from you.

√ **I'm looking forward to hearing some good news from you.**

News is an uncountable noun.

next 1 × I have some spare time this week but the next week I'll have to start work.

√ **I have some spare time this week but next week I'll have to start work.**

Do not use **the** in time expressions with **next** when the point or period of time is being considered in relation to the present.
Compare: 'Next Friday we're going fishing.' (in relation to the present)
'The next afternoon they took us to see the National Gallery.' (in relation to the day before the trip to the National Gallery)

2 × I am looking forward to seeing you on next Sunday.

√ **I am looking forward to seeing you next Sunday.**

Do not use a preposition to begin a time expression with **next** when the point or period of time is being considered in relation to the present.
See also ON 1

3 × The next post office is opposite the bus station.

√ **The nearest post office is opposite the bus station.**

Do not use **next** to mean **nearest**.

nice × Most people like to come home to a nice and tidy house.

√ **Most people like to come home to a house that is nice and tidy.**

Two-part adjectival phrases with **nice** such as 'nice and tidy', 'nice and clean', and 'nice and smart' are ALWAYS placed after the noun they modify.

night 1 × He suddenly realized that it was getting dark
and it would soon be the night.
✓ **He suddenly realized that it was getting dark
and it would soon be night.**

When **night** means 'the period when it is dark' (as
opposed to **day,** 'the period when it is light'), it is
usually used WITHOUT **the:** 'It would soon be night.' (= It
would soon be dark.)

2 × It was about nine o'clock in the night when we
heard a noise outside.
✓ **It was about nine o'clock at night when we
heard a noise outside.**

ten o'clock **in the morning,** two o'clock **in the
afternoon,** half-past seven **in the evening,** BUT nine
o'clock **at night**

3 × Night was falling and it started to rain.
✓ **It was getting dark and it started to rain.**

'Night was falling' is not really incorrect but is only
used in a literary context.

no × The boy was scared and asked me no to tell
his parents.
✓ **The boy was scared and asked me not to tell
his parents.**

no = (1) not any: 'He has no money.'
(2) the opposite of **yes**
Not is used to make a sentence or part of a sentence
negative.

nobody 1 × Nobody have complained about the noise.
✓ **Nobody has complained about the noise.**
× When I arrived, there were nobody at all in the
house.
✓ **When I arrived, there was nobody at all in the
house.**

nobody/no one + singular verb

2 × He closed the door quietly so that nobody
wouldn't hear him.
✓ **He closed the door quietly so that nobody
would hear him.**

× Nobody never arrived late.
✓ **Nobody ever arrived late.**
Do not use **not/never/rarely** etc. after **nobody** or **no one**.

3   × Nobody of the children was hurt, but the driver of the car died.
✓ **None of/not one of the children was hurt, but the driver of the car died.**
Nobody and **no one** cannot be followed by **of** unless the phrase introduced by **of** modifies the preceding noun: 'Nobody/no one of importance attended the meeting.'

4   × We didn't know where to go, and there was no body to ask.
✓ **We didn't know where to go, and there was nobody to ask.**
Nobody (pronoun) is ALWAYS one word.

noise   × I turned on the radio but there was no noise.
✓ **I turned on the radio but there was no sound.**
noise = loud unpleasant sounds: 'The noise of the traffic gave me a headache.'
sound = something noticed by the ear: 'the sound of a guitar', 'the sound of a car engine'

no matter 1   × No matter he tries hard, he never succeeds in passing.
✓ **No matter how hard he tries, he never succeeds in passing.**
no matter how much he studies/often he goes/well he plays etc. + main clause

2   × No matter the recession, sales remained high.
✓ **In spite of the recession, sales remained high.**
No matter is ALWAYS followed by a **wh-** word: 'No matter what they did, they couldn't put the fire out.'

nominate × Mr Tong was nominated manager of the company in 1984.
√ **Mr Tong was appointed manager of the company in 1984.**

nominate = suggest someone for election or selection (for a job or position)
appoint = give someone a job or position

no more × My wife had left the hotel and I no more needed a double room.
√ **My wife had left the hotel and I no longer needed a double room.**

When talking about time, use **no longer**, NOT **no more**. Note the alternative: 'My wife had left the hotel and I didn't need a double room any more.'

none 1 × None visited the old man for over a week.
√ **Nobody visited the old man for over a week.**

Unlike **nobody** and **no one**, **none** cannot be used of people unless it refers to people who have already been mentioned OR it is followed by **of**: 'I invited three guests but none (of them) accepted.' 'None of my friends can speak English.'

2 × I told the police officer that in my opinion none of the two drivers was responsible.
√ **I told the police officer that in my opinion neither of the two drivers was responsible.**

When talking about two people or things, use **neither**. For three or more, use **none**.

no one See NOBODY 1, 2, 3

North × I am now living in North England.
√ **I am now living in the north of England.**

North/South/East/West etc. are usually only used in the names of countries and their internal divisions: 'North America', 'South Carolina'.
To refer to approximate locations, use **the north/south of ...** or **northern/southern** etc.

no sooner   × No sooner we had arrived than it began to rain.

✓ **No sooner had we arrived than it began to rain.**

When **no sooner** is placed at the beginning of a sentence, the subject and (auxiliary) verb change places.

not 1   × My father asked me to not go out that night.

✓ **My father asked me not to go out that night.**

Do not split a **to** infinitive with **not/never**.

2   × We stayed not long enough to see the whole exhibition.

✓ **We didn't stay long enough to see the whole exhibition.**

When there is no auxiliary verb, a negative is usually made with **do** (in the appropriate tense) + **not**.
Compare: 'She may arrive tomorrow–she may not arrive tomorrow.' (**may** is the auxiliary verb)
'She arrived yesterday–she didn't arrive yesterday.'

3   See THINK 2

nothing   × I haven't got nothing more to tell you in this letter.

✓ **I haven't got anything more to tell you in this letter.**

✓ **I have got nothing more to tell you in this letter.**

Do not use two negatives (such as **haven't** and **nothing**) in the same clause.

notice 1   × I wrote him a notice saying that the package
            had arrived.
          √ **I wrote him a note saying that the package
            had arrived.**

notice = a short written statement giving information
or directions, usually found in a public place: 'There
was a notice on the wall saying "Private property. No
parking." '
note = a short informal letter or written message from
one person to another

2   × The machine still didn't work, so I re-read the
        notice.
      √ **The machine still didn't work, so I re-read the
        instructions.**

notice = a sign giving information or directions, often
on a wall in a public place: 'The notice said "No
smoking!" '
instructions = a series of directions provided with a
new piece of equipment

3   × It was so dark that at first I didn't take any
        notice of him.
      √ **It was so dark that at first I didn't notice him.**

take notice of = pay attention to: 'Nobody took any
notice of what I was saying.'
notice = become aware of

not only 1   × She not only made her own dresses but also
              her own hats.
            √ **She made not only her own dresses but also
              her own hats.**

The position of **not only** should be the same as the
position of **but also** (i.e. immediately before an object,
immediately before a main verb, etc.).
Compare: 'He injured not only his shoulder but also
his elbow.' ('his shoulder' and 'his elbow' are both
noun phrases)
'He not only injured his back but also hurt his head.'
('injured' and 'hurt' are both verbs)

2   × Not only I passed the test, but I got a distinction.

✓ **Not only did I pass the test, but I got a distinction.**

When **not only** is used at the beginning of a sentence, the subject and (supplied) auxiliary verb change places (as in the question form): 'I passed' becomes 'did I pass'.

nowadays 1   × Nowaday it is very difficult to find a good job.

✓ **Nowadays it is very difficult to find a good job.**

nowadays (WITH **s**)

2   × Although she is not very young, she still likes to wear nowadays clothes.

✓ **Although she is not very young, she still likes to wear modern/fashionable clothes.**

Nowadays (= currently) is an adverb, NOT an adjective.

number 1   × The number of thieves are increasing.

✓ **The number of thieves is increasing.**

the number of ... + singular verb

2   × A large number of cars was parked outside the school.

✓ **A large number of cars were parked outside the school.**

a number of ... + plural verb

3   × Harsher punishments will not reduce the number of crime.

✓ **Harsher punishments will not reduce the number of crimes.**

the number of + plural form of a countable noun

4   See BIG 1

obey   × He was a very good boy and obeyed to his parents all the time.

✓ **He was a very good boy and obeyed his parents all the time.**

obey someone WITHOUT **to**

obligation   × My obligations include doing the housework and picking up the children from school.
√ **My duties include doing the housework and picking up the children from school.**

obligation = moral duty or responsibility: 'Since they had invited us to their wedding, we felt under an obligation to invite them to ours.' (countable)
'You can try the computer in our showroom without any obligation.' (uncountable)
duty = what you must do in your job or because you think it is right: 'a moral duty'

oblige   × In order to pay the hospital bill, it obliged me to sell my car.
√ **In order to pay the hospital bill, I was obliged to sell my car.**

be obliged + to-v

observance   × This experiment requires very careful observance.
√ **This experiment requires very careful observation.**

observance = (1) the obeying of (a law or rule): 'the observance of a speed limit'
(2) the keeping of (a custom or ceremony): 'the observance of religious holidays'
observation = the act of watching carefully; the act of studying and making detailed notes: 'The patient was kept under observation for several weeks.'

obvious   × The lack of freedom and social justice is obvious for everyone.
√ **The lack of freedom and social justice is obvious to everyone.**

obvious to someone, NOT **for**

occasion   × The scholarship provided me with my first occasion to travel overseas.
√ **The scholarship provided me with my first opportunity to travel overseas.**

occasion = the time when an event happens: 'I've been to Rome on several occasions.' (= several times)
opportunity = a time when it becomes possible to do something

occur 1   × The incident occured at 11 p.m.
√ **The incident occurred at 11 p.m.**
occur (ONLY ONE **r**)
occurring, occurred (DOUBLE **r**)

2   × The concert will occur at eight o'clock next
Tuesday.
√ **The concert will take place at eight o'clock
next Tuesday.**
Occur is usually used of unplanned events: 'The
accident occurred last night shortly before ten.'
For planned events, use **take place**.

o'clock 1   × It was twenty past four o'clock when the train
arrived.
√ **It was twenty past four when the train arrived.**
O'clock may be used in telling the time ONLY for full
hours (WITHOUT any minutes following). Compare: 'It's
four o'clock.' 'It's ten past four.'

2   × I start work at 9.00 o'clock.
√ **I start work at 9 o'clock.**
'9 p.m./9.00 p.m.', '10 p.m./10.00 p.m.' BUT '9 o'clock',
'10 o'clock'

3   × By seven o'clock p.m. the child had been
found.
√ **By seven p.m. the child had been found.**
√ **By seven o'clock (in the evening) the child
had been found.**
Use either **o'clock** OR **a.m./p.m.**, NOT both.

of 1   × I tried to open the door but the handle came of
in my hand.
√ **I tried to open the door but the handle came off
in my hand.**
Compare: 'The handle of the drawer came off in my
hand.'

2   × The old man didn't give me a minute of peace.
√ **The old man didn't give me a minute's peace.**
Time expressions are usually formed with **-'s** or **-s'**:
'last week's news', 'three months' leave', etc.

3   × This coat isn't mine. It's of a friend.
      √ **This coat isn't mine. It's a friend's.**
      To express human ownership, use **-'s** (NOT **of**).
      Compare: 'John's garden' BUT 'the roof of the house'

4   × They are both friends of him.
      √ **They are both friends of his.**
      a friend **of mine/yours/his/hers/ours/theirs** = one of
      my/your/his/her/our/their friends
      Compare: 'That's a photograph of him.' (= showing
      him)
      'That's a photograph of his.' (= belonging to or taken
      by him)

5   × I don't think the watch is of gold.
      √ **I don't think the watch is made of gold.**
      (be) made of gold/wood/plastic etc.

6   × Arlon is one of the oldest towns of Belgium.
      √ **Arlon is one of the oldest towns in Belgium.**
      a town **in** Belgium, a village **in** France, NOT **of**

7   × I arrived in London on 25th of November.
      √ **I arrived in London on 25th November.**
      Say 'the 25th of November' or 'November the 25th' BUT
      write '25th November' or 'November 25th' WITHOUT **the**
      or **of**.

8   × The scenery reminded her of a painting of
        Renoir.
      √ **The scenery reminded her of a painting by**
        Renoir.
      a painting of Renoir = a picture that someone painted
      of Renoir
      a painting by Renoir = a picture that Renoir painted

9   × The magazine contains six pages of
photographs of the Cup Final of Europe.
√ **The magazine contains six pages of
photographs of the European Cup Final.**

A phrase beginning with **of** should not be used to
modify a noun when there is an adjective available:
'Do you like English cheese?' NOT 'Do you like the
cheese of England?'

10   See BEHIND

off 1   × My company gave all the staff an off day to
celebrate its fiftieth anniversary.
√ **My company gave all the staff a day off to
celebrate its fiftieth anniversary.**

off (adjective) = not as good as usual: 'He'll win
easily, unless it's one of his off days.' (= a day when
he does not play as well as he usually plays)
off (adverb) = spent or to be spent as a holiday

2   × Don't forget to off the lights before you go out.
√ **Don't forget to turn/switch off the lights before
you go out.**

There is no such verb as 'to off'.

3   × The glass fell off of the table.
√ **The glass fell off the table.**

Off is NEVER followed by **of**.

offer 1   × I took out my cigarettes and offerred him one.
√ **I took out my cigarettes and offered him one.**
offer, offering, offered, offered (ONLY ONE **r**)

2   × The old man then offered something to eat to
the little boy.
√ **The old man then offered the little boy
something to eat.**

With **offer**, the indirect object ('the little boy') comes
before the direct object ('something to eat') UNLESS the
direct object is a pronoun or is much shorter than the
indirect object: 'I offered the apple to the little girl
sitting in the corner.'

3 × An old man offered me to go to his house.
    ✓ **An old man invited me to go to his house.**

offer to do something (for someone) = express
willingness to do something: 'She offered to help me.'
invite (someone) to (do) something = ask (someone) to
a social occasion: 'He invited her to the party.'

4 × The coat had been offered to me by my wife
    on my birthday.
    ✓ **The coat had been given to me by my wife on
    my birthday.**

Something that is **offered** may or may not be accepted:
'I offered her a cigarette, but she didn't want one.'
Something that is **given** (such as a birthday present) is
accepted: 'I gave her a cigarette and then lit it for her.'

officer × Most of my friends got jobs as shop assistants
    or officers.
    ✓ **Most of my friends got jobs as shop assistants
    or office workers.**

officer = a person having a position of rank or
authority: 'an army officer', 'a police officer', 'a local
government officer'
office worker = a person who works in an office

official × She is good at organizing people without
    seeming arrogant or official.
    ✓ **She is good at organizing people without
    seeming arrogant or officious.**

official = done by or related to a person or group in
authority; formal: 'an official letter', 'an official inquiry',
'official approval'
officious (usually derogatory) = too eager to give
orders or exercise authority

old 1 × He fell in love with a young girl of nineteen
    years old.
    ✓ **He fell in love with a young girl of nineteen.**

'a child of five', 'a man of sixty' WITHOUT **years old**
Compare: 'The girl was nineteen years old.'

2 × Rollo Martins is a fifty years-old writer.
   ✓ **Rollo Martins is a fifty-year-old writer.**

Note two hyphens, NOT one.
Nouns of measurement ('week', 'gram', 'year', etc.) are always singular when used in compound adjectives: 'a ten-second silence', 'a six-minute wait', 'a five-mile race'.

old-fashioned × This shirt is rather old-fashion.
   ✓ **This shirt is rather old-fashioned.**
   old-fashioned, NOT **old-fashion**

on 1 × On the next morning he got up and walked down to the river to wash himself.
   ✓ **The next morning he got up and walked down to the river to wash himself.**

Do not use a preposition to begin a time expression with **next** when the point of time is being considered in relation to the present: 'the next morning', 'the next afternoon'.

2 See THING 1, TOP

3 See AFTERNOON 2

once 1 × You may remember that we had once a long talk in the hotel bar.
   ✓ **You may remember that we once had a long talk in the hotel bar.**

When there is no auxiliary verb, **once** (= on a single occasion in the past) is placed immediately before the main verb: 'She once told me she had been married.' Otherwise it goes immediately after the (first) auxiliary verb: 'They had once lived in Chile.' **Once** can also go at the beginning or end of the clause: 'Once they had lived in Chile.' 'They had lived in Chile once.'

2 × I hope to see you once next month.
   ✓ **I hope to see you some time next month.**
   once = on a single occasion in the past, NOT in the future

3 × Once it will stop raining, we can go out.
✓ **Once it stops raining, we can go out.**
✓ **Once it has stopped raining, we can go out.**

After **when/whenever/once/until/after/if**, use the present simple (or present perfect) tense for future reference, NOT **shall/will** + verb.

one 1 × Outside the house I was stopped by one of my mother's friend.
✓ **Outside the house I was stopped by one of my mother's friends.**

The noun following **one of** has a plural form: 'one of my friends', 'one of her sisters', 'one of my brother's teachers'.

2 × That hat isn't Angela's—the one of Angela is blue.
✓ **That hat isn't Angela's–Angela's is blue.**

When talking about possession, use **-'s/-s'**, NOT **the one of**.

3 × After we had been to Helen's house, we decided to go to Paul's one.
✓ **After we had been to Helen's house, we decided to go to Paul's.**
× If you can carry those books, I'll bring these ones.
✓ **If you can carry those books, I'll bring these.**

One/ones should not follow words which can themselves be used as pronouns (except in informal conversation).

4 × One of the eggs were bad.
✓ **One of the eggs was bad.**

A phrase beginning with **one of** takes a singular verb.

5   × I'm sharing a flat with one friend who also comes from Hong Kong.
   √ **I'm sharing a flat with a friend who also comes from Hong Kong.**

Do not use **one** instead of **a** or **an** unless it is used for emphasis. Compare: 'Would you like a cigarette?' 'I said you could take one cigarette, not two!'

6   × One mustn't waste ones time when there is so much to do.
   √ **One mustn't waste one's time when there is so much to do.**

Use **one's** as the possessive form of **one**. Note, however, that there is no apostrophe in **its** (the possessive form of **it**).

7   × One cannot succeed unless he works hard.
   √ **One cannot succeed unless one works hard.**

In British English (unlike American English) it is not usually acceptable to change from **one** to **he**, **him**, etc. However, most speakers find the repetition of **one** awkward, and try to avoid it: 'One cannot succeed without working hard.'

8   See EVERYONE 1

ones   × I understand you have already been to Sweden ones.
   √ **I understand you have already been to Sweden once.**

Ones /wʌnz/ is the plural form of **one** (a pronoun).
Once /wʌns/ means 'on a single occasion in the past'.

only 1   × The level of pollution can only be reduced by the introduction of new laws.
   √ **The level of pollution can be reduced only by the introduction of new laws.**

To avoid confusion, **only** should be placed as near as possible to the word or phrase that it modifies.

2   × Only when it started to rain he noticed that he had left his raincoat somewhere.
    ✓ **Only when it started to rain did he notice that he had left his raincoat somewhere.**

After phrases and clauses beginning with **only**, the subject and (supplied) auxiliary verb change places (as in the question form): 'he noticed' becomes 'did he notice'.
Compare: (1) 'After five days the letter arrived.' 'Only after five days did the letter arrive.'
(2) 'When it stopped raining, we set off.' 'Only when it stopped raining did we set off.'

3   × If you only would stay longer, your English would improve.
    ✓ **If only you would stay longer, your English would improve.**
    ✓ **If you would only stay longer, your English would improve.**

Only is rarely placed between the subject and the auxiliary verb.

4   × The sea is not the only that is affected by pollution.
    ✓ **The sea is not the only thing that is affected by pollution.**
    × Bob wasn't the only who disagreed with the decision.
    ✓ **Bob wasn't the only one who disagreed with the decision.**

Only cannot be used as a pronoun.

5   See NOT ONLY

open 1   × John knocked on the door and his grandfather opened.
    ✓ **John knocked on the door and his grandfather opened it.**

Compare: (1) 'He opened the door.' 'The door opened.'
(2) 'She suddenly opened her eyes.' 'Her eyes suddenly opened.'

2 × I got out of bed and opened the radio to listen to the news.
✓ **I got out of bed and turned/switched on the radio to listen to the news.**

turn on/off OR **switch on/off** a light/radio/television, NOT **open**

3 × If someone tried to open a new topic, she would immediately interrupt.
✓ **If someone tried to introduce a new topic, she would immediately interrupt.**

introduce a (new) topic/subject/argument, NOT **open**

opened × I couldn't buy a newspaper because the shop wasn't opened.
✓ **I couldn't buy a newspaper because the shop wasn't open.**

The opposite of **closed** (adjective) is **open** (adjective).
Compare: 'The shop was opened by Mary this morning because the manager was ill.'

opinion × According to Henry's opinion, less money should be spent on weapons.
✓ **According to Henry, less money should be spent on weapons.**
✓ **In Henry's opinion, less money should be spent on weapons.**

According to is NOT used with **opinion**.

opportunity 1 × After ten years I finally had an opportunity for visiting America.
✓ **After ten years I finally had an opportunity to visit America.**

have/get/be **an opportunity** + to-v

2 × There is an opportunity that David's father will come tonight.
✓ **There is a chance that David's father will come tonight.**

There is a chance that ... is used to talk about a possibility.

Use **opportunity** when the possibility is a favourable one: 'Winning the scholarship gave her the opportunity to visit Paris.'

opposite 1   × I used to think that 'tall' was opposite 'low'.
✓ **I used to think that 'tall' was the opposite of 'low'.**

Compare: 'The bank is opposite (= facing) the post office.'

2   × The opposite woman was knitting a cardigan.
✓ **The woman opposite was knitting a cardigan.**

Opposite (= facing the speaker or facing the person being talked about) comes after the noun it modifies.

3   × Hiroko's mother was opposite to her marriage to Koichi.
✓ **Hiroko's mother was opposed to her marriage to Koichi.**

opposite = (1) showing the greatest possible difference: 'The two men went off in opposite directions.' (= one went to the left and one to the right)
(2) being on the other side of; facing: 'Her mother lives in the house opposite (mine).'
opposed to = not in favour of; against

or 1   × At night we used to go out with our friends or stayed at home listening to music.
✓ **At night we used to go out with our friends or stay at home listening to music.**

When you use **or** with two verbs, both verbs should have the same form. Compare: 'We used to go to the cinema or watch the television.' 'We went to the cinema or watched the television.'

2   × I think the microphone or the recording mechanism are broken.
✓ **I think the microphone or the recording mechanism is broken.**

When each of the nouns joined by **or** is singular, the verb is usually singular.

3 × If you want to see it, you must come or on Monday or on Friday afternoon.

✓ **If you want to see it, you must come either on Monday or on Friday afternoon.**

either ... or ... , NOT **or ... or ...**
Note the alternative: 'If you want to see it, you must come on Monday or Friday afternoon.'

4 See NEITHER 1

oral × Her oral English is very fluent and clear.

✓ **Her spoken English is very fluent and clear.**

The use of **oral** to mean 'spoken' is restricted to certain phrases in education: 'oral skills', 'an oral examination', etc.

order 1 × Turning on the radio, I noticed immediately that it was out of order.

✓ **Turning on the radio, I noticed immediately that it was not working properly.**

The phrase **out of order** is used mostly on notices stating that things such as public telephones, ticket machines, etc. are not working.

2 × I was so excited that I forgot to order them to check that the camera was working properly.

✓ **I was so excited that I forgot to ask them to check that the camera was working properly.**

A speaker cannot **order** someone to do something unless he or she has the authority to do so. Compare: 'The teacher ordered the child to sit down.' 'The soldiers were ordered to attack.'

originate × One of our teachers originates from Scotland.

✓ **One of our teachers comes from Scotland.**

Originate is not usually used of people.

other 1   × 'Go and play with some others children,' she said.

✓ **'Go and play with some other children,' she said.**

When used before a noun, **other** has no **s**. **Others** is a pronoun. Compare: 'Do you have any other shoes besides the brown ones?' 'Besides the brown shoes, do you have any others?'

2   × They had stolen not just my car but an other car as well.

✓ **They had stolen not just my car but another car as well.**

Another (= an other) is ALWAYS one word.

3   × When Lillian and Janet arrived, I ordered two other cups of coffee.

✓ **When Lillian and Janet arrived, I ordered two more cups of coffee.**

Other means 'more and also different'.

otherwise   × She'll have to wait for us, or otherwise she won't know where to go.

✓ **She'll have to wait for us; otherwise she won't know where to go.**

otherwise (= if not) WITHOUT **or**

ought   × 'Ought we go now?' she asked me. 'It's getting late.'

✓ **'Ought we to go now?' she asked me. 'It's getting late.'**

ought + to-v

out 1   × She suddenly stood up and ran out from the room.

✓ **She suddenly stood up and ran out of the room.**

out of, NOT **from**

2 × I felt very cold when I went out the room.
  √ **I felt very cold when I went out of the room.**
  Out is an adverb: 'Alan went out, leaving just the two of us in the room.'
  Out of is a preposition.
  Note that in informal conversation, **out** is sometimes used instead of **out of**: 'I saw someone jump out the window.'

outdoor × She makes the dog stay outdoor during the summer.
  √ **She makes the dog stay outdoors during the summer.**
  Outdoor is an adjective: 'He enjoys the outdoor life.'
  Outdoors is an adverb: 'He likes to work outdoors.'

outside √ **AmE She was listening outside of the door.**
  √ **BrE She was listening outside the door.**
  Outside is used in both American and British English.
  Outside of can be used in informal American English but not in British English.

outskirts × I have to take the train because the house is on the outskirt of London.
  √ **I have to take the train because the house is on the outskirts of London.**
  Outskirts is a plural noun. There is no singular form.

overdue × I suddenly realized that my driving licence was overdue.
  √ **I suddenly realized that my driving licence had expired.**
  Be/become overdue is used of a bill, payment, library book, etc.
  Expire is used of a licence, contract, library ticket, etc.

overjoyed × We overjoyed ourselves when we heard the news.
  √ **We were overjoyed when we heard the news.**
  Overjoyed is an adjective. There is no such verb as 'overjoy yourself'.

overwork   × He had managed to save a lot of money by
overworking.
√ **He had managed to save a lot of money by
working overtime.**

overwork = work too hard: 'The doctor advised him
not to overwork.'
work overtime = work beyond the usual time for extra
pay

own   × I now have enough money to buy an own car.
√ **I now have enough money to buy my own car.**

Own (determiner/pronoun) ALWAYS follows a possessive
form: 'their own children', 'her own flat', 'Tina's own
radio'.

pace   × In the silence he thought he heard paces
outside the window.
√ **In the silence he thought he heard footsteps
outside the window.**

pace = (the distance moved by taking) a single step:
'The trees were planted ten paces apart.'
footstep = the mark or sound made by a person's step

painful   × The operation was successful but I still feel
very painful.
√ **The operation was successful but I still feel
a lot of pain.**

painful = giving pain: 'The finger I trapped in the door
is still very painful.'

pair   × The old pair stood up and started to dance.
√ **The old couple stood up and started to dance.**

couple = husband and wife, boyfriend and girlfriend,
etc.

pants   √ **AmE The man was wearing red shoes and
bright green pants.**
√ **BrE The man was wearing red shoes and
bright green trousers.**

pants (American English) = trousers
pants (British English) = short underclothes covering
the lower part of the body; underpants; knickers

paper 1   × Each of us was given a clean paper to write on.

✓ **Each of us was given a clean piece/sheet of paper to write on.**

Paper is an uncountable noun.

2   × The last paper of the book was missing.

✓ **The last page of the book was missing.**

page = a printed sheet in a book, magazine, etc.

pardon   × I asked the teacher if I could be pardoned for a few minutes.

✓ **I asked the teacher if I could be excused for a few minutes.**

pardon (formal) = forgive: 'I'm sure they will pardon the occasional mistake.'

excuse = allow (someone) to leave (a classroom, meeting, etc.)

parking   × Several cars were parking outside the building.

✓ **Several cars were parked outside the building.**

park (a vehicle) (of a driver) BUT **be parked** (of a stationary vehicle)

Compare: 'She parks her car outside my house. It is parked there all night.'

part 1   × A part of the difficulty was caused by her poor English.

✓ **Part of the difficulty was caused by her poor English.**

It is unusual to use **a** before **part of** unless **part of** is modified by an adjective. Compare: 'Lack of money was part of the problem.' 'Lack of money was a large part of the problem.'

2   × Nowadays a large part of women go out to work.

✓ **Nowadays a large number of women go out to work.**

(a) part of + uncountable noun/singular form of a countable noun

Compare: 'A large part of the population is unemployed.' 'A large number of workers are unemployed.'

3 × He refused to part from his old camera.
✓ **He refused to part with his old camera.**

part from (a person): 'The two sisters were parted from each other when they were sent to different schools.'
BUT **part with** (a thing)

party × The party was being made at a friend's house.
✓ **The party was being held at a friend's house.**

give/hold/throw a party, NOT **make**

pass 1 × We were glad to hear that you had passed in your examination.
✓ **We were glad to hear that you had passed your examination.**

pass an examination WITHOUT **in**

2 × We like to pass our holidays near the sea.
✓ **We like to spend our holidays near the sea.**

spend your **holidays** somewhere, NOT **pass**

3 × We passed the night at a cheap hotel.
✓ **We spent the night at a cheap hotel.**

Pass is usually intransitive when used of time: 'Two weeks passed and there was still no reply.'

4 × I am going to pass my music examination on Thursday.
✓ **I am going to take my music examination on Thursday.**

pass (a test or examination) = succeed in
take (a test or examination) = undergo: 'Of those who took the exam, only fifty per cent passed.'

passed × I bought the car with the money I've earned during the passed twelve months.
√ **I bought the car with the money I've earned during the past twelve months.**

Passed is the past tense and past participle of the verb **pass**.
Compare: 'This year has passed quickly.' 'I've been very busy over the past year.'

past × I was very glad to hear that you past your exams.
√ **I was very glad to hear that you passed your exams.**
× Several taxis past me without stopping.
√ **Several taxis passed me without stopping.**

Past is (1) an adjective: 'For the past week he's been ill in bed.'
(2) a preposition: 'She walked past me very quickly.'
(3) an adverb: 'She walked past very quickly.'
(4) a noun: 'He never speaks about his past.'
Note that **past** is NOT used as a verb.
Passed is the past tense and past participle of the verb **pass**.

pay 1 × It's quite a new coat and I payed a lot for it.
√ **It's quite a new coat and I paid a lot for it.**
pay, paying, paid, paid

2 × 'Who paid the tickets?' I asked.
√ **'Who paid for the tickets?' I asked.**
pay an amount BUT **pay for** something

3 × Very few office workers get a good pay.
√ **Very few office workers get good pay.**
Pay is an uncountable noun.

payment × Dr Schneider charges a high payment but he is very good.
√ **Dr Schneider charges a high fee but he is very good.**
payment = (1) the act of paying: 'Here is a cheque in payment of the invoice.'

(2) an amount of money (to be) paid
fee = a sum of money paid to a doctor, lawyer, or other professional person

peculiar × She said she liked the jumper because the colour was very peculiar.
✓ **She said she liked the jumper because the colour was very unusual.**
peculiar (usually derogatory) = odd or strange
unusual = uncommon or rare

people 1 × Peoples come from all over the world to visit the city.
✓ **People come from all over the world to visit the city.**
a people (countable) = a race
people (plural noun) = men, women, and children

2 × There was few people at the funeral.
✓ **There were few people at the funeral.**
× I think people who does these things should be punished.
✓ **I think people who do these things should be punished.**
People is a plural noun.

3 × Our teacher is quite a young people.
✓ **Our teacher is quite a young person.**
People is the plural of **person**.

per cent × A large per cent of the population were against nuclear weapons.
✓ **A large percentage of the population were against nuclear weapons.**
Compare: 'Seventy per cent of the population were against nuclear weapons.'

percentage × Only a small percentage of the windmills still works.
✓ **Only a small percentage of the windmills still work.**
A ... percentage of does not affect the noun and verb that follow: 'windmills' is plural and so 'work' is also plural.

perfect 1   × Each day the weather seemed to become more
perfect.
√ **Each day the weather seemed to improve.**

Something can be **absolutely perfect** but NOT
very/more/somewhat (etc.) **perfect**. There are no
degrees of perfection.

2   × I am pleased to say that the tape recorder
now works perfect.
√ **I am pleased to say that the tape recorder
now works perfectly.**

Perfect is an adjective.
Perfectly is an adverb.

perhaps   × If it isn't in the bedroom, perhaps would you
have a look in the dining room.
√ **If it isn't in the bedroom, perhaps you would
have a look in the dining room.**

√ **If it isn't in the bedroom, would you have a look
in the dining room perhaps.**

In the interrogative clause, perhaps is usually placed
immediately before the main verb or at the end (NOT
before the auxiliary verb). Note the alternative: 'If it isn't
in the bedroom, perhaps you would have a look in the
dining room.'

period   × In the long period, this will have the effect of
increasing the price of food.
√ **In the long term, this will have the effect of
increasing the price of food.**

in the long/short term = over a long/short period of
time stretching from the present into the future

permission 1   × To get a job in Switzerland, foreigners need
a special permission.
√ **To get a job in Switzerland, foreigners need
special permission.**

Permission is an uncountable noun.

2   × If you wish to enter another country, you will
have to take permission from the authorities.
√ **If you wish to enter another country, you will
have to get/obtain permission from the
authorities.**

get/obtain permission, NOT **take**

person   × Her husband talked so much that all the other
persons in the room had to keep quiet.
√ **Her husband talked so much that all the other
people in the room had to keep quiet.**

Person is singular.
People is plural.
Note that **persons** is rarely used except in public
notices and other formal contexts: 'Seating capacity:
twelve persons.'

personage   × She is the main personage in Shaw's play
'Arms and the Man'.
√ **She is the main character in Shaw's play
'Arms and the Man'.**

personage (formal; often slightly mocking) = a well-known
or important person
character = a person in a play, novel, etc.

personal   × The meals can be improved if the canteen
personal agree to co-operate.
√ **The meals can be improved if the canteen
personnel agree to co-operate.**

personal (adjective) = concerning or belonging to one
person in particular; individual; private: 'a personal
opinion', 'personal reasons'
personnel (noun) = all the people employed in a
company, office, etc.

personality   × He is a man of strong personality who will
fight for what is right.
√ **He is a man of strong character who will fight
for what is right.**

When talking about a person's moral quality, use
character, NOT **personality**.
Compare: 'For a career in sales, you need a forceful
personality.' 'People of character and integrity never
turn their backs on the truth.'

phenomena   × There has never been a serious study of this phenomena.
✓ **There has never been a serious study of this phenomenon.**
✓ **There has never been a serious study of these phenomena.**
Phenomenon is singular.
Phenomena is plural.

phenomenon   × I like reading about ghosts and similar mysterious phenomenons.
✓ **I like reading about ghosts and similar mysterious phenomena.**
Phenomenon is singular.
Phenomena is plural.

phone 1   ✓ **AmE I talked to him for a long time by phone last night.**
✓ **BrE I talked to him for a long time on/over the phone last night.**
In American English, use **talk/speak** to someone **by/on/over the phone**.
In British English, use **talk/speak** to someone **on/over the phone**, NOT **by phone**.

2   × She phoned to the hospital to ask about her husband.
✓ **She phoned the hospital to ask about her husband.**
phone someone/somewhere WITHOUT **to**

piano   See PLAY 3

piece   × The pencils were free and so I took two pieces.
✓ **The pencils were free and so I took two.**
Piece is NOT used with countable nouns.
Compare: 'a piece of cheese', 'a piece of furniture', 'a piece of luck'.

pitiful × We both felt pitiful when we saw how lonely she was.
√ **We both felt pity for her when we saw how lonely she was.**

pity (noun) = sorrow for the suffering of others
pitiful (adjective) = deserving or arousing pity: 'He had lost all his hair in the fire and was a pitiful sight.'

pity × She expected me to feel pity on her and help her.
√ **She expected me to take pity on her and help her.**
√ **She expected me to feel pity for her and help her.**

take pity on BUT **feel pity for**

place 1 × He was looking for a place where to spend the night.
√ **He was looking for somewhere to spend the night.**

look for/find etc. **somewhere** + to-v: 'She is looking for somewhere to live.' Compare: 'He was looking for a place where he could spend the night.' 'She's looking for a place where she can live.'

2 × When I lived at home, my father did not let me go to any place on my own.
√ **When I lived at home, my father did not let me go anywhere on my own.**
Use **anywhere** when you mean 'in/to any place'.

3 × I left the coat in my room but it may not be in that place any longer.
√ **I left the coat in my room but it may not be there any longer.**
Use **there** when you mean 'in/to that place'.

4   × The old man laughed and answered, 'There's enough place in the wardrobe for all your clothes.'

✓ **The old man laughed and answered, 'There's enough room in the wardrobe for all your clothes.'**

place = a position or particular part of some space: 'The best place to sit is right in front of the stage.'
room = a space which is big enough for something: 'There's room in the back seat for all three of you.'

play 1   × My favourite play is chess.

✓ **My favourite game is chess.**

play (verb) = take part in (a sport or game): 'She plays tennis every Saturday.'
game (noun) = something you do for enjoyment or sport
Compare: 'Which game would you like to play, chess or draughts?'

2   × At the cinema they were playing a Walt Disney film.

✓ **At the cinema they were showing a Walt Disney film.**

show a film, NOT **play**

3   ✓ **AmE I've been playing piano since I was eight.**

✓ **BrE I've been playing the piano since I was eight.**

In American English **the** is optional when talking about musical instruments..
In British English, use **play** football/tennis/chess BUT **play the** piano/guitar/violin.

please   × Please, as soon as the radio has been repaired, let me know.

✓ **As soon as the radio has been repaired, please let me know.**

Please is NEVER used before a subordinate clause. Note the common patterns: 'Please let me know as soon as you can.' 'Will you please let me know as soon as you can?' 'Will you let me know as soon as you can, please?'

pleasure 1 × As mayor of this town, it gives me a great
pleasure to welcome you.
✓ **As mayor of this town, it gives me great
pleasure to welcome you.**
give someone **(great) pleasure** WITHOUT **a**
Compare: 'It is a great pleasure for me to welcome
you.'

2 × A lot of people work for their pleasure, not
because of financial obligations.
✓ **A lot of people work for pleasure, not because
of financial obligations.**
do something **for pleasure** WITHOUT **his/our/their** etc.

3 × It's the first time that I've had the pleasure to
meet her.
✓ **It's the first time that I've had the pleasure of
meeting her.**
be pleased + to-v BUT **have the pleasure of** + v-ing

p.m. 1 × The fight will be shown on television at 7.30
p.m. in the evening.
✓ **The fight will be shown on television at 7.30
p.m.**
✓ **The fight will be shown on television at 7.30
in the evening.**
'at 7.30 p.m.' OR 'at 7.30 in the evening'

2 See O'CLOCK 3

pocket × He was leaning against the wall with his hands
in the pockets.
✓ **He was leaning against the wall with his
hands in his pockets.**
When talking about the position of a person's hands,
use **my/your/his** etc. (NOT **the**) with **pocket**.

poetry × In my spare time I like writing poetries.
✓ **In my spare time I like writing poetry.**
Poetry is an uncountable noun.

point 1 × The meal was terrible but it was no point in complaining.
✓ **The meal was terrible but there was no point in complaining.**
there is little/no point (in) + v-ing, NOT **it**

2 × There is no point to complain about the service.
✓ **There is no point (in) complaining about the service.**
there is little/no point (in) + v-ing

3 × I had to spend forty-eight hours listening to him with a gun pointed to my head.
✓ **I had to spend forty-eight hours listening to him with a gun pointed at my head.**
point at (NOT **to**) = aim (something) in a particular direction

point of view 1 × My point of view is that married women with young children should be able to work if they wish.
✓ **My opinion/view is that married women with young children should be able to work if they wish.**
point of view = the position or angle from which someone approaches a problem or situation: 'A good salesman should try to see things from the customer's point of view.'
opinion/view = what a person thinks about something
Note that **point of view** is usually used when referring to other people's opinions, NOT your own.
Compare: 'in her opinion/from her point of view' BUT 'in my opinion'

2 × In her point of view, there is only one solution.
✓ **From her point of view, there is only one solution.**
in her view/opinion BUT **from her point of view**

police 1 × The police was not able to find anything.
✓ **The police were not able to find anything.**
Police is ALWAYS used with a plural verb.

2 × He was charged with shooting a police.
✓ **He was charged with shooting a policeman.**
policeman = a member of the police force
police = the police force in general

3 × The woman took the lost child to the nearest police office.
✓ **The woman took the lost child to the nearest police station.**
police station, NOT **office**

politics × One of the main politics of the government is to reduce unemployment.
✓ **One of the main policies of the government is to reduce unemployment.**
politics = (1) the art and science of governing a country: 'He has chosen a career in politics.'
(2) political affairs: 'I'm not interested in politics.'
(3) political opinions: 'Nobody knows much about his politics.'
policy = a plan or course of action (taken by a government, political party, business, etc.)

pollution × There is a pollution everywhere, even in the countryside.
✓ **There is pollution everywhere, even in the countryside.**
Pollution is an uncountable noun.

ponder × It is a very delicate question and we have to ponder the advantages against the disadvantages.
✓ **It is a very delicate question and we have to weigh the advantages against the disadvantages.**
ponder = spend time considering: 'He was standing by the car, pondering how to get into it without a key.'
weigh = compare or measure

position   × I should like to explain our government's
            position about nuclear weapons.
            √ **I should like to explain our government's
            position on nuclear weapons.**
            position on something, NOT **about**

possibility 1   × We are considering the possibility to do the
            job ourselves.
            √ **We are considering the possibility of doing the
            job ourselves.**
            be possible + to-v: 'It may be possible to do the job
            ourselves.' BUT **the possibility of** + v-ing

        2   × My visit to Tokyo was a good possibility for me
            to learn Japanese.
            √ **My visit to Tokyo gave me a good opportunity
            to learn Japanese.**
            × A person who wants to go out to work should
            be given the possibility to do so.
            √ **A person who wants to go out to work should
            be given the opportunity to do so.**
            Use **opportunity** to talk about a favourable moment or
            occasion to do something.
            Compare: 'There's a possibility that I'll be late.'

possible 1   × If you find my book, could you possible return
            it to me?
            √ **If you find my book, could you possibly return
            it to me?**
            Possible is an adjective.
            Possibly is an adverb.

        2   × Is it possible that you can send me the coat
            this week?
            √ **Is it possible for you to send me the coat this
            week?**
            possible (for someone) + to-v

        3   See EVER 3

possibly × I asked the doctor to come as soon as possibly.
√ **I asked the doctor to come as soon as possible.**

as ... as possible, NOT **possibly**

post × I refused to return the book unless they agreed to pay the cost of the post.
√ **I refused to return the book unless they agreed to pay the cost of the postage.**

post (British English)/**mail** (American English) = the official system for sending letters and parcels
postage = the charge for sending a letter or parcel by post

power × The illness has left her with very little power.
√ **The illness has left her with very little strength/ energy.**

A person's **power** refers to their social or political influence, NOT to their physical **strength**. Compare: 'The British royal family has very little power these days.' 'I seem to have lost all the strength in my left arm, doctor.'

practice √ **AmE I had to practice for half an hour every evening.**
√ **BrE I had to practise for half an hour every evening.**

In American English **practice** (**ce**) is the most usual form for both noun and verb. However, **practise** (**se**) may also be used for both.
In British English **practise** (**se**) is the verb and **practice** (**ce**) is the noun.

prefer 1 × I told her I prefered to sit next to the window.
√ **I told her I preferred to sit next to the window.**
prefer (ONLY ONE **r**)
preferring, preferred (DOUBLE **r**)

2 × I preferred to stay out in the cold rather than spending the night there.
   √ **I preferred to stay out in the cold rather than spend the night there.**
   prefer to do A **(rather) than** do B

3 × Why do you prefer the theatre than the cinema?
   √ **Why do you prefer the theatre to the cinema?**
   × I prefer drawing than painting.
   √ **I prefer drawing to painting.**
   prefer A **to** B, NOT **than**

4 × He prefers living in Hong Kong more than living in Taiwan.
   √ **He prefers living in Hong Kong to living in Taiwan.**
   Prefer is NOT used with **more than**.

preferable × Going swimming is more preferable than playing football.
   √ **Going swimming is preferable to playing football.**
   An adjective which contains the sense 'more' as part of its meaning cannot be used with **more**.

present 1 × This tie was a present of my wife.
   √ **This tie was a present from my wife.**
   (receive) a present from somebody, NOT **of**

2 × Before leaving the examination room we had to present our answer papers.
   √ **Before leaving the examination room we had to hand in our answer papers.**
   present = give or award, especially in a formal or ceremonial way: 'The prizes are usually presented by the headmaster.'
   hand in = give (something) to another person, especially by passing it to them by hand

3   × It was the first time I had been present to a
         road accident.
      ✓ **It was the first time I had been present at a
         road accident.**

      be present at an event, NOT **to**

presently   ✓ **AmE Presently, nearly every machine used in
                 the home is made of plastic.**
             ✓ **BrE At present, nearly every machine used in
                 the home is made of plastic.**

      Presently can mean 'soon' in both British and
      American English: 'The car will arrive presently to take
      Her Majesty back to the palace.'
      Note that in American English **presently** can also mean
      'at present; currently': 'The President is presently
      undergoing minor surgery.'
      The American usage is gradually becoming accepted
      outside the USA, although careful users of British
      English consider it to be non-standard.

prevent 1   × His parents tried to prevent him to join the
                 army.
             ✓ **His parents tried to prevent him from joining
                 the army.**

      prevent someone **(from)** + v-ing

2   × Stricter punishments would prevent people
         from doing these things.
      ✓ **Stricter punishments would deter people from
         doing these things.**

      prevent = stop (someone doing something): 'They
      locked all the doors to prevent him escaping.'
      deter = discourage

3   × Stricter punishments may help to prevent
         society from serious crime.
      ✓ **Stricter punishments may help to protect
         society from serious crime.**

      prevent = stop (something happening): 'Bad weather
      prevented the plane from taking off.' 'Good tyres help
      to prevent accidents.'
      protect = guard or keep safe

prevention   × I decided to take a big stick with me, just as a
                    prevention.
                 √ **I decided to take a big stick with me, just as a
                    precaution.**

                 prevention = the act of preventing (stopping something
                 from happening): 'The police are concerned with the
                 prevention of crime.'
                 precaution = an action taken in an attempt to avoid
                 possible danger, injury, etc.

price   × The price of keeping a person in prison for a
               year is enormous.
            √ **The cost of keeping a person in prison for a
               year is enormous.**

            cost = the expense of doing something or having
            something done
            price = the amount of money asked for something
            which is for sale

principle   × I was introduced to several senior lecturers,
                   but not the principle.
                √ **I was introduced to several senior lecturers,
                   but not the principal.**

                principle = a general truth, rule, or standard of
                behaviour
                principal = a head of a school or college

print   × The magazine is printed every month.
            √ **The magazine is published every month.**

            print = produce many copies of a book, newspaper,
            etc. by using machines: 'Due to increased demand,
            another six thousand copies are to be printed.'
            publish = produce and distribute (a book, newspaper,
            etc.) for sale to the public

prison   × Sending people to the prison is not the way to
                reduce crime.
             √ **Sending people to prison is not the way to
                reduce crime.**

             Use go **to prison**, send someone **to prison,** be put **in
             prison** WITHOUT **the.**
             Only use **the** when talking about a particular prison:
             'The prison in this town is a big one.'

probably   × They probably will understand and try to help you.

    ✓ **They will probably understand and try to help you.**

Probably usually goes immediately after the (first) auxiliary verb: 'They have probably finished the meeting.' When there is no auxiliary verb, **probably** is usually placed immediately before the main verb: 'She probably knows.' However, when the main verb is **be**, **probably** is placed immediately after it: 'He is probably ill.' Note that **probably** can also come at the beginning of a sentence, though this is less common.

problem 1   × I experienced problems to find the right accommodation.

    ✓ **I experienced problems in finding the right accommodation.**

a problem/problems in + v-ing

2   × If their children are at school all day, I see no problem why both parents should not go to work if they want to.

    ✓ **If their children are at school all day, I see no reason why both parents should not go to work if they want to.**

reason why, NOT problem

proceed   × The main film was proceeded by a short cartoon.

    ✓ **The main film was preceded by a short cartoon.**

proceed = begin and continue: 'After a five-minute delay, the lecture proceeded.'
precede = come, go, or happen (immediately) before

professor   × He has applied for a job as a professor in a language school.

    ✓ **He has applied for a job as a teacher in a language school.**

professor = the most senior teacher in a university

program   ✓ AmE Every Friday we receive a program of
the following week's events.
✓ BrE Every Friday we receive a programme of
the following week's events.

Program is the usual American English spelling.
Programme is the British English spelling.
Note, however, that **a computer program** has the same
spelling in both American and British English.

progress   ✗ I did little progress at the start of the course.
✓ **I made little progress at the start of the
course.**

make progress, NOT **do**

prohibit   ✗ Even the teachers were prohibited to walk on
the lawn.
✓ **Even the teachers were prohibited from walking
on the lawn.**

prohibit someone **from** + v-ing

promise   ✗ Jimmy promised to his parents not to run
away again.
✓ **Jimmy promised his parents not to run away
again.**

promise someone something WITHOUT **to**

pronunciation   ✗ The language lab helps me improve my
pronounciation.
✓ **The language lab helps me improve my
pronunciation.**

Do not confuse the spelling of the noun **pronunciation**
(**un**) with that of the verb **pronounce** (**oun**).

proof   ✗ Today we have scientific proofs that tobacco is
harmful.
✓ **Today we have scientific proof that tobacco is
harmful.**

Proof is an uncountable noun.

propaganda × The television company receives most of its money from propaganda.
  √ **The television company receives most of its money from advertising.**
  Propaganda is used in a political context.
  Advertising is used in a commercial context.

properties × The police eventually found most of the stolen properties.
  √ **The police eventually found most of the stolen property.**
  Property (= possessions or belongings) is an uncountable noun.

propose × It was proposed all members of staff to start work an hour earlier.
  √ **It was proposed that all members of staff (should) start work an hour earlier.**
  propose that someone **(should) do** something

prospect × There were very few prospects to get a job.
  √ **There were very few prospects of getting a job.**
  prospects of + v-ing

protection × Wanting a military protection is not the same as wanting a war.
  √ **Wanting military protection is not the same as wanting a war.**
  Protection is an uncountable noun.

protest × She told the shop assistant that she wanted to protest about the cardigan she had bought.
  √ **She told the shop assistant that she wanted to complain about the cardigan she had bought.**
  Protest is used when a person feels very strongly that something is wrong or unjust: 'The crowds were protesting about the government's purchase of nuclear weapons.'
  Customers **complain** about faulty goods.

prove × This new engine has not been properly proved.
  ✓ **This new engine has not been properly tested.**

prove = provide proof or be proof of (something): 'Can you prove to the court that you are telling the truth?'
test = try; do experiments on (something) in order to discover how good or bad it is

provide 1 × My job provides me the opportunity to meet new people every day.
  ✓ **My job provides me with the opportunity to meet new people every day.**

provide someone **with** (a chance or opportunity to do something)
Note the alternative: 'My job gives me the opportunity to meet new people every day.'

2 × In my view, a father should provide his family.
  ✓ **In my view, a father should provide for his family.**

provide for someone = support someone (buy their food, clothes, etc.)

3 × I was very pleased with the room you provided to me.
  ✓ **I was very pleased with the room you provided for me.**
  ✓ **I was very pleased with the room you provided me with.**

provide (a room, accommodation, etc.) **for** someone
OR **provide** someone **with** (a room, accommodation, etc.), NOT **to**

public × The play was so boring that some of the public got up and left.
  ✓ **The play was so boring that some of the audience got up and left.**

public = people in general: 'The British public has been shocked by the incident.'
audience = people who (pay to) attend a performance at a cinema, theatre, etc.

punishment   × For certain crimes, the punishment should be very strong.
√ **For certain crimes, the punishment should be very severe.**
a **severe/harsh punishment**, NOT **strong**

put off   × Once indoors, he immediately put off his wet clothes and dried himself.
√ **Once indoors, he immediately took off his wet clothes and dried himself.**
take off your clothes, NOT **put off**

qualification   × I am taking another course to improve my qualification.
√ **I am taking another course to improve my qualifications.**
qualifications = the necessary ability, examination passes, experience, etc. (for a particular job): 'We decided to appoint her because she had the right qualifications for the job.'
qualification = a BA, MSc, or other examination pass

quality   × Switzerland produces goods with a very high quality.
√ **Switzerland produces goods of a very high quality.**
of (a) high/low/poor **quality**, NOT **with**

quarrel   × At the end of the quarrel Paul was badly hurt and I had to take him to hospital.
√ **At the end of the fight Paul was badly hurt and I had to take him to hospital.**
quarrel = an argument; a verbal conflict
fight = a physical conflict involving the use of violence, weapons, blows, etc.

question   × Today it is out of the question that the first years of a child's life are very important.
✓ **Today it is beyond question that the first years of a child's life are very important.**

out of the question (used especially of proposals) = completely impossible: 'To ask the men to work seven days a week is out of the question.'
beyond question = beyond doubt

quick   × We were expected to answer each question very quick.
✓ **We were expected to answer each question very quickly.**

Quick is an adjective.
Quickly is an adverb.

quiet 1   × I went up the stairs as quiet as I could.
✓ **I went up the stairs as quietly as I could.**

Quiet is an adjective.
Quietly is an adverb.

2   × I quiet agree with you.
✓ **I quite agree with you.**
× The girl he married was quiet tall.
✓ **The girl he married was quite tall.**

Quiet (et) is an adjective (opposite **loud**): 'Her voice was so quiet I couldn't hear what she was saying.'
Quite (te) is an adverb.

quite 1   × One night when the house was quite Peter got out of bed and ran away.
✓ **One night when the house was quiet Peter got out of bed and ran away.**

Quite (te) is an adverb: 'quite clever' (= fairly clever) 'I quite agree' (= I completely agree)
Quiet (et) is an adjective meaning 'with little noise' (opposite **loud**).

2   × I've quite grown used to living on my own.
✓ **I've grown quite used to living on my own.**

Quite is placed immediately before the word or phrase it modifies.

3 × In the circumstances, it was a quite rude
answer.
✓ **In the circumstances, it was quite a rude
answer.**

quite + **a/an** + adjective + noun

4 × This year the work at university is quite harder
than last year.
✓ **This year the work at university is rather
harder than last year.**

Quite is NOT used before comparative adjectives/
adverbs.

radio × I was listening to the news in the radio.
✓ **I was listening to the news on the radio.**
on the radio/television, NOT **in**

raincoat × It's a black rain coat with red buttons.
✓ **It's a black raincoat with red buttons.**
Raincoat is ALWAYS one word.

raise 1 ✓ **AmE My husband has just been given a big
raise.**
✓ **BrE My husband has just been given a big
pay rise.**
When the meaning is 'an increase in wages', use **raise**
in American English and **rise** in British English.

2 See CRITICISM

rare × Water is very rare in some parts of the
country.
✓ **Water is very scarce in some parts of the
country.**
rare (of unusual things and events) = uncommon: 'a
rare coin', 'a rare bird', 'a rare visit'
scarce (of things which are usually common) = in
short supply

rarely See NEVER 5, 6

rather 1   × I told her I would rather to go by train than to fly.

✓ **I told her I would rather go by train than fly.**

would rather + infinitive WITHOUT **to**

2   × I would rather you shouldn't invite too many people.

✓ **I would rather you didn't invite too many people.**

Do not follow **would rather** with **should/would**.

reach 1   × When the blue car reached to the corner, it stopped.

✓ **When the blue car reached the corner, it stopped.**

reach somewhere/something WITHOUT **to**

2   See AIM 2

real   ✓ **AmE I'm real sorry to hear that.**

✓ **BrE I'm really sorry to hear that.**

When the meaning is 'very', use **really** (NOT **real**) in British English.

In American English, both **really** and **real** are possible but **real** is more informal.

realize 1   × The headmaster realized his threat and sent the children home.

✓ **The headmaster carried out his threat and sent the children home.**

Realize (= to make something happen or become real) is usually used with words such as 'hope', 'ambition', and 'intention'.

2   × Nobody realized whether he was coming.

✓ **Nobody knew whether he was coming.**

Realize (= to become aware of) is used when talking about something which is factual or certain, NOT something uncertain.

Compare: 'Nobody realized that he was coming.' (He was coming but nobody was aware of it.)

really 1   × It was only a short trip but we had really a good time.

✓ **It was only a short trip but we had a really good time.**

✓ **It was only a short trip but we really had a good time.**

Really (= very; extremely) usually comes immediately before the adjective or adverb it qualifies. Otherwise its position is a matter of emphasis. It is commonly placed immediately before the verb. When a verb has several parts, **really** is usually placed immediately after the (first) auxiliary: 'We're really enjoying ourselves.'

2   × To his great amazement, little Nicola really won the race.

✓ **To his great amazement, little Nicola actually won the race.**

Really and **actually** are sometimes interchangeable, but NOT when the meaning is 'strange as it may seem'. For this meaning, use **actually**.

reason 1   × The reason I didn't buy the car was because I thought it was too expensive.

✓ **The reason I didn't buy the car was that I thought it was too expensive.**

The use of a **because** clause after **reason** is regarded by careful users as non-standard.

2   × There are many good reasons to thinking this.

✓ **There are many good reasons for thinking this.**

× What is the reason of your long silence?

✓ **What is the reason for your long silence?**

reason for (doing) something, NOT **to** OR **of**

reasonable   × I was far too upset and emotional to make a reasonable decision.

✓ **I was far too upset and emotional to make a rational decision.**

reasonable = fair, sensible, or acceptable: 'a reasonable offer/suggestion'
rational = produced by means of careful, logical thinking: 'a rational conclusion/argument/explanation'

recall   × May I recall you what happened that day?
             ✓ **May I remind you (of) what happened that day?**
             recall (fairly formal) = remember: 'I really can't recall what his wife looks like.'
             remind = cause (someone) to remember

receive   × I recieved both letters on the same day.
             ✓ **I received both letters on the same day.**
             receive (e BEFORE **i)**

recognize × On the plane home, I suddenly recognized that I had left my coat at the hotel.
             ✓ **On the plane home, I suddenly realized that I had left my coat at the hotel.**
             recognize = know again (someone or something you have seen, heard, or met before): 'She had changed so much over the years that I hardly recognized her.'
             realize = be/become aware of something

recommend × I recommend you a walk along the Seine.
             ✓ **I recommend a walk along the Seine.**
             ✓ **I recommend (that) you take a walk along the Seine.**
             ✓ **I recommend taking a walk along the Seine.**
             Recommend is used in the following patterns to mean 'advise or suggest': 'recommend a person/thing', 'recommend (that) someone (should) do something', 'recommend doing something'.
              Note that in British English there is also the pattern 'recommend someone to do something'. However, this pattern can sound awkward and is less common.

refer   × She refered to a dictionary if she didn't know a word.
             ✓ **She always referred to a dictionary if she didn't know a word.**
             referred (DOUBLE **r)**

refrain   × We all refrained telling her what we really thought.
             ✓ **We all refrained from telling her what we really thought.**
             refrain from + v-ing

refuse × I expect that the younger generation will refuse these old-fashioned ideas.
√ **I expect that the younger generation will reject these old-fashioned ideas.**

refuse an invitation = decline an invitation
refuse/reject an offer = decline an offer
reject an idea/philosophy = dismiss an idea/philosophy because you are not in agreement with it

regard 1 × Please give your sister my warmest regard.
√ **Please give your sister my warmest regards.**

regard = (1) consideration
(2) respect: 'He had a high regard for his teacher.' 'I hold her in the highest regard.'
regards = greetings; good wishes

2 × He shows no regard to other people.
√ **He shows no regard for other people.**

regard for (the feelings of) someone, NOT **to**

3 × He is generally regarded to be one of the world's finest physicists.
√ **He is generally regarded as one of the world's finest physicists.**

regard a person or thing **as** (being) something, NOT **to be**

regret × He soon began to regret to have run away from home.
√ **He soon began to regret having run away from home.**

regret + v-ing

regretful 1 × I made several regretful mistakes.
√ **I made several regrettable mistakes.**

regretful = feeling or expressing regret
regrettable = to be regretted

2   × I am regretful to inform you that your
    application has been unsuccessful.
    √ **I regret to inform you that your application has
    been unsuccessful.**

Regretful is usually used to describe real feelings: 'I
felt rather regretful that I couldn't go with them.' 'She
gave me a regretful look.'
I/We regret to ... is a polite expression used chiefly in
formal letters.

related   × All the other problems are related with the
    economic one.
    √ **All the other problems are related to the
    economic one.**

A is **related to** B, NOT **with**

relax   × I usually relax myself by taking a hot bath.
    √ **I usually relax by taking a hot bath.**

Relax is NOT a reflexive verb.

relieve   × His fear immediately changed to relieve.
    √ **His fear immediately changed to relief.**

Relieve is a verb.
Relief is a noun.

remember 1   × I am remembering leaving a map of Rome in
    the pocket.
    √ **I remember leaving a map of Rome in the
    pocket.**

Remember is NOT used in progressive tenses.

2   × I did not remember to meet her before but I
    pretended I knew her.
    √ **I did not remember meeting her before but I
    pretended I knew her.**

remember + to-v = not forget: 'Please remember to
feed the cat.'
remember + v-ing = recall

3 × I would like to remember you that the machine is still under guarantee.
✓ **I would like to remind you that the machine is still under guarantee.**

remind someone = cause someone to remember

remind 1 × The flowers reminded him his garden.
✓ **The flowers reminded him of his garden.**

remind someone **of** something = cause someone to think about something

2 × I wish you had reminded me of phoning her.
✓ **I wish you had reminded me to phone her.**

remind someone **to do** something = tell someone that there is something he or she ought to do

3 × I remind the happy days we spent together at college.
✓ **I remember the happy days we spent together at college.**

remind = cause (someone) to remember
Compare: 'I was reminded of the happy days we spent together at college.' (= something caused me to remember ...)

remove × My family removed to Kamakura when I was five years old.
✓ **My family moved to Kamakura when I was five years old.**

Some people used to use **remove** when talking about people moving to another house but this is now considered very old-fashioned.

rent × If you like riding, there are horses you can rent.
✓ **If you like riding, there are horses you can hire.**

In British English, **hire** usually refers to a single payment made for the temporary use of something: 'hire a tennis racket/wedding dress/car'.
Rent usually refers to a regular series of payments made over a long period of time: 'rent a house/flat'. Note, however, that in American English, a person **rents** a car.

replace × I told him he would have to replace the broken lid by a new one.
  √ **I told him he would have to replace the broken lid with a new one.**
  replace something **with** something else, NOT **by**

request × We had to request for more help.
  √ **We had to request more help.**
  request something WITHOUT **for**

research 1 × I'm doing some researches on the industrial development of my country.
  √ **I'm doing some research on the industrial development of my country.**
  Research is an uncountable noun.

2 × A lot of money is spent on research against the causes of cancer.
  √ **A lot of money is spent on research into the causes of cancer.**
  (do) **research into** something, NOT **against**

3 × More police were sent to join in the research but the child was never found.
  √ **More police were sent to join in the search but the child was never found.**
  research = advanced study which aims to discover new knowledge: 'cancer research', 'She's doing research into the causes of crime.'
  search = the act of looking for (someone or something) by carefully examining a place or area

resist × She couldn't resist his rudeness any longer and walked out of the room.
  √ **She couldn't tolerate his rudeness any longer and walked out of the room.**
  resist = fight against; oppose: 'resist an enemy attack'
  tolerate = stand; bear; put up with

respectful   × Some former prisoners are now respectful
citizens.
✓ **Some former prisoners are now respectable
citizens.**
× If you want to make a good impression, you'll
have to look a bit more respectful.
✓ **If you want to make a good impression, you'll
have to look a bit more respectable.**

respectful = having or showing respect: 'a respectful
attitude'
respectable = displaying socially acceptable standards
in appearance or behaviour; deserving respect

responsibility   × People with children have a lot of
responsabilities.
✓ **People with children have a lot of
responsibilities.**

responsibilities (WITH **sib**)

responsible 1   × I'm writing to you as you are the responsible
person for customer relations.
✓ **I'm writing to you as you are the person
responsible for customer relations.**

a responsible person = a trustworthy person
the person responsible (for something) = the person
whose duty it is to deal with or look after something

2   × I am also responsible to decide on the best
way to manufacture a product.
✓ **I am also responsible for deciding on the best
way to manufacture a product.**

responsible for + v-ing

3   × The dealer is responsible of any fault in the
product.
✓ **The dealer is responsible for any fault in the
product.**

responsible for something, NOT **of**

rest × Whenever we rest in Milan, we always go to the opera.
√ **Whenever we stay in Milan, we always go to the opera.**

rest = stop an activity in order to recover your energy: 'After climbing for two hours, we decided to stop and rest.'
stay = spend time (in a place), especially one or more nights

result × Nowadays we hear a lot about pollution and its results on our health.
√ **Nowadays we hear a lot about pollution and its effects on our health.**

result = the outcome of an action or state of affairs: 'His poverty was the result of gambling.' 'Her first book was the result of a trip to Africa.' 'The anti-smoking campaign has produced excellent results.'
effect (on someone/something) = a change in condition brought about by a cause: 'The drug had no effect on him.' (= there was no change in his condition)
'Wine always has an effect on me—it makes me want to sing.'

return 1 × She returned back after half an hour.
√ **She returned after half an hour.**
× When are you going to return back the money you owe me?
√ **When are you going to return the money you owe me?**

Back is NOT used with **return** because **return** means 'come/go/give/send back'.

2 × In my opinion the government should return capital punishment.
√ **In my opinion the government should restore/bring back/reintroduce capital punishment.**

return = give or send back: 'Please return the photographs as soon as possible.'

3 See HOME

reward × Two of the German films were given rewards.
            ✓ **Two of the German films were given awards.**
            reward = a sum of money offered for helping the
            police, finding and returning lost possessions, etc.:
            'The bank is offering a reward of a thousand pounds.'
            award = a prize given for merit

ride   × He spends all his time riding his new car.
            ✓ **He spends all his time driving his new car.**
            ride a horse/bicycle BUT **drive** a car/van/train

ring 1 × He rung the bell and the door opened.
            ✓ **He rang the bell and the door opened.**
            ring, ringing, rang, rung

2   × I rang to the college to explain my absence.
            ✓ **I rang the college to explain my absence.**
            ring a person/place WITHOUT **to**

rise   × Many firms try to survive by rising productivity.
            ✓ **Many firms try to survive by raising**
              productivity.
            Rise is an intransitive verb: 'Prices rose.' (= Prices
            increased.)
            Raise is a transitive verb: 'They raised the prices.'
            (= They increased the prices.)

risk   × Not one of us would risk to go out on our own.
            ✓ **Not one of us would risk going out on our**
              own.
            risk + v-ing

rob   × While he was asleep, she robbed him his
              watch.
            ✓ **While he was asleep, she stole his watch.**
            ✓ **While he was asleep, she robbed him of his**
              watch.
            × The wicked old man robbed all my money.
            ✓ **The wicked old man stole all my money.**
            ✓ **The wicked old man robbed me of all my**
              money.
            steal something (**from** someone) OR (less common) **rob**
            someone (**of** something)

round   × The accident happened round three o'clock.
             √ **The accident happened around three o'clock.**
             around (NOT **round**) = (at) about/approximately

rude   × The shop assistant was very rude with me.
             √ **The shop assistant was very rude to me.**
             (be) **rude to** someone, NOT **with**

run 1   × A lot of people run to see what had happened.
             √ **A lot of people ran to see what had happened.**
             run, running, ran, run

2   × The car was running too fast for me to see the
               number plate.
             √ **The car was moving too fast for me to see the
               number plate.**
             A vehicle **travels**, **moves**, or **goes** at a certain speed in
             a certain direction.

's 1   × The shopkeeper said the fault was the
               manufacturers responsibility.
             √ **The shopkeeper said the fault was the
               manufacturer's responsibility.**
             When talking about something which is possessed by
             or connected with someone, use an apostrophe.

2   × Some of the tree's leaves had fallen on top of
               the car.
             √ **Some of the leaves from the tree had fallen
               on top of the car.**
             Compare: 'All her father's tools were missing,' (NOT
             'tools of her father')
             'The handles of the tools were made of wood' (NOT
             ' ... tools' handles ... ').
             The possessive **'s/s'** is commonly used with human
             and animal nouns but not with inanimate nouns.

sack 1 × When I took the two oranges out of the sack, I discovered that one of them was bad.
√ **When I took the two oranges out of the bag, I discovered that one of them was bad.**

sack = a very large strong bag: 'a sack of coal'
bag = a container made of cloth, paper, leather, etc.: 'a bag of sweets', 'a shopping bag'

2 × My new coat has a belt and two large sacks.
√ **My new coat has a belt and two large pockets.**

sack = a very large strong bag
pocket = a small flat cloth bag sewn into or onto a garment, used for keeping small items in

salary × His salary is about a hundred and fifty pounds a week.
√ **His wage is about a hundred and fifty pounds a week.**

A **salary** is usually paid monthly but a **wage** is usually paid weekly.

sale × I bought both pairs of shoes on a sale.
√ **I bought both pairs of shoes in a sale.**

buy something **in a sale**, NOT **on**

salute × A group of officials were at the airport to salute the visitors.
√ **A group of officials were at the airport to greet/welcome the visitors.**

salute (of members of the armed forces) = make a formal sign of respect, especially by raising the right arm: 'Always salute a superior officer.'
greet/welcome = express pleasure on meeting someone

same 1 × Paris has the same level of pollution with Los Angeles.
√ **Paris has the same level of pollution as Los Angeles.**

× The belt is made of the same material like the coat.

✓ **The belt is made of the same material as the coat.**

the same ... as, NOT **with** or **like**

2   See THAN 1

sat   × She was sat on a chair at the table, having her lunch.

✓ **She was sitting on a chair at the table, having her lunch.**

The use of **sat** with **be** is considered non-standard.

satisfactory   × For many people, a part-time job can be very satisfactory.

✓ **For many people, a part-time job can be very satisfying.**

satisfactory = good enough to satisfy or be acceptable: 'Some of the students are asked to leave the college if their work is not satisfactory.'
satisfying = giving pleasure or contentment

satisfied   × I was completely satisfied of the quality of her work.

✓ **I was completely satisfied with the quality of her work.**

satisfied with someone/something, NOT **of**

save   × The police telephoned his parents to tell them that he was save.

✓ **The police telephoned his parents to tell them that he was safe.**

Save is a verb.
Safe is an adjective.

say 1   × When he arrived, they said him that his friend had died.

✓ **When he arrived, they told him that his friend had died.**

✓ **When he arrived, they said that his friend had died.**

tell someone that BUT **say** that

2 × A policeman said me to go with him to the police station.
    ✓ **A policeman told me to go with him to the police station.**
    × He was tired of people saying him what to do.
    ✓ **He was tired of people telling him what to do.**
    tell someone to do something, NOT **say**

3 × The magazine also says about English football.
    ✓ **The magazine also talks about English football.**
    talk about (= discuss), NOT **say about**

4 × No one likes to be said a liar.
    ✓ **No one likes to be called a liar.**
    call someone a liar/thief/cheat etc., NOT **say**

5 See JOKE, LIE

scarce × If you are interested in scarce birds, you should visit the bird garden.
    ✓ **If you are interested in rare birds, you should visit the bird garden.**
    × Chocolate was very rare during the war.
    ✓ **Chocolate was very scarce during the war.**
    scarce (of things which are usually common) = in short supply
    rare (of unusual things and events) = uncommon

scarcely See NEVER 6

scarf × There was a white silk scarve in one of the pockets.
    ✓ **There was a white silk scarf in one of the pockets.**
    Scarf is singular.
    Scarves is plural.

scene 1   × From the window, there was a beautiful scene of the lake.
✓ **From the window, there was a beautiful view of the lake.**

scene = a view presented by a particular situation or setting; picture
view = the area within your vision when you are in a particular place

2   × The driver stopped now and again so that we could enjoy the scene.
✓ **The driver stopped now and again so that we could enjoy the scenery.**

scene = a view presented by a particular situation or setting; picture: 'The old man chasing the dog made a very amusing scene.'
scenery = the natural features of the countryside

scenery   × What a beautiful scenery!
✓ **What beautiful scenery!**
Scenery is an uncountable noun.

school 1   ✓ **AmE Most Norwegians speak English quite well because everybody has to learn English in school.**
✓ **BrE Most Norwegians speak English quite well because everybody has to learn English at school.**

In American English, use **in/at school**.
In British English, use **at school**, NOT **in**.

2   × She said that her daughter wanted to leave the school and get married.
✓ **She said that her daughter wanted to leave school and get married.**
× He still isn't old enough to go to a school.
✓ **He still isn't old enough to go to school.**

Use **leave school**, **start school**, **go to school** (WITHOUT **a** or **the**) when referring to school as an institution and not to one school in particular. Compare: 'She goes to a very good school.'

scissors   × First cut along the dotted line with a scissors.
   √ **First cut along the dotted line with a pair of scissors.**
   √ **First cut along the dotted line with some scissors.**

Scissors is a plural noun.

search 1   × A police patrol was organized to search him.
   √ **A police patrol was organized to search for him.**
   × An old lady saw Tom and realized that he was the little boy who was searched by the police.
   √ **An old lady saw Tom and realized that he was the little boy that the police were searching for.**
   √ **An old lady saw Tom and realized that he was the little boy who was sought by the police.**

search someone = examine someone's clothing or pockets to discover whether he or she is carrying a gun, drugs, stolen goods, etc.: 'They searched him but couldn't find the film.'
search for or **seek** (formal) = try to find someone/something

   2   × I searched my passport everywhere but couldn't find it.
   √ **I searched for my passport everywhere but couldn't find it.**

search a place = examine a place carefully to try to find something: 'I searched the room but couldn't find my passport.'
search for something = try to find something (usually something that has been lost or hidden)

second   See MONTH

see 1   × I saw a large blue car to drive past on the other side of the road.
   √ **I saw a large blue car drive past on the other side of the road.**

see a person/thing + infinitive WITHOUT **to**

2   × He sat seeing the planes taking off.
   √ **He sat watching the planes taking off.**
   × The lecturer asked us to see carefully what he
      was doing.
   √ **The lecturer asked us to look carefully at what
      he was doing.**

see = experience with the eyes (without concentrating
or paying attention): 'Did you see anyone go out?'
'Turn the light on if you can't see.'
watch = use the eyes to observe something, especially
for a long time
look at = use the eyes to observe something, usually
for a short time

3   × I have sent you the magazine so you can see
      by yourself how beautiful our country is.
   √ **I have sent you the magazine so you can see
      for yourself how beautiful our country is.**

see for yourself (NOT **by**) = see (something) with your
own eyes
Compare: 'If everybody is busy, you'll have to go by
yourself.' (= alone)

4   See DREAM 3

seek 1   × He sat nearer the tree, seeking for protection.
   √ **He sat nearer the tree, seeking protection.**

seek someone/something WITHOUT **for**

2   × We are often accused of seeking for to destroy
      the countryside.
   √ **We are often accused of seeking to destroy
      the countryside.**

seek to do something WITHOUT **for**

seem 1   × London seemed him to be marvellous.
   √ **London seemed marvellous to him.**

seem + adjective + **to** someone

2   × The woman who was shouting seemed the owner of the car.
    ✓ **The woman who was shouting seemed to be the owner of the car.**

When the noun phrase following **seem** does not contain an adjective, **seem** is usually followed by **to be**. Compare: 'She seemed (to be) angry.' 'She seemed (to be) an intelligent woman.' 'She seemed to be the leader of the group.'

3   × You should give help to anyone who seems that he needs it.
    ✓ **You should give help to anyone who seems to need it.**

it (preparatory subject) + **seem** + **that** clause
This is the only pattern in which **seem** may be followed by a **that** clause. Compare: 'It seems that John needs help.' 'John seems to need help.'

seldom   See NEVER 6

semester   ✓ **AmE Last semester there were a lot of complaints.**
    ✓ **BrE Last term there were a lot of complaints.**

The American school year is usually divided into two **semesters**, although it is also sometimes divided into three or four **terms**.
In Britain, the school year is usually divided into three **terms**.

send   × If you can't find the magazine in Corsica, write to me and I'll sent it to you.
    ✓ **If you can't find the magazine in Corsica, write to me and I'll send it to you.**

send, sending, sent, sent

separate   × My parents seperated when I was still at school.
    ✓ **My parents separated when I was still at school.**

separate (**a** AFTER **p**)

serious   × If we're serious in reducing the amount of crime, there should be stricter punishments.
   ✓ **If we're serious about reducing the amount of crime, there should be stricter punishments.**
be serious about (doing) something, NOT **in**

shadow   × If the sun is too hot, perhaps you would like to sit in the shadow?
   ✓ **If the sun is too hot, perhaps you would like to sit in the shade?**
shade = any area sheltered from the sun
shadow = a clear shape made by the shade of a particular person or thing
Compare: 'The leafy branches provide plenty of shade.'
'The little boy saw his shadow on the ground.'

shake   × They stood inside the door and shaked hands with each of the guests.
   ✓ **They stood inside the door and shook hands with each of the guests.**
shake, shaking, shook, shaken

shall 1   × The next meeting of the heads of state shall take place in Vienna.
   ✓ **The next meeting of the heads of state will take place in Vienna.**
For future reference, use **will** with the second and third person. **Shall** is used only with the first person (I/we).

2   × I shall be very grateful if you could help me with my problem.
   ✓ **I should be very grateful if you could help me with my problem.**
I should/would/'d be very grateful/pleased etc. if you could ... , NOT **shall**

3   × Finally, I'll like to thank you again for your hospitality.
   ✓ **Finally, I'd like to thank you again for your hospitality.**
I should/would/'d like to thank/ask etc. (polite) = I want to thank/ask etc.

4 See AFTER 6, AS LONG AS 1, CASE 2, IF 1, IMMEDIATELY 2, MOMENT 2, ONCE 3, UNTIL 2, WHEN 1, WHENEVER

shaved   × He had a clean-shaved face.
√ **He had a clean-shaven face.**

The adjective, especially when used in compounds, is **shaven**. The past participle is usually **shaved**: 'Have you shaved today?'

she   See THEY 1

sheep   × A lot of cows and sheeps died because of the polluted water.
√ **A lot of cows and sheep died because of the polluted water.**

Sheep is the singular AND plural form.

shopping 1   × This morning I went for shopping.
√ **This morning I went shopping.**

go + v-ing
Compare: 'go fishing', 'go swimming', etc.

2   × It happened in the supermarket while I was doing my shoppings.
√ **It happened in the supermarket while I was doing my shopping.**

Shopping is an uncountable noun.

shortly 1   × She spoke very shortly about how they had lived during the war.
√ **She spoke very briefly about how they had lived during the war.**

shortly = impatiently; not politely: 'He answered rather shortly that he was not the slightest bit interested.'
briefly = for a short time

2   × Shortly, he said that the repair was not his responsibility.
√ **In short, he said that the repair was not his responsibility.**

shortly = soon: 'I'll be back shortly.'
in short = to sum up in a few words

shorts   × He packed two shirts and a shorts.
     √ **He packed two shirts and a pair of shorts.**

Shorts is a plural noun. Note the alternative: 'some shorts'.

should 1   × I have friends who should love to stay at home, but they have to go to work.
     √ **I have friends who would love to stay at home, but they have to go to work.**

first person conditional = **should/would** + infinitive
second and third person conditional = **would** + infinitive (NOT **should**)

2   See BETTER 4

shout   × She made me so annoyed I felt like shouting to her.
     √ **She made me so annoyed I felt like shouting at her.**

shout to someone = call someone to attract their attention
shout at someone = speak to someone in a very loud voice, especially when angry

side 1   × On the back side of the coat there were some dirty marks.
     √ **On the back of the coat there were some dirty marks.**
   × You will find my name and address on the back side of this sheet.
     √ **You will find my name and address on the back of this sheet.**

on the back/front of something (WITHOUT **side**)
Note that if a thing has only two sides it is possible to say **on the other side**: 'My favourite songs are on the other side (of the record).'

2   × On the other side, I can understand why she feels disappointed.
     √ **On the other hand, I can understand why she feels disappointed.**

on the one hand ... /on the other hand ... , NOT **side**

sightseeing   × We are going to do a sightseeing tomorrow.
✓ **We are going to do some sightseeing tomorrow.**
Sightseeing is an uncountable noun.

sign   × One of her hobbies is collecting the signs of famous singers.
✓ **One of her hobbies is collecting the signatures of famous singers.**
sign = something which is understood as having a particular meaning: 'a road sign'
signature = a person's name written in that person's own handwriting on a cheque, formal letter, etc.

since 1   × I am studying law since 1982.
✓ **I have been studying law since 1982.**
× Since that journey, I never sailed again.
✓ **Since that journey, I have never sailed again.**
When talking about an action or state which began in the past and continues into the present, use a present perfect tense.

2   × I have been living in London since four weeks now.
✓ **I have been living in London for four weeks now.**
since + beginning of period
for + length of period
Compare: 'I have been living in London for almost two years, since October 1986.'

3   × I stayed in your hotel for three nights, since 23rd November to 26th November.
✓ **I stayed in your hotel for three nights, from 23rd November to 26th November.**
from ... to ... : 'from Monday to Wednesday', 'from 7 a.m. to 3 p.m.', 'from 1947 to 1966'

4 × Since the last few years, unemployment has been increasing.

✓ **Over/during the last few years, unemployment has been increasing.**

Since is used to indicate a point of time in the past (i.e. the starting point for an action or state which is still continuing in the present): 'I've been living in Paris since July.'
Use **over/during** to talk about the period of time within which an action happens.

sincerely × Dear John, ... Yours sincerely ...

✓ **Dear John, ... Yours/With love/With best wishes ...**

When writing to a friend or relative, do not end your letter **Yours sincerely** or **Yours faithfully**. These phrases are usually used in more formal letters.

sit 1 × I looked for an empty sit at the other end of the plane.

✓ **I looked for an empty seat at the other end of the plane.**

Seat /siːt/ is a noun.
Sit /sɪt/ is a verb.

2 See ARMCHAIR

skilful × 'You are lucky to have such skilful children,' she said.

✓ **'You are lucky to have such talented children,' she said.**

skilful = having or showing skill (gained from instruction and experience)
talented = having or showing a natural ability to do something well

sleep 1 × I slept at ten o'clock last night.

✓ **I went to sleep at ten o'clock last night.**

sleep = remain in the state of being asleep
go to sleep = fall asleep (i.e. enter the state of being asleep)
Compare: 'I went to bed at nine, went to sleep at ten, and slept until six this morning.'

2 × After showing the conductor my ticket, I
started sleeping again.
  ✓ **After showing the conductor my ticket, I went
back to sleep.**

go back to sleep = fall asleep again (after an
interruption)

3 × I felt warm and relaxed and was almost
sleeping when suddenly the telephone rang.
  ✓ **I felt warm and relaxed and was almost
asleep when suddenly the telephone rang.**

Asleep (adjective) can be used with **almost, nearly**,
etc. when talking about a partial state.
Sleep (verb) always refers to a complete state and
cannot be qualified in this way.

4 × I started sleeping and didn't wake up till the
next morning.
  ✓ **I fell asleep and didn't wake up till the next
morning.**

Fall asleep and **go to sleep** are the usual expressions.

5 × The child fell into sleep as soon as he got into
bed.
  ✓ **The child fell asleep as soon as he got into
bed.**

fall asleep, NOT **into**

slide × One or two cars were sliding when they tried
to stop because of the ice.
  ✓ **One or two cars were skidding when they
tried to stop because of the ice.**

slide = to go smoothly over a surface: 'The children
were happily sliding on the ice.'
skid = to slide out of control, especially of a vehicle
when the driver tries to stop quickly

small × Even his wife said he was a selfish, bad-
tempered small man.
  ✓ **Even his wife said he was a selfish, bad-
tempered little man.**

Unlike **small**, **little** can be used to express approval or
disapproval: 'a nasty little man', 'a beautiful little car'.

smash × He ran out of the house and smashed the door behind him.
          ✓ **He ran out of the house and slammed the door behind him.**

smash = break into pieces: 'I'm amazed that the plate didn't smash when you dropped it.' 'Those naughty children have smashed the window with their cricket ball.'
slam = (of a door, drawer, etc.) shut violently with a bang

smell 1 × Travelling can be very unpleasant, especially if the person sitting next to you smells garlic and old cheese.
            ✓ **Travelling can be very unpleasant, especially if the person sitting next to you smells of garlic and old cheese.**

smell = perceive or recognize something by means of the nose: 'I can smell smoke.'
smell of (onions etc.) = have or give off the smell of (onions etc.)

2 See SOUND 4

smile × She smiled to me as if she knew me.
          ✓ **She smiled at me as if she knew me.**
          × I thought I saw him smile on her.
          ✓ **I thought I saw him smile at her.**

smile at someone, NOT **to** OR **on**

smoke × We could see a thick black smoke coming out of the window.
          ✓ **We could see thick black smoke coming out of the window.**

Smoke is an uncountable noun.

so 1 × The coat is new and is so in very good condition.
          ✓ **The coat is new and so is in very good condition.**

When used as a conjunction, **so** must be placed at the beginning of the clause. Note the alternative: 'The coat is new and is therefore in very good condition.'

2   × If you find the wallet, I should be so grateful if
you would return it to the above address.

   ✓ **If you find the wallet, I should be very/extremely
   grateful if you would return it to the above
   address.**

In the pattern **so** + adjective + **if**, the adverb **so**
expresses an extreme degree of personal emotion.
The pattern is usually used when trying hard to
persuade someone to do something. 'I'd be so grateful
if you could spare just a moment.' 'We'd be so
pleased if you and your wife could come.'

3   × My English is so poor so my wife has to
translate everything.

   ✓ **My English is so poor that my wife has to
   translate everything.**

so + adjective/adverb + **that** clause: 'She was so clever
that all the universities wanted her.' 'The pianist
played so badly that the audience walked out.'
Compare: 'My English is very poor so my wife has to
translate everything.'

4   × It was a so beautiful day that we decided to go
to the beach.

   ✓ **It was such a beautiful day that we decided to
   go to the beach.**

such + **a/an** + adjective + noun + **that**
Compare: 'The weather was so beautiful that ... '
(**so** + adjective + **that**)

5   × I'm sure you'd never find so bad food in any
other canteen.

   ✓ **I'm sure you'd never find such bad food in any
   other canteen.**

So cannot be used before an adjective which is
immediately followed by a noun.
Compare: 'The food was so bad that nobody could eat
it.' 'Nobody had ever tasted such bad food.'

6   See THAT 4

social 1 × The next election was won by the Social Party.
             √ **The next election was won by the Socialist Party.**

social = concerning (life in a) society: 'The two children have different social backgrounds.'
socialist = concerning socialism (the political system that favours equality of opportunity and public as opposed to private ownership)

2 × Our new neighbours are not very social.
       √ **Our new neighbours are not very sociable.**

social = concerning (life in a) society
sociable = friendly

socialist × Socialists and psychologists have studied the problem at great length.
               √ **Sociologists and psychologists have studied the problem at great length.**

socialist (in politics) = a person who believes in socialism
sociologist (in sociology) = a person who studies societies and group behaviour

society × I was asked to give a talk about women and their role in the society.
             √ **I was asked to give a talk about women and their role in society.**

Do not use **the** with **society** when it means 'people in general, considered as a single group'. Compare: 'He joined the drama society.' (= a particular organization)

soft × She spoke very soft and nobody could hear her.
          √ **She spoke very softly and nobody could hear her.**

Soft is an adjective.
Softly is an adverb.

solution × The ideal solution of this problem is for his wife to get a part-time job.
✓ **The ideal solution to this problem is for his wife to get a part-time job.**

a solution to a problem, NOT **of**

some 1 × The rewind button worked properly for only some hours.
✓ **The rewind button worked properly for only a few hours.**

some = several
a few = not many

2 × Do you have some questions?
✓ **Do you have any questions?**

In questions and negative sentences, use **any**, NOT **some**.

somebody See SOMEONE

someone 1 × There are someones who aren't afraid of punishment at all.
✓ **There are some people who aren't afraid of punishment at all.**

Someone and **somebody** do NOT have plural forms.

2 × She hadn't seen someone for over a week.
✓ **She hadn't seen anyone for over a week.**
× Somehow he had to get on the train without being seen by someone.
✓ **Somehow he had to get on the train without being seen by anyone.**

In a negative context, use **anyone/anybody**, NOT **someone/somebody**.

3 × I ran over to the car to see if someone was injured.
✓ **I ran over to the car to see if anyone was injured.**

When talking about something unknown or uncertain, use **anyone/anybody**, NOT **someone/somebody**: 'Did you see anyone?' 'I doubt if anybody will object.'

4 × Perhaps someone of your staff has already
found it.
✓ **Perhaps one of your staff has already found it.**

one of + plural countable noun, NOT **someone of**
Note the alternative: 'Perhaps someone on your staff
has already found it.'

something 1 × By six o'clock I am too tired to do something
else.
✓ **By six o'clock I am too tired to do anything
else.**

Note that **anything** is used in affirmative sentences
which actually express a negative meaning: 'By six
o'clock I am too tired to do anything else.' (= By six
o'clock I am so tired that I cannot do anything else.)
Compare: 'too ill to eat any food', 'too busy to see
anyone'

2 × At first we couldn't see something suspicious.
✓ **At first we couldn't see anything suspicious.**
× Does your country export something?
✓ **Does your country export anything?**

Something is usually used in affirmative sentences:
'We could see something.'
Anything is usually used in negative sentences and
questions: 'We couldn't see anything.' 'Can you see
anything?'

3 × If the cassette is stuck, you'll have to use a
knife or something like that.
✓ **If the cassette is stuck, you'll have to use a
knife or something.**

... or something is an informal expression meaning
' ... or something like that': 'Why don't you buy her a
book or something?'

somewhere × The bus service is so bad that it's almost
impossible to get somewhere.
✓ **The bus service is so bad that it's almost
impossible to get anywhere.**

Use **anywhere** (NOT **somewhere**) in a negative context.

soon   × As it soon will be Christmas, I'm anxious to get the television repaired as quickly as possible.
✓ **As it will soon be Christmas, I'm anxious to get the television repaired as quickly as possible.**

Soon is usually placed immediately after the (first) auxiliary verb: 'Ann said she would soon have enough money to go on holiday.' When there is no auxiliary verb, **soon** is usually placed immediately before the main verb: 'She soon had enough money.' However, when the main verb is **be**, **soon** is placed immediately after it: 'She was soon fit and well again.'

sooner   See NO SOONER

sorry   × I really sorry about all the trouble I have caused you.
✓ **I am really sorry about all the trouble I have caused you.**

Sorry is an adjective, NOT a verb: 'be sorry', 'feel sorry', 'look sorry', etc.

so that   × He hadn't taken any warm clothes so that he felt cold.
✓ **He hadn't taken any warm clothes so he felt cold.**

So that is used to express purpose: 'He took some warm clothes so that he wouldn't be cold.'
So is used to talk about the result of an action.

sound 1   × I turned the volume right up but there were still no sounds.
✓ **I turned the volume right up but there was still no sound.**

a sound (countable) = something that is received by your sense of hearing: 'The first time I went snorkelling I heard sounds I had never heard before.'
sound (uncountable) = everything that is received by your sense of hearing

2 × The engine was old and was making a lot of sound.

✓ **The engine was old and was making a lot of noise.**

noise = (usually) loud or unpleasant sound

3 × I heard a noise which sounded to be a helicopter.

✓ **I heard a noise which sounded like a helicopter.**

sound like something

4 × Her voice sounded more seriously than before.

✓ **Her voice sounded more serious than before.**

Sound belongs to a group of verbs (including **be**, **feel**, **look**, **seem**, **smell**, and **taste**) that are followed by adjectives rather than adverbs.

South See NORTH

sow × I thanked her for sowing the button back on.

✓ **I thanked her for sewing the button back on.**

sow = put (seed) in the ground
sew = attach, mend, or stitch by means of a needle and thread

space × There are hundreds of millions of stars in the space.

✓ **There are hundreds of millions of stars in space.**

Do not use **the** when using **space** to mean 'everything beyond the Earth's atmosphere'.

spare × They spare as much money as they can for their holidays.

✓ **They save as much money as they can for their holidays.**

spare = (1) have in excess and available: 'Do we have any money to spare this week? The baby could do with some new clothes.'
(2) afford (to give): 'I'd like to watch the film but I can't spare the time.'
save = set aside

speak 1   × Only eight per cent of all Swiss are speaking Italian.
          ✓ **Only eight per cent of all Swiss speak Italian.**

Use the present simple tense for habitual actions.

2   × Neither of my parents speaks in English.
          ✓ **Neither of my parents speaks English.**

speak (English) = know (English) and use it habitually
speak in (English) = use (English) to communicate on a particular occasion
Compare: 'The guide speaks English, German, and Spanish but he'll be speaking in Spanish this afternoon because most of the visitors are from Spain.'

3   × She spoke that she would visit England in July.
          ✓ **She said that she would visit England in July.**

Speak is NOT used as a reporting verb.

4   × I could hear her speaking with herself in the kitchen.
          ✓ **I could hear her talking to herself in the kitchen.**

talk to yourself, NOT **speak with**

5   See LIE

specially   × I was surprised that she was late, specially since she usually arrived early.
          ✓ **I was surprised that she was late, especially since she usually arrived early.**
          × A woman who works sometimes neglects her family, specially the children.
          ✓ **A woman who works sometimes neglects her family, especially the children.**

specially = for a single special purpose: 'The course has been specially prepared for young beginners.' 'I came here specially to see you.'
especially = (1) particularly: 'You need extra heating in the house—especially during the winter months.'
(2) to an exceptional degree: 'The film will be especially interesting to those who are fond of water sports.'

spectacle   × On the first day of the holiday I broke my spectacle.

✓ **On the first day of the holiday I broke my spectacles.**

Spectacles (= glasses) is a plural noun.
Compare: 'a pair of spectacles'.

speech   × I was invited to make a speech on the radio.

✓ **I was invited to give a talk on the radio.**

A **speech** is usually made by a politician or by an important person at a meeting, social occasion, or dinner: 'The Prime Minister's speech included a fierce attack on the unions.'
A **talk** is usually informative, and often given by a lecturer: 'The subject of Dr Chase's talk is "Solar Energy and the Nuclear Debate".'

speed 1   × Despite the traffic lights ahead, the car continued with the same speed.

✓ **Despite the traffic lights ahead, the car continued at the same speed.**

travel/move etc. **at** (a certain) speed, NOT **with**

2   × The police stopped several drivers for overspeeding.

✓ **The police stopped several drivers for speeding.**

speeding = driving faster than the speed limit
There is no such verb as 'overspeed'.

spend 1   × They don't have any money to spend for luxuries.

✓ **They don't have any money to spend on luxuries.**

spend (an amount of) money **on** something, NOT **for**

2   × Thank you for spending so much time to listen to our complaints.

✓ **Thank you for spending so much time listening to our complaints.**

spend time + v-ing

3 × We went to the cinema to spend the time until the train arrived.

√ **We went to the cinema to pass the time until the train arrived.**

pass (the) time = do something in order to avoid doing nothing and being bored: 'On long train journeys the children pass the time by playing cards.'

4 × Yesterday we spend the whole day visiting museums.

√ **Yesterday we spent the whole day visiting museums.**

× I had to spent all my time looking after the old lady.

√ **I had to spend all my time looking after the old lady.**

spend, spending, spent, spent

5 × She spends most of her free time on reading.

√ **She spends most of her free time reading.**

× We spent the whole day in shopping.

√ **We spent the whole day shopping.**

spend (a period of) **time** + v-ing WITHOUT **on** OR **in**

6 × We spent a very good time in New York.

√ **We had a very good time in New York.**

have a good time (= enjoy yourself), NOT **spend**

spite 1 × Inspite of our advice, she agreed to marry him.

√ **In spite of our advice, she agreed to marry him.**

In spite of is ALWAYS three words.

2 × They refused to play in the rain in spite of the crowd protested.

√ **They refused to play in the rain in spite of the crowd's protests.**

In spite of is a preposition (NOT a conjunction) and cannot be followed by a subject and verb.

3   × I believe that every crime, in spite of the
circumstances, should be severely punished.
√ **I believe that every crime, regardless of the
circumstances, should be severely punished.**

in spite of = despite: 'The plane took off in spite of the
bad weather.' (= although the weather was bad)
regardless of = without considering or taking notice of:
'The plane will take off, regardless of the weather.'
(= no matter whether the weather is good or bad)

sport 1   × The magazine is about sports.
√ **The magazine is about sport.**

sport/s (countable) = a particular type of sport:
'Football and tennis are popular sports.'
sport (uncountable) = sport in general: 'Sport is good
for your health.'

2   × She bought a bright red sport car.
√ **She bought a bright red sports car.**

In most compounds, use **sports**, NOT **sport**: 'sports
centre', 'sports jacket'.
Note, however, that in some American English
compounds, both are possible: 'sport(s) center',
'sport(s) jacket'.

spring   See SUMMER

staff   × There are over eighty staffs at the new
college.
√ **There are over eighty members of staff at the
new college.**

Staff refers not to a single person but to a group.
Note the alternative: 'The new college has a staff of
over eighty.'

stand 1   × We spent the morning standing by the
swimming pool.
√ **We spent the morning (sitting/lying) by the
swimming pool.**

stand (of people) = be on your feet in an upright
position (as opposed to sitting, lying, etc.)

2   × She's always very impatient and can't stand
        to have to wait.
        ✓ **She's always very impatient and can't stand
        having to wait.**
        can't/couldn't stand + v-ing

start   See SLEEP 2, 4

stationery   × The traffic remained stationery so that the
        ambulance could pass.
        ✓ **The traffic remained stationary so that the
        ambulance could pass.**
        stationery (**e** BEFORE **r**) = writing materials, such as
        paper, envelopes, etc.
        stationary (**a** BEFORE **r**) = still; not moving

statistic   × Many statistic studies show that the more
        sophisticated a society, the smaller the
        number of housewives.
        ✓ **Many statistical studies show that the more
        sophisticated a society, the smaller the
        number of housewives.**
        Statistic is a noun.
        Statistical is an adjective.

steal 1   × They can't afford to buy food and so they steal
        people.
        ✓ **They can't afford to buy food and so they steal
        from people.**
        Note the alternative: 'They can't afford to buy food and
        so they steal.'

2   × The bank in our town has been stolen twice
        this year.
        ✓ **The bank in our town has been robbed twice
        this year.**
        steal money, a watch, etc. BUT **rob** a person, a bank,
        or a post office

stick   × When I tried to rewind the tape, it stucked.
        ✓ **When I tried to rewind the tape, it stuck.**
        ✓ **When I tried to rewind the tape, it got stuck.**
        stick, sticking, stuck, stuck

still   × It is my first time abroad and so I feel still
             excited and confused.
           ✓ **It is my first time abroad and so I still feel
             excited and confused.**
           × My country still is not very rich, but at least
             everyone has enough food to eat.
           ✓ **My country is still not very rich, but at least
             everyone has enough food to eat.**

When there is no auxiliary verb, **still** is placed
immediately before the main verb: 'I still feel excited.'
If the main verb is **be**, **still** is placed immediately after
it: 'It's still dark outside.' Otherwise **still** goes
immediately after the (first) auxiliary verb: 'You can't
still be feeling tired.'

stimulus   × Coffee is quite a strong stimulus.
              ✓ **Coffee is quite a strong stimulant.**

stimulus (non-medical) = something which causes or
encourages activity or greater effort: 'The new textbook
provided a good stimulus for both teachers and
students.'
stimulant (medical) = a drug, medicine, etc. which
causes or encourages activity in the mind or body

stood   × He was stood there for more than an hour.
           ✓ **He was standing there for more than an hour.**
The use of **stood** with **be** is considered non-standard.

stop 1   × The train stoped at Birmingham.
            ✓ **The train stopped at Birmingham.**
stop (ONLY ONE **p**)
stopping, stopped (DOUBLE **p**)

2   × He was very tired but that didn't stop him
         to walk even further.
       ✓ **He was very tired but that didn't stop him
         from walking even further.**
stop someone **(from)** + v-ing = prevent someone (from)
doing something

3 × The child couldn't stop from talking.
   ✓ **The child couldn't stop talking.**

   stop + v-ing (WITHOUT **from**) = cease an activity: 'I've stopped smoking.'
   Compare: 'The rain stopped us from going out.'
   (= prevented us from going out)

4 × I stopped to play the piano at the age of eight.
   ✓ **I stopped playing the piano at the age of eight.**
   × He loved toys and couldn't stop to look at them.
   ✓ **He loved toys and couldn't stop looking at them.**

   stop + v-ing = cease or discontinue an activity
   stop + to-v = halt or pause (in order to do something)·
   'Although I was in a hurry, I stopped to talk to him.'

storey × They live on the second storey.
   ✓ **They live on the second floor.**

   A building has (a number of) **storeys** or **floors**.
   However, it is usual to say that a person lives on a particular **floor**, NOT **storey**: 'My flat is on the seventh floor.'
   Note the American spelling: **story**.

strange × I'm sure you will recognize the coat because it is very strange.
   ✓ **I'm sure you will recognize the coat because it is very unusual.**

   strange (usually derogatory) = odd; peculiar
   unusual = uncommon; rare

stranger × There are a lot of strangers visiting England.
   ✓ **There are a lot of foreigners visiting England.**

   stranger = a person you have never met before:
   'Although he was a total stranger, he started asking me for money!'
   foreigner = a person from another country

street × The street from Kuala Lumpur to Singapore is now very good.
✓ **The road from Kuala Lumpur to Singapore is now very good.**

To refer to the long narrow stretch of land connecting two towns, villages, etc., use **road** (NOT **street**).
A **street** is usually inside a town or village and has buildings on at least one side.

strong See PUNISHMENT

strongly 1 × All the students began to work more strongly in the weeks before the examination.
✓ **All the students began to work harder in the weeks before the examination.**

Compare: 'I would strongly recommend that you work harder.'

2 × When the plane took off, she held my hand strongly and began to cry.
✓ **When the plane took off, she held my hand tightly and began to cry.**

hold/grasp/grip something **tightly**, NOT **strongly**
strongly =(1) noticeably: 'He smelt strongly of beer.'
=(2) urgently: 'I strongly advise you to think again.'

studio ✓ **AmE She lives in a small studio in London.**
✓ **BrE She lives in a small bedsitter in London.**

studio (American English)/**bedsitter** (British English) = a single rented room in which a person lives and sleeps
Note that in British English **studio** means 'a room where a painter or photographer works' or '(a part of) a building where a film is made.'

subconscious × The driver of the car was taken to hospital subconscious.
✓ **The driver of the car was taken to hospital unconscious.**

subconscious (of thoughts or desires) = existing or occurring in the mind without the person being aware of it:
'His dream about crossing the ocean single-handed probably arose from a subconscious desire for fame.'
unconscious (of a person) = without consciousness

subject ✗ The subject of my thesis is about women in the popular press.
✓ **The subject of my thesis is women in the popular press.**
Subject is NOT followed by **about**.
Note the alternative: 'My thesis is about women in the popular press.'

succeed ✗ Not many of us succeed to achieve our ambitions.
✓ **Not many of us succeed in achieving our ambitions.**
manage + to-v BUT **succeed in** + v-ing

successful ✗ Has the regime been successful to reform the society?
✓ **Has the regime been successful in reforming the society?**
(be) successful in + v-ing

such 1 ✗ I was such in a hurry that I forgot my coat.
✓ **I was in such a hurry that I forgot my coat.**
When used as a predeterminer, **such** is placed immediately before **a/an**. It NEVER comes before a preposition.

2 ✗ She was always a such intelligent woman.
✓ **She was always such an intelligent woman.**
such + **a/an** + adjective + noun

suddenly ✗ Late one evening, as I was getting into the bath, suddenly I heard a strange noise.
✓ **Late one evening, as I was getting into the bath, I suddenly heard a strange noise.**
When there is no auxiliary verb, **suddenly** is placed immediately before the main verb: 'He suddenly stopped talking.' If the main verb is **be**, **suddenly** is placed immediately after it: 'He was suddenly all alone.'
Otherwise **suddenly** goes immediately after the (first) auxiliary verb: 'He has suddenly stopped smoking.'

Note also the use of **suddenly** at the beginning of a sentence, where it tends to have a more dramatic effect: 'Suddenly, there was a loud crash.' 'Suddenly, two strange men appeared in the room.'

suffer × The woman was so unpleasant that not one of us could suffer her.
√ **The woman was so unpleasant that not one of us could tolerate her.**

Suffer is no longer used with the meaning 'tolerate' except in a literary or religious context.

suggest 1 × She suggested to go to the zoo.
√ **She suggested going to the zoo.**
suggest + v-ing

2 × I suggest you buying the magazine too.
√ **I suggest you buy the magazine too.**
× I suggest you to take more exercise.
√ **I suggest you take more exercise.**
suggest (that) someone **do** something

suit 1 × All the rooms in the hotel were occupied except for the honeymoon suit.
√ **All the rooms in the hotel were occupied except for the honeymoon suite.**
a suit /suːt/ **of clothes** BUT **a suite** /swiːt/ **of rooms** (in a hotel)

2 × This type of work suits to many people.
√ **This type of work suits many people.**
something **suits** someone WITHOUT **to**

suitable × I did not feel suitable to a career in medicine.
√ **I did not feel suited to a career in medicine.**
suitable (for) = right or appropriate: 'The film isn't really suitable for children.' 'We would like to give her the job but her qualifications aren't suitable.'
(be/feel) suited to = (be/feel) the right or appropriate person for a particular situation: 'He's not suited to life in a big city.'

summer   × In Norway the weather in the summers is usually about the same as in England.
√ **In Norway the weather in (the) summer is usually about the same as in England.**
in (the) spring/summer/autumn/winter = each spring/summer/autumn/winter

sunken   × Within three minutes the ship had sunken.
√ **Within three minutes the ship had sunk.**
sink, sinking, sank, sunk
Sunken is the adjective: 'a sunken ship'.

superior 1   × The second hotel was superior than the first one.
√ **The second hotel was superior to the first one.**
superior to something, NOT **than**

2   × It was difficult to decide which of the designs was more superior.
√ **It was difficult to decide which of the designs was superior.**
Superior has no comparative form.

supply   × We shall supply you everything you need.
√ **We shall supply you with everything you need.**
supply someone **with** something

support   × He couldn't support the way his father used to shout at him.
√ **He couldn't tolerate the way his father used to shout at him.**
Support is NOT used with the meaning 'tolerate' or 'put up with'.

suppose 1   × My wife supposes to have left her coat in the cloakroom.
√ **My wife supposes that she has left her coat in the cloakroom.**
suppose + **that** clause

2   × All their products are suppose to be
     guaranteed for six months.
     ✓ **All their products are supposed to be
     guaranteed for six months.**
     be supposed (WITH final **d**) to be/do something

3   × It is a very unusual coat so I suppose you will not
     have any trouble finding it.
     ✓ **It is a very unusual coat so I don't suppose you
     will have any trouble finding it.**
     When the clause following **suppose** contains a negative
     idea, **suppose** is made negative and the verb that
     follows is positive.

4   × Since the machine is still under guarantee, I
     suppose I won't be charged for the repairs.
     ✓ **Since the machine is still under guarantee, I
     assume I won't be charged for the repairs.**
     suppose = think something is likely; imagine: 'If she's
     lost her umbrella, I suppose I'll have to lend her mine.'
     assume = accept that something is true (without being
     told) and behave or act accordingly

sure   × I always buy my ticket in advance to make
         sure about getting a seat.
         ✓ **I always buy my ticket in advance to make
         sure of getting a seat.**
         make sure of (doing) something, NOT **about**

surely 1   × It was an absolutely terrible flight. The next
             time I go to Rio, I will surely go by train.
             ✓ **It was an absolutely terrible flight. The next
             time I go to Rio, I will definitely go by train.**
             Surely is used to express a strong belief (or disbelief)
             in the likelihood of something and often to encourage
             the listener to express agreement: 'Surely they should
             have arrived by now!' 'A twenty-dollar parking fine!
             Surely someone's made a mistake!' 'Surely a man like
             Harry couldn't have done such a terrible thing!'
             Definitely expresses a sense of certainty about a fact
             or facts.

2 × He said he felt nervous because of all the recent air disasters. Surely I became worried too.

✓ **He said he felt nervous because of all the recent air disasters. Naturally I became worried too.**

surely = I feel sure that
naturally = as one would expect; of course

surprise 1 × The young woman looked very surprise to see me.

✓ **The young woman looked very surprised to see me.**

Surprise is a verb and a noun.
Surprised is an adjective.

2 × That these people commit crimes is not surprising me.

✓ **That these people commit crimes does not surprise me.**

The verb **surprise** is NOT used in progressive tenses.
Compare: 'That these people commit crimes is not surprising.'
Surprising is an adjective.

3 × At my surprise, the whole house was empty.

✓ **To my surprise, the whole house was empty.**

to my/his/their etc. **surprise**, NOT **at**

surprised × I was very surprised learning that you had decided to go to medical school.

✓ **I was very surprised to learn that you had decided to go to medical school.**

be surprised + to-v

sympathetic × He's a selfish, greedy man and not at all sympathetic.

✓ **He's a selfish, greedy man and not at all likeable.**

sympathetic = feeling or showing sympathy: 'He expected people to be sympathetic because he was an orphan.'
likeable = easy to like

take 1   × A few minutes later an ambulance arrived and took the injured man.

✓ **A few minutes later an ambulance arrived and took the injured man away.**

Take (= carry, lead, or move) is used with adverbs such as **away**, **out**, etc., or with a phrase that refers to a place: 'I took her to the cinema.'
Note the alternative: 'A few minutes later an ambulance arrived and collected the injured man.'

2   × Unfortunately my studies take a lot of time.

✓ **Unfortunately my studies take up a lot of time.**

take up an amount of time or space = occupy an amount of time or space

3   × When you come to dinner on Sunday, take your fiancée with you so I can meet her.

✓ **When you come to dinner on Sunday, bring your fiancée with you so I can meet her.**

Bring is used for movement towards the place where the speaker is, was, or intends to be (or towards the person being talked about): 'She asked the nurse to bring her a drink of water.'
Take is used for movement in other directions.

4   See DINNER, MEAL, PERMISSION 2

take notice of   See NOTICE 3

take up   × As soon as the plane took up, I realized I had forgotten my coat.

✓ **As soon as the plane took off, I realized I had forgotten my coat.**

take off (of an aeroplane) = leave the ground, NOT **take up**

talk 1   ✓ **AmE I didn't want to talk with him because I was in a hurry.**

✓ **BrE I didn't want to talk to him because I was in a hurry.**

In British English, use **talk to** someone (**about** something), NOT **with**.
In American English, both **to** and **with** are possible.

2   × He talked that he had just arrived from Beijing.
✓ **He said that he had just arrived from Beijing.**
Talk is NOT used as a reporting verb.

tall   × I prefer rooms with tall ceilings.
✓ **I prefer rooms with high ceilings.**
tall = the distance from bottom to top: 'a tall person',
'a tall tree'
high = the distance (of the uppermost point) above the
ground: 'a high shelf', 'a high altitude', 'a high
mountain'

taste 1   × I buy all my family's clothes because my
husband has such a bad taste.
✓ **I buy all my family's clothes because my
husband has such bad taste.**
(have/show) **excellent/good/poor taste** WITHOUT **a**

2   See SOUND 4

tasteful   × The food was excellent and very tasteful.
✓ **The food was excellent and very tasty.**
tasteful = approved by people with good taste (i.e.
people who have the ability to choose or recognize
good art, music, clothes, style, behaviour, etc.): 'The
design of the room was very tasteful—pale colours,
matching fabrics, and soft corner lighting.'
tasty (of food) = having a pleasant taste (i.e. a
pleasant sensation on the tongue): 'a tasty meal'

tax   × Too many people are given taxes instead of
being sent to prison.
✓ **Too many people are given fines instead of
being sent to prison.**
tax = a sum of money paid to the government
according to the amount a person earns and the things
a person buys: 'The tax on wine has been increased.'
'income tax'
fine = a sum of money paid as a penalty by a person
who breaks the law: 'a parking fine'

teach 1 ✗ Mr Brown has never teached our class.
✓ **Mr Brown has never taught our class.**
teach, teaching, taught, taught

2 ✗ We are taught in reading, writing, and in English grammar.
✓ **We are taught reading, writing, and English grammar.**
be taught something WITHOUT **in**

technique ✗ The main cause of unemployment is modern technique.
✓ **The main cause of unemployment is modern technology.**
technique = a (skilled) way of doing something
technology = all the scientific theories, methods, and processes that are used in industry

telephone See PHONE

television See RADIO

tell 1 ✗ He told that he hadn't eaten anything for over a week.
✓ **He told them that he hadn't eaten anything for over a week.**
✓ **He said that he hadn't eaten anything for over a week.**
✗ He had been married twice, he told, and had four children.
✓ **He had been married twice, he told me, and had four children.**
✓ **He had been married twice, he said, and had four children.**
Unlike **say**, **tell** (as a reporting verb) is used with an indirect object.

2 ✗ John said that he was trying to get to London. 'That's where I'm going,' told the man.
✓ **John said that he was trying to get to London. 'That's where I'm going,' said the man.**

Tell must be followed by a grammatical object and is usually used with indirect (reported) speech: 'The man told John (that) he was going to London.'

3   × Please tell to Mr Young that I am looking forward to meeting him.
     ✓ **Please tell Mr Young that I am looking forward to meeting him.**

tell something **to** someone: 'Please tell the news to Mrs Patel.' BUT **tell** someone something WITHOUT **to**: 'They've told Mrs Patel the news.'

4   × Can you tell me where should I go to buy a ticket?
     ✓ **Can you tell me where I should go to buy a ticket?**

When the object of the sentence is a **wh-** clause, the subject and verb in the **wh-** clause do NOT change places.

5   × My teacher told me not feel shy.
     ✓ **My teacher told me not to feel shy.**

tell someone **(not) to do** something

6   × Kiri was always telling about herself and her problems.
     ✓ **Kiri was always talking about herself and her problems.**

tell someone **about** something BUT **talk about** something

tempo   × He stopped running when he saw the dog and then continued in a slower tempo.
            ✓ **He stopped running when he saw the dog and then continued at a slower pace.**

tempo = the speed at which a piece of music is/should be played: 'Suddenly the band broke into a faster tempo.'
pace = the speed at which a person walks or runs

term   See SEMESTER

test   × On my first day at the school, I had to make a test.

   √ **On my first day at the school, I had to take a test.**

   take/do a test, NOT **make**

testament   × He was worried because his father had died without making a testament.

   √ **He was worried because his father had died without making a will.**

   testament (formal) = (1) proof: 'The new school buildings, which were financed by Sir Harold, are a testament to his generosity.'
   (2) will (This usage occurs only in the phrase 'last will and testament'.)

text   × She said she was writing a text about France for her local newspaper.

   √ **She said she was writing an article about France for her local newspaper.**

   text = (1) the words in a book, magazine, etc. (as opposed to the illustrations): 'Alongside each drawing there were several lines of text.'
   (2) the written version of a play, speech, etc.: 'Critics would be well advised to stick to the text.'
   article = a piece of writing in a newspaper or magazine

than 1   × Women have the same abilities than men.
   √ **Women have the same abilities as men.**
   the same ... as, NOT **than**

2   See PREFER 3, 4

thank 1   × I thank you very much for your last letter.
   √ **Thank you very much for your last letter.**
   I and **we** are used with **thank** only in a rather formal context: 'I should like to thank you for all your help.' 'We can't thank you enough.'

2 × First, I thank you for answering my letter.
✓ **First, I should like to thank you for answering my letter.**
✓ **First, may I thank you for answering my letter.**
Note the less formal alternative: 'Thank you for answering my letter.'

3 × Thank you for agree to listen.
✓ **Thank you for agreeing to listen.**
× Thank you very much that you have agreed to help us.
✓ **Thank you very much for agreeing to help us.**
thank someone **for** + v-ing

thanks × First of all, thanks for your most interesting question.
✓ **First of all, thank you for your most interesting question.**
Thanks is informal.
Thank you is more formal.

that 1 × The weather has been very good, except for two days that it rained.
✓ **The weather has been very good, except for two days when it rained.**
When the meaning is 'on/in/during which' (referring to time), use **when**, NOT **that**. Compare: 'I shall always remember the two days that I spent in Paris.'

2 × I was shocked by the sight that I could hardly speak.
✓ **I was so shocked by the sight that I could hardly speak.**
so + adjective/adverb + **that** clause: 'I'm so tired that I can't keep awake.' 'He spoke so quickly that nobody could understand him.'

3 × He closed the door quietly that nobody would hear him.
✓ **He closed the door quietly so that nobody would hear him.**
Use **so that** to express purpose, NOT **that**.

(that) 4   × Children are not as easy to please nowadays
that they were in the past.
✓ **Children are not as easy to please nowadays
as they were in the past.**

When making a comparison, use **(not) as/so ... as** (NOT
that): 'It's as hard to get into university today as it was
ten years ago.'

5   × It worried me that the letter had not arrived,
especially that it had never happened before.
✓ **It worried me that the letter had not arrived,
especially since/as it had never happened
before.**

When giving a reason for something, use **since** or **as**,
NOT **that**

6   × It is two months now that I left Germany.
✓ **It is two months now since I left Germany.**

Note, however, that you can sometimes use **that** with
ago: 'It was ten years ago that I first came to England.'

7   × Next to me was an old lady that seemed to be
sound asleep.
✓ **Next to me was an old lady who seemed to be
sound asleep.**

That can only be used to introduce an identifying
relative clause (one which identifies, defines, or
restricts the preceding noun): 'The woman that is
sitting behind us is Tom's mother.' 'The man that I
marry will have lots of money.' **That** cannot be used to
introduce a non-identifying relative clause (one which
simply adds more information about the noun and
which is preceded by a comma).

8   × If you haven't sent it yet, I'd be pleased if you
would do that as soon as possible.
✓ **If you haven't sent it yet, I'd be pleased if you
would do so as soon as possible.**

To make a precise reference to a previously
mentioned action, use **do so**, NOT **do that**.

the 1 × She is arriving on March the 25th.
   ✓ **She is arriving on March 25th.**

   When speaking, use 'March the twenty-fifth' OR 'the twenty-fifth of March'.
   When writing, use 'March 25th' OR '25th March' (WITHOUT **the** and **of**).

2 × Very few people can speak the English well in Japan.
   ✓ **Very few people can speak English well in Japan.**

   Do not use **the** with the names of languages: 'speak English', 'learn French', 'understand Chinese', etc.
   Use **the** when talking about the people who live in a particular country: 'the English', 'the French', 'the Chinese'.

3 × I have just seen a new magazine about the computers.
   ✓ **I have just seen a new magazine about computers.**

   Do not use **the** with the plural form of a countable noun when used in a general sense.
   Compare: 'She likes cats.' (= cats in general)
   'The cats we saw in Venice looked very hungry.' (= a particular group of cats)

4 × Some people have more contact with the violence and it becomes a part of their lives.
   ✓ **Some people have more contact with violence and it becomes a part of their lives.**
   × Nowadays the pollution is a very serious problem.
   ✓ **Nowadays pollution is a very serious problem.**

   Do not use **the** with an uncountable noun when talking in a general sense: 'He hates dishonesty.' 'Power doesn't interest him.'
   The is used when the sense is restricted: 'She hates the dishonesty of the man.' 'The power enjoyed by politicians doesn't interest him.'

(the) 5   × Our plane arrived at the Gatwick Airport.
√ **Our plane arrived at Gatwick Airport.**

Do not use **the** before the names of airports and railway stations: 'Charles de Gaulle (Airport)', 'Narita (Airport)', 'Charing Cross (Station)'.

6   × The language school is situated in a big building in the Malibu Street.
√ **The language school is situated in a big building in Malibu Street.**

Do not use **the** with the names of streets and roads: 'Oxford Street', 'Fifth Avenue', 'Fir Tree Avenue', 'Blue Pool Road'.

7   × Climbing the Mount Fuji in winter can be very dangerous.
√ **Climbing Mount Fuji in winter can be very dangerous.**

Do not use **the** with the name of a mountain: 'Mount Everest', 'Mount Fuji', 'Mount Olympus'. Note, however, that **the** is used with the names of groups of mountains: 'the Alps', 'the Andes', 'the Himalayas'.

8   × Yellow River has caused many terrible floods.
√ **The Yellow River has caused many terrible floods.**

Always use **the** with the names of canals, rivers, and seas: 'the Suez Canal', 'the Ganges', 'the Thames', 'the Atlantic', 'the Mediterranean'.

9   × It is more than ten years since I visited West Indies.
√ **It is more than ten years since I visited the West Indies.**

Most plural proper nouns begin with **the**: 'the Bahamas', 'the Himalayas', 'the United States'.

10   × This is my second visit to UK.
√ **This is my second visit to the UK.**

Use **the** with any country whose name includes 'state', 'union', 'republic', etc.: 'the UK', 'the United Kingdom', 'the USA', 'the United States', 'the USSR', 'the Union of Soviet Socialist Republics'.

11 × Only very wealthy tourists can afford to stay at Imperial Hotel.

✓ **Only very wealthy tourists can afford to stay at the Imperial Hotel.**

The is usually used with the names of hotels and restaurants unless the name is a possessive form. Compare: 'the Hilton', 'the Mandarin', 'the Sheraton' BUT 'Claridge's', 'Salvo's', 'Tiffany's'

12 See CHURCH, COLLEGE, HALF 1, HOSPITAL, PLAY 3, SCHOOL 2

their × I had been sitting their for almost half an hour.

✓ **I had been sitting there for almost half an hour.**

their = belonging to them
there = to, at, or in that place

them See ME 1

then 1 × We took a bus to the city centre then caught a train to London.

✓ **We took a bus to the city centre and then caught a train to London.**

Then is NOT a conjunction.

2 × After my father retires, then I shall help him financially.

✓ **After my father retires, I shall help him financially.**

Then (= at that time) is only used after a time clause when it introduces a result or consequence. Compare: 'When you've seen the trees, then you'll know why I came to live here.' (= as a result of seeing the trees)

there 1 × People over sixty should be able to choose when to give up there jobs.

✓ **People over sixty should be able to choose when to give up their jobs.**

there = in, at, or to that place: 'Put the book over there.' 'We went to Italy last year and we're going there again this year.'
their = of or belonging to them: 'Have you met their daughter?'

2 × My sister often goes to a swimming pool at the end of the road but I don't like going to there.

✓ **My sister often goes to a swimming pool at the end of the road but I don't like going there.**

There and **here** cannot follow **to** unless the speaker is indicating or pointing to something: 'When the tide comes in, the water reaches right up to there.'

3 × There was four people in the car.

✓ **There were four people in the car.**

there is/was + EITHER the singular form of a countable noun OR an uncountable noun: 'There was a letter on the mat.' 'There was smoke coming under the door.'
there are/were + the plural forms of a countable noun: 'There were babies crying in every room.'

4 × Suddenly he remembered the little lake, there his mother used to take him.

✓ **Suddenly he remembered the little lake, where his mother used to take him.**

There is an adverb.
Where is a conjunction.

5 × There are exactly two weeks since I last went to New York.

✓ **It is exactly two weeks since I last went to New York.**

it is + time phrase + **since** + clause

6 See GOOD 2

7 See WHERE

therefore × It is therefor essential that every child has a good education.

✓ **It is therefore essential that every child has a good education.**

therefore (WITH final **e**)

they 1 × As far as I can see, the two wheels which are supposed to turn round they do not turn round.
√ **As far as I can see, the two wheels which are supposed to turn round do not turn round.**

Do not repeat the subject (by using a pronoun) after a relative clause. The subject of 'do not turn round' is 'the two wheels'.

2 × They are several activities arranged for you.
√ **There are several activities arranged for you.**

In many sentences the verb **be** is used to express a state or fact. If the subject has not been mentioned before, it is placed immediately after the verb and the sentence begins with **there** (NOT **they** or **it**): 'There are too many chairs in the room.' 'There's a bottle of wine in the cupboard.'

thing 1 × The only bad thing on him was that he never stopped talking.
√ **The only bad thing about him was that he never stopped talking.**

a good/bad thing about someone/something, NOT **on**

2 See EVERY 2

think 1 × I am often thinking about these problems.
√ **I often think about these problems.**

Use the present simple tense when talking about an action which happens regularly or often. **Think** (= give thought to) is not usually used in the progressive unless it refers to a current activity: 'Be quiet. I'm thinking.'

2 × I think she didn't understand what you said.
√ **I don't think she understood what you said.**

Note that when the clause following **think** contains a negative idea, **think** is made negative and the verb that follows is positive.

(think) 3 × We should spend more time thinking why people do such terrible things.
✓ **We should spend more time thinking about why people do such terrible things.**
think about = consider

4 × People without a job try not to think on the future.
✓ **People without a job try not to think about/of the future.**
think about/of someone/something = form ideas in your mind about someone/something

5 × I am thinking to make another trip to Italy next year.
✓ **I am thinking of making another trip to Italy next year.**
× I was thinking to wear the trousers so I took them out of the suitcase.
✓ **I was thinking of wearing the trousers so I took them out of the suitcase.**
think of + v-ing = intend or plan

6 × 'I must be getting old', I thought myself.
✓ **'I must be getting old', I thought to myself.**
× 'I can't stay here all night,' he thought by himself.
✓ **'I can't stay here all night,' he thought to himself.**
think to yourself, NOT **by**

7 × I was thinking if you would like to have lunch before visiting the museum.
✓ **I was wondering if you would like to have lunch before visiting the museum.**
I was wondering if/whether is often used to introduce polite invitations and requests: 'I was wondering if you'd like to play tennis on Saturday.' 'I was wondering whether you could give me some advice.'

this   × During this next five weeks I will be staying with an English family.
  ✓ **During these next five weeks I will be staying with an English family.**

This /ðɪs/ is singular.
These /ðiːz/ is plural.
The use of **this** or **these** depends upon whether the noun that follows is singular or plural. Compare: 'this book' BUT 'these books'

thousand 1   × There were more than thousand people in the audience.
  ✓ **There were more than a thousand people in the audience.**

Hundred, thousand, million, etc. cannot be used in the singular without **a** or **one.**

2   ✓ **AmE We received exactly two thousand thirty replies.**
  ✓ **BrE We received exactly two thousand and thirty replies.**

In British English, use 'one thousand and nine', 'eight thousand and sixty-two' BUT 'five thousand six hundred', 'three thousand two hundred and nine'.

3   See HUNDRED

threaten 1   × She threatened leaving without him if he didn't hurry.
  ✓ **She threatened to leave without him if he didn't hurry.**

threaten + to-v

2   × He heard his father threatening his mother of leaving her.
  ✓ **He heard his father threatening his mother with leaving her.**

threaten someone **with** something, NOT **of**

thunder   × I heard a terribly loud noise, like a thunder, as the vehicles crashed into each other.
√ **I heard a terribly loud noise, like thunder, as the vehicles crashed into each other.**
Thunder is an uncountable noun.

till   × I managed to drive the car till the nearest hospital.
√ **I managed to drive the car to the nearest hospital.**
√ **I managed to drive the car as far as the nearest hospital.**
Till and **until** are usually used when talking about time, NOT distance, area, or scope.

time 1   × They walked along the beach for long time.
√ **They walked along the beach for a long time.**
a long time WITH **a**

2   × I'm sorry I've not had a time to write to you until now.
√ **I'm sorry I've not had time to write to you until now.**
(not) have time (to do something) WITHOUT **a**

3   × The course in electrical engineering takes four years time.
√ **The course in electrical engineering takes four years.**
When talking about how long something takes or lasts, do not use **time** with a time phrase: 'Each letter took one hour to write.' 'The battery will last seven days.' Note, however, that in phrases which begin with **in**, the word **time** may be included: 'I'll have finished my course in four years' time.' 'Bill is due to arrive in three weeks' time.'

4   × Parents should spend more time to look after their children.
√ **Parents should spend more time looking after their children.**
spend time + v-ing

5 × On the last time I went shopping I bought a cassette recorder.
✓ **The last time I went shopping I bought a cassette recorder.**

the next time, the first time, etc. WITHOUT **on**

6 × The fire brigade arrived just on time, before the fire could spread.
✓ **The fire brigade arrived just in time, before the fire could spread.**

on time = (arriving) at the right time; punctual(ly): 'The train arrived at 17.28; it was exactly on time.'
in time = not late; early enough: 'Make sure you arrive in time to see the beginning of the film.'

7 × It didn't take a long time before we were back home again.
✓ **It didn't take long before we were back home again.**

not take long WITHOUT **time** OR **a**

times × He couldn't see where he was going and fell down many times.
✓ **He couldn't see where he was going and kept falling down.**

'To do something many times' (= keep doing something) is not actually wrong but sounds unnatural.

tired × By the time we arrived in Rio I was feeling completely tired.
✓ **By the time we arrived in Rio I was feeling completely exhausted.**

Although usage varies, an adjective which does not contain the sense 'very', 'extremely', or '100%' as part of its meaning is NOT usually used with **absolutely** or **completely**. To intensify such adjectives, use **very** or **extremely**.
Compare: 'completely exhausted' BUT 'very tired' (**exhausted** = 'very tired')
'completely soaked' BUT 'very wet' (**soaked** = 'very wet')
'absolutely filthy' BUT 'very dirty' (**filthy** = 'very dirty')
'absolutely frantic' BUT 'very anxious' (**frantic** = 'very anxious')

tiresome × The flight from Hong Kong to London was very tiresome.
✓ **The flight from Hong Kong to London was very tiring.**

tiresome = annoying or irritating: 'That tiresome child never gives me a minute's peace.'
tiring = causing tiredness; exhausting

title 1 × The new magazine is titled 'Computer News'.
✓ **The new magazine is called 'Computer News'.**
Title is a noun, NOT a verb.

2 × The newspaper titles were all about the earthquake.
✓ **The newspaper headlines were all about the earthquake.**

title = name of a book, play, painting, piece of music, etc.
headline = heading above a story in a newspaper

to 1 × If your English is to poor, nobody understands you.
✓ **If your English is too poor, nobody understands you.**
× He had been drinking to much.
✓ **He had been drinking too much.**

To is (1) a preposition: 'I'm going to the cinema tonight.'
(2) an adverb: 'Push the door to. It's cold in here.'
(mainly British English usage)
(3) the first part of a full infinitive: 'I want to ask you something.'
Too means 'more than enough' or 'more than is good'.
See also TOO

2 × She said she'd be back in to minutes.
✓ **She said she'd be back in two minutes.**
To is a preposition, adverb, and first part of a full infinitive.
Two means 'the number two/2'.

3   × At that moment he noticed a man running
        to him.
        ✓ **At that moment he noticed a man running
        towards him.**

Use **to** when you want to emphasize the destination.
Use **towards** when you want to emphasize the
direction.
Compare: 'John drove to the station.' (We know he
stopped at the station.)
'John drove towards the station.' (We don't know
where he stopped.)

4   × He came into the shop and went to the woman
        behind the counter.
        ✓ **He came into the shop and went up/over to
        the woman behind the counter.**
        × The old lady stood up, went to John, and
        asked him what he was doing there.
        ✓ **The old lady stood up, went up/over to John,
        and asked him what he was doing there.**

To describe the action of deliberately moving towards
and stopping in front of a person, use **go up/over to**,
NOT **go to**.

5   × Each time I tried to close my eyes and to relax,
        the young man said something to me.
        ✓ **Each time I tried to close my eyes and relax,
        the young man said something to me.**

When two infinitives are joined by **and**, **to** is usually
used only before the first one.

6   See NOT 1

toast   × I usually have a cup of coffee and a toast for
        breakfast.
        ✓ **I usually have a cup of coffee and a piece of
        toast for breakfast.**

Toast is an uncountable noun.

tobacco × Don't offer him a tobacco if he's trying to stop smoking.
✓ **Don't offer him a cigarette if he's trying to stop smoking.**

tobacco (uncountable) = the dried leaves of a plant from which cigarettes, cigars, etc. are made

today × As I told you in our today's telephone conversation, I think I left my coat at your hotel.
✓ **As I told you in today's telephone conversation, I think I left my coat at your hotel.**

Do not use a determiner before **today's, yesterday's**, etc. Note the alternative: 'As I told you (earlier) today in our telephone conversation ... '

too 1 × In my opinion, this is a too traditional approach.
✓ **In my opinion, this is too traditional an approach.**

too + adjective + **a/an** + noun

2 × I was too happy when I received your letter today.
✓ **I was very happy when I received your letter today.**

too = more than enough; more than is good or acceptable: 'You are driving too fast! Stop and let me get out.' 'The meat was too tough to eat.'
very = extremely
Compare: 'It was very cold but not too cold to go out.'

3 × I don't like football and my brother doesn't too.
✓ **I don't like football and my brother doesn't either.**

When using **too** and **either** as adverbs, use **too** in affirmative statements and **either** in negative statements. Compare: 'I can read and my sister can too.' 'I can't swim and my sister can't either.'

4 × Too, I would like to know more about the
British way of life.
✓ **Also, I would like to know more about the
British way of life.**

Unlike **also** and **in addition**, **too** is NEVER used at the
beginning of a sentence. Compare: 'I would like to
know more about the British way of life, too.'

5 See MUCH 6

too many × It's an interesting magazine with too many
good ideas.
✓ **It's an interesting magazine with a lot of good
ideas.**

too many = more than is acceptable or required

too much 1 × 'If you are too much selfish, nobody will like
you,' she said.
✓ **'If you are too selfish, nobody will like you,'
she said.**

too + adjective WITHOUT **much**

2 × I noticed that he had had a couple of drinks
too much.
✓ **I noticed that he had had a couple of drinks
too many.**

countable noun + **too many**

3 See MUCH 6

top × You will find my address on top of the letter.
✓ **You will find my address at the top of the
letter.**

Compare: 'The book is on top of the television.'
(= resting on the surface of the television)

touch 1 × People living in the city were not touched by
the famine.
✓ **People living in the city were not affected by
the famine.**

Use **affect** (NOT **touch**) when you mean 'have an effect
on'.

2   × It is good for a person to go out to work
because they get in touch with other people.
√ **It is good for a person to go out to work
because they come into contact with other
people.**

get in touch with = communicate with (someone) by
letter or telephone: 'Don't wait until Christmas before
you get in touch.'
come into contact with = meet

translate   × The magazine has just been translated to
Greek.
√ **The magazine has just been translated into
Greek.**

translate something (from one language) **into** another,
NOT **to**

travel   × He began to tell me about the first travel he
had done by plane.
√ **He began to tell me about the first journey he
had made by plane.**

travel (uncountable) = the general activity of moving
about the world or from place to place: 'She enjoys
foreign travel.'
journey (countable) = a trip from one place to another

trouble   × I'm sorry to cause you so many troubles.
√ **I'm sorry to cause you so much trouble.**
Trouble is an uncountable noun here.

trousers   × He bought himself a new trousers.
√ **He bought himself some new trousers.**
Trousers is a plural noun. Compare: 'a new pair of
trousers.'

true   × I hope my dream becomes true.
√ **I hope my dream comes true.**
come true, NOT **become**

truly   × Yours truely
√ **Yours truly**
true (WITH **e**) BUT **truly** (WITHOUT **e**)

trust × After he was caught stealing, nobody trusted in him.
  √ **After he was caught stealing, nobody trusted him.**

trust in = have faith in: 'trust in God'
trust = rely on someone to be honest

try × I tryed to tell her my name, but she couldn't hear me.
  √ **I tried to tell her my name, but she couldn't hear me.**

try, trying, tried, tried

turn back × Hearing a crash, I quickly turned back and saw that a car had hit a lamp post.
  √ **Hearing a crash, I quickly turned round and saw that a car had hit a lamp post.**
  × Having woken up, he sat up in his seat and turned back to see who was making all the noise.
  √ **Having woken up, he sat up in his seat and turned round to see who was making all the noise.**

turn back = stop and begin to return to the place you started from: 'If the bridge has been destroyed, we'll have to turn back.'
turn round = move so that you face in the opposite direction

turn up × George turned up to be the father of one of my old schoolfriends.
  √ **George turned out to be the father of one of my old schoolfriends.**

turn up = arrive, appear, or be found: 'He turned up at the party dressed in pink pyjamas!' 'I can't find my keys, but I expect they'll turn up somewhere.'
turn out = prove to be: 'After a bad start, the party turned out to be a great success.'

two See BOTH 4

type   × The manager of the shop told me that he **was** not responsible for these type of fault.
     √ **The manager of the shop told me that he was not responsible for these types of fault.**

these types of fault (OR **these types of faults**) BUT **this type of fault**
Note the alternative: 'faults of this type'

UK   × I have an uncle who lives in UK.
     √ **I have an uncle who lives in the UK.**
See note at THE 10

ultimately   × Ultimately there has been another increase in the number of violent crimes.
     √ **Lately there has been another increase in the number of violent crimes.**

ultimately = in the end: 'Naturally I can give you some advice but ultimately it's your decision.'
lately = in the recent past

un-   See IMPOLITE

understand 1   × Until I saw the clock I hadn't understood how late it was.
     √ **Until I saw the clock I hadn't realized how late it was.**

understand = know or grasp the meaning of something: 'I found the lecture hard to understand.'
realize = become aware (of something)

2   × As you understand, I don't have much free time.
     √ **As you know, I don't have much free time.**
as you (will) know/appreciate/realize/gather, NOT **understand**

unfortunately   × Unfortunatly there was nowhere to sit.
     √ **Unfortunately there was nowhere to sit.**
unfortunately (e BEFORE l)

unique × It is one of the most unique pieces of architecture in Spain.

✓ **It is one of the rarest pieces of architecture in Spain.**

Something can be **absolutely unique** or **totally unique** but NOT **very/more/most/somewhat** (etc.) **unique**. There are no degrees of uniqueness when **unique** means 'the only one of its kind'.

United States × I met people from Canada and United States.

✓ **I met people from Canada and the United States.**

See note at THE 10

university × I am about to start studying at the Leeds University.

✓ **I am about to start studying at Leeds University.**

Leeds University BUT **the University of Leeds**
London University BUT **the University of London**
Note that the usual written form is 'the University of Leeds/London etc.'.

unless 1 × I will lend you my copy unless if you want me to buy two.

✓ **I will lend you my copy unless you want me to buy two.**

Unless is NOT used with **if**.

2 × It would have been a wonderful holiday unless Ali had come with us.

✓ **It would have been a wonderful holiday if Ali hadn't come with us.**

Unless cannot introduce an impossible condition.
Compare: 'I'll go out tonight if it doesn't rain.' OR 'I'll go out tonight unless it rains.' (It is possible that it may rain.)
'I'd go out tonight if I didn't have so much work to do. (NOT **unless**)
'I'd have gone out last night if I hadn't had so much work to do.' (NOT **unless**)

until 1   × I shall be staying here untill Christmas.
√ **I shall be staying here until Christmas.**
until (ONLY ONE **l**)

2   × I shall wait here until you will return.
√ **I shall wait here until you return.**
After **until/when/whenever/once/after/if**, use the
present simple tense (or present perfect) for future
reference, NOT **shall/will** + verb.

3   × I will have finished this book until tomorrow.
√ **I will have finished this book by tomorrow.**
Until is used for an action or state continuing up to a
certain time.
By is used for an action which happens at or before a
certain time. Compare: 'I have to keep writing until the
end of next year.' 'My book will be finished by the end
of next year.'

4   × The magazine covers everything from politics
until what's happening in Hollywood.
√ **The magazine covers everything from politics
to what's happening in Hollywood.**
Until and **till** are usually used when talking about time,
NOT distance, area, or scope.

upstairs   See DOWNSTAIRS

us   See ME 1

USA   × I was travelling on a flight from USA to Paris.
√ **I was travelling on a flight from the USA to
Paris.**
See note at THE 10

use 1   × In my previous job I use to travel a lot.
√ **In my previous job I used to travel a lot.**
used to (WITH silent **d**)
Compare: 'I used to use a fountain pen.'

2   × It took a long time for me to get use to the
local accent.

✓ **It took a long time for me to get used to the
local accent.**

get used to something (WITH silent **d**) = become
accustomed to something

used 1   × The shoes under the bed were used and had
holes in them.

✓ **The shoes under the bed were worn-out and
had holes in them.**

used = not brand new; second-hand: 'He is looking for
a good, used car for his daughter.'
worn-out = reduced to an unusable state by
continuous use or wear

2   × People are used to consider women inferior to
men.

✓ **People are used to considering women
inferior to men.**

used to do something = did something regularly in the
past but not any more
be used to doing something = be in the habit of doing
something

usual 1   × In Finland it is very usual that women go out
to work.

✓ **In Finland it is very usual for women to go out
to work.**

usual for someone **to do** something, NOT **that**

2   × I thought it was just a usual parcel but then it
began to move across the table.

✓ **I thought it was just an ordinary parcel but
then it began to move across the table.**

usual (opposite **unusual**) = customary: 'We arranged to
meet at the usual time.' 'It's usual to thank people for
their help.'
ordinary (opposite **special**) = without any special
features or qualities

usually   × As usually, he arrived five minutes late.
              ✓ **As usual, he arrived five minutes late.**
              Note the fixed phrase: **as usual**.

variety   × We would like to see a greater variety in
                dishes on the menu.
              ✓ **We would like to see a greater variety of
                dishes on the menu.**
              variety of, NOT **in**

vegetable × I buy a lot of fresh fruit and vegetable.
               ✓ **I buy a lot of fresh fruit and vegetables.**
               Unlike **fruit**, **vegetable** is a countable noun.

very 1   × He looked very funny that I couldn't help
                laughing.
              ✓ **He looked so funny that I couldn't help
                laughing.**
              so + adjective/adverb + **that** clause

      2   × She was very admired and respected by all
                the pupils' parents.
              ✓ **She was greatly/much admired and respected
                by all the pupils' parents.**
              Past participles with a strongly passive meaning are
              usually modified by **greatly** or **much**, NOT **very**. Note
              that **very** is chiefly used with past participles that are
              like adjectives and refer to a state of mind or
              emotional condition: 'very
              bored/worried/interested/pleased'.

      3   × Although he was very in love with Marianne,
                he wanted to marry a rich heiress.
              ✓ **Although he was deeply in love with
                Marianne, he wanted to marry a rich heiress.**
              Very cannot usually be used before a phrase
              beginning with a preposition (such as 'in love with', 'in
              need of', 'at odds with', etc.). However, in such cases
              it is often possible to use **very much**: 'Although he was
              very much in love with Marianne, he wanted to marry
              a rich heiress.'

      4   See note at CERTAIN 1

very much   × I like very much beaches.
✓ **I like beaches very much.**
A verb and its direct object are not usually separated by an adverb or adverbial phrase.

victim   × Only two people died in the fire but there were a lot of victims.
✓ **Only two people died in the fire but there were a lot of casualties.**
If you wish to refer only to those people who are *injured* in an accident, use **casualties**. If you wish to refer to all the people who suffer in an accident, both the dead and injured, use **victims**.

view 1   × The view of all the blood on the ground made her feel ill.
✓ **The sight of all the blood on the ground made her feel ill.**
Note that **view** is usually used of something distant: 'To get a better view of the valley, we climbed to the top of the hill.'

2   See POINT OF VIEW

visit   × We decided to do another visit the next day.
✓ **We decided to pay another visit the next day.**
pay (someone/something) **a visit** OR **pay a visit** (to someone/something), NOT **do**

voice 1   × He continued speaking with a very loud voice.
✓ **He continued speaking in a very loud voice.**
speak/talk in a loud/quiet voice, NOT **with**

2   × The film was very interesting, even though there was no voice.
✓ **The film was very interesting, even though there was no sound.**
voice = the sound produced by a person when speaking or singing
sound = something that is heard
Compare: 'The only sound I could hear was a child's voice.'

wait   × I stopped and waited the truck to pass.
         ✓ **I stopped and waited for the truck to pass.**
         wait for a person/thing (to do something)

wake   × He waked up early the next morning feeling
           very cold.
         ✓ **He woke up early the next morning feeling
           very cold.**
         wake, waking, woke, woken

want 1 × My parents wanted that I should go to a
           different university.
         ✓ **My parents wanted me to go to a different
           university.**
          × 'Do you want I take you to his house?' she
           asked
         ✓ **'Do you want me to take you to his house?'
           she asked.**
         want someone to do something

   2   × I want you to send me the coat if you find it.
         ✓ **I would like you to send me the coat if you
           find it.**
         'I want you to send me the coat' is grammatically
         correct but in many situations it would be considered
         to be too direct. 'I would like you to ... ' is more polite.

   3   × The whole house wanted to be painted.
         ✓ **The whole house wanted painting.**
         Want is followed by v-ing when it is used with the
         meaning 'need': 'The grass wants cutting once a
         week.'

   4   × Just as he wanted to leave the bank, a
           detective grabbed him by the arm.
         ✓ **Just as he was about to leave the bank, a
           detective grabbed him by the arm.**
         be about + to-v (NOT **want**) = be on the point of doing
         something

watch 1 × The purpose of the trip was to watch the ancient Egyptian temples.

✓ **The purpose of the trip was to see the ancient Egyptian temples.**

watch = observe an activity or event (i.e. something which includes motion or change): 'We sat on the beach and watched the sun go down.'
see = experience something visually: 'Have you ever seen a giant turtle?'

2 × We spent the afternoon watching paintings.

✓ **We spent the afternoon looking at paintings.**

watch = observe an activity or event
look at = direct your gaze at; examine

way 1 × In the way to the airport we got caught in a traffic jam.

✓ **On the way to the airport we got caught in a traffic jam.**

on the way to a place, NOT **in**

2 × For some people, crime is just another way to make a living.

✓ **For some people, crime is just another way of making a living.**

a way (= means) **of** + v-ing

wear × The old man had white hair and he worn glasses.

✓ **The old man had white hair and he wore glasses.**

Wore is the past tense.
Worn is the past participle.

weather × We had a miserable weather while on holiday.

✓ **We had miserable weather while on holiday.**

Weather is an uncountable noun.

week 1   × We knew that a four weeks holiday would bring us closer together.
✓ **We knew that a four-week holiday would bring us closer together.**
See note at MONTH

2   See IN 6

welcome 1   × As mayor, I would like to welcome you all in our town.
✓ **As mayor, I would like to welcome you all to our town.**
welcome someone **to** a place, NOT **in**

2   × You can bring as many friends to the party as you like. Everyone is welcomed.
✓ **You can bring as many friends to the party as you like. Everyone is welcome.**
welcome (verb) = greet a guest or visitor in a friendly way when he or she arrives
welcome (adjective) = warmly invited

well 1   × Everything was well until somebody came and sat in the seat next to mine.
✓ **Everything was fine until somebody came and sat in the seat next to mine.**
× His table manners were not very well.
✓ **His table manners were not very good.**
Well is usually used as an adverb: 'The team played well on Saturday.' As an adjective, **well** usually means 'in good health': 'George can't come because he's not very well.' 'You're looking well after your holiday.'

2   × He knew well where he wanted to go.
✓ **He knew exactly/precisely where he wanted to go.**
know someone/something **well** = be fully familiar with: 'After living in Florence for two years, I know the city very well.'

well-known   × Both these singers are very well-known.
√ **Both these singers are very well known.**
Compare: 'a well-known singer' (hyphenated before a
noun) BUT 'the singer is well known' (two separate
words when used predicatively)

were 1   × I still write to the friends I made while I were
in Hamburg.
√ **I still write to the friends I made while I was in
Hamburg.**
Were is used with **I** only in this type of conditional
clause: 'If I were you, I'd accept the offer.'

2   × They raised the ladder until they reached the
floor were the fire was.
√ **They raised the ladder until they reached the
floor where the fire was.**
Were is a past tense form of **be**: 'They were sick after
eating too much.'
Where means 'the place in which or to which': 'This is
a photograph of the hotel where we stayed.'

West   See NORTH

what 1   × 'What means this strange sign?' she asked.
√ **'What does this strange sign mean?' she
asked.**
what + auxiliary verb + subject + main verb (unless the
main verb is **be**: 'What's your name?')

2   × She told him that she didn't want to marry
him, what in my opinion was very silly of her.
√ **She told him that she didn't want to marry
him, which in my opinion was very silly of her.**
What is NOT used as a relative pronoun.

when 1   × When I'll return home, I'll look for a better job.
√ **When I return home, I'll look for a better job.**
After **when/whenever/once/until/after/if**, use the
present simple (or present perfect) tense for future
reference, NOT **shall/will** + verb.

2   × When arriving home, I wrote down everything I
had seen.
✓ **On/Upon arriving home, I wrote down
everything I had seen.**

To express the meaning 'immediately after (doing
something)' use **on/upon** + v-ing, NOT **when**.

whenever   × Whenever you'll hear about this place, you'll
want to come back.
✓ **Whenever you hear about this place, you'll
want to come back.**

See note at WHEN 1

where   × He wanted to get to Paris, where he had an
uncle living there.
✓ **He wanted to get to Paris, where he had an
uncle living.**

When **where** is used as a relative pronoun, it is NOT
followed by **there**. Compare: 'He lives in London. He
has a house there.' 'He lives in London, where he has
a house.'

whether   × The whether was cloudy so we took our
raincoats with us.
✓ **The weather was cloudy so we took our
raincoats with us.**

whether (WITH **he**) = if: 'I don't know whether I should
go.'
weather (WITH **ea**) = wind, rain, sunshine, snow, etc.

which 1   × The magazine has a hundred and fifty pages
which they are full of photographs.
✓ **The magazine has a hundred and fifty pages
which are full of photographs.**

Do not repeat the subject after a relative pronoun.
Compare: 'The magazine has a hundred and fifty
pages. They are full of photographs.' 'The magazine
has a hundred and fifty pages which are full of
photographs.'

2 × The coat has two pockets, of which one of them
contains a wallet.
✓ **The coat has two pockets, one of which
contains a wallet.**

Compare: 'The coat has two pockets. One of them
contains a wallet.'

3 × We spent a week in Malta, a small sunny
island which inhabitants are very friendly.
✓ **We spent a week in Malta, a small sunny
island whose inhabitants are very friendly.**

whose = of which/of whom

4 × I decided to visit an old friend which I had not
seen for a long time.
✓ **I decided to visit an old friend that/whom I had
not seen for a long time.**
× He went to New York because he had an uncle
which was living there.
✓ **He went to New York because he had an
uncle that/who was living there.**

Which cannot be used to refer to people.

who × The car smashed into the side of a bus, who
was going very fast.
✓ **The car smashed into the side of a bus, which
was going very fast.**

Who cannot be used to refer to things.

whole × As a whole, I am very happy here.
✓ **On the whole, I am very happy here.**

as a whole = considered as a single body or unit:
'The college as a whole supports the principal.'
on the whole = taking all things into consideration: 'On
the whole, the results are very good.'

why See AS 5

wife × Nowadays many husbands and wifes share the housework.

✓ **Nowadays many husbands and wives share the housework.**

Wife is singular.
Wives is plural.

will 1 × When capital punishment was abolished, people thought that murders will become more numerous.

✓ **When capital punishment was abolished, people thought that murders would become more numerous.**

When the reporting verb is in the past tense ('thought'), **will** becomes **would**. Compare: 'Murders will become more numerous.'

2 See AFTER 6, AS LONG AS 1, CASE 3, IF 1, IMMEDIATELY 1, MOMENT 2, ONCE 3, UNLESS 2, UNTIL 2, WHEN 1, WHENEVER

winter See SUMMER

wish 1 × He wishes he can drive a car; taxis are so expensive.

✓ **He wishes he could drive a car; taxis are so expensive.**

With **wish**, a past tense is used to express a present meaning: 'I wish I knew how to play the guitar.'

2 × I wished him to go away because I was tired and needed some sleep.

✓ **I wanted him to go away because I was tired and needed some sleep.**

✓ **I wished that he would go away because I was tired and needed some sleep.**

want someone **to do** something BUT **wish (that)** someone **would do** something

3   × I wish you will have an enjoyable and unforgettable stay.
  ✓ **I hope you (will) have an enjoyable and unforgettable stay.**

To express hopes and wishes for the future, do not use **wish** followed by **will** + verb. However, **wish** can be followed by a noun or noun phrase: 'I wish you an enjoyable and unforgettable stay.' 'We'd like to wish you a very merry Christmas.'

with 1 × I finally opened the can with using a screwdriver.
 ✓ **I finally opened the can by using a screwdriver.**

by + v-ing, NOT **with**
Compare: 'I finally opened the can with a screwdriver.'

2   See SAME 1

within × I promised to return the record within next weekend.
 ✓ **I promised to return the record by next weekend.**

within = before (a day, week, etc.) is over: 'I promised to return the record within a week.'
by = no later than
Note that **within** is followed by an expression which describes a period of time (a day, five hours, etc.) whereas **by** is followed by a time or date.

without × The problem was to get on one of the boats without be seen by anyone.
 ✓ **The problem was to get on one of the boats without being seen by anyone.**

without + v-ing

women × In my opinion, a married women ought to stay at home with her children.
 ✓ **In my opinion, a married woman ought to stay at home with her children.**

Woman /wʊmən/ is singular.
Women /wɪmɪn/ is plural.

wonder   × I wonder that the machine has other faults I
haven't noticed.
√ **I wonder whether the machine has other faults
I haven't noticed.**

wonder whether/if except in the colloquial pattern **it's
no wonder that** (= it is hardly surprising that): 'It's no
wonder that you're tired–you didn't go to bed last
night.'

wonderful   × The weather yesterday was wonderfull.
√ **The weather yesterday was wonderful.**
wonderful (ONLY ONE **l**): 'delightful', 'beautiful', 'grateful'

wood   × The coat has a leather belt and three brown
wood buttons.
√ **The coat has a leather belt and three brown
wooden buttons.**
The adjective meaning 'made of wood' is usually
wooden, NOT **wood**.

work 1   × Without a full-time work, some people think it
is not worth living.
√ **Without full-time work, some people think it is
not worth living.**
√ **Without a full-time job, some people think it is
not worth living.**
× I have come to England to do a research work
in civil engineering.
√ **I have come to England to do research work
in civil engineering.**
Work is an uncountable noun.

2   × I got up and got ready to go to my work.
√ **I got up and got ready to go to work.**
go to work WITHOUT **my/your/his** etc.
Compare: 'go to school', 'go to church'

3   × These days a lot of women go to work outside.
√ **These days a lot of women go out to work.**
go out to work = have a job outside your home

world 1   × The sewing machine is one of the most widely used products of the world.
√ **The sewing machine is one of the most widely used products in the world.**
superlative adjective + **in the world**, NOT **of**

2   × Rio is known in the world for its beautiful beaches.
√ **Rio is known throughout the world for its beautiful beaches.**
known/spoken/understood etc. **throughout the world**, NOT **in**

worse   × It was the worse journey I have ever made.
√ **It was the worst journey I have ever made.**
× People's lack of responsibility makes the problem even more worse.
√ **People's lack of responsibility makes the problem even worse.**
bad, worse, worst

worst   × The next time I saw her she looked even worst.
√ **The next time I saw her she looked even worse.**
bad, worse, worst

worth 1   × The missing ring worths about two thousand pounds.
√ **The missing ring is worth about two thousand pounds.**
Worth is an adjective/preposition, NOT a verb.

2   × That new magazine is certainly worth its money.
√ **That new magazine is certainly worth the money.**
be worth the money, NOT **its**

3   × That ring has great sentimental worth.
√ **That ring has great sentimental value.**
Compare: 'That watch is worth fifty pounds.' 'That watch has a value of fifty pounds.'

would 1 × Some people might argue that a woman wouldn't work if she has children.
✓ **Some people might argue that a woman shouldn't work if she has children.**

Use **should** (NOT **would**) to express obligation or duty.

2 × If you would have any more questions, I'll do my best to answer them.
✓ **If you should have any more questions, I'll do my best to answer them.**

When talking about something which is unlikely or improbable, use **if ... should**, NOT **if ... would**.

wound × Only the driver was wounded in the accident.
✓ **Only the driver was injured/hurt in the accident.**

wound = cause injury to (someone) by using a weapon

write 1 × I'm writting to tell you how I'm getting on with my course.
✓ **I'm writing to tell you how I'm getting on with my course.**

write, writing, wrote (ONLY ONE **t**)
written (DOUBLE **t**)

2 ✓ **AmE I want to apologize for not having written you before.**
✓ **BrE I want to apologize for not having written to you before.**

write to a person or place (British English)
write (to) a person or place (American English)

3 × Dear ... I write to you to ask for your advice.
✓ **Dear ... I am writing to you to ask for your advice.**

The present progressive tense is used for actions which are happening at the time when they are mentioned.

year 1 × Robert was a little boy of ten years.
✓ **Robert was a little boy of ten.**

'a child of six', 'a man of fifty', etc. WITHOUT **years**
Compare: 'Robert was ten years old.'
See also OLD

2 See IN 6

yet 1 ✗ He left the house at five in the morning, when the family was yet asleep.
✓ **He left the house at five in the morning, when the family was still asleep.**

Yet is mainly used in questions and negative sentences and is used to ask whether something has happened: 'Have they woken up yet?' (= Are they still asleep?) or to say that something has not happened: 'They haven't woken up yet.' (= They are still asleep.)
Still is mainly used to talk about actions or states which are continuing in the present: 'I'm still hungry.' 'She still goes to the same school.' However, **still** can also be used with a negative verb to say that something has not happened: 'I still haven't passed my driving test.' (= It's taking a long time.)

2 ✗ I remember that you used to be fond of water sports. Are you yet?
✓ **I remember that you used to be fond of water sports. Are you still?**

Use **still** when talking about something which is continuing. Compare: 'I'm still reading the book you lent me.' 'Haven't you finished it yet?'

3 See ALTHOUGH 1

you See ME 1

yours 1 ✗ Dear Sir, ... Yours,
✓ **Dear Sir, ... Yours faithfully,**

When writing a formal letter beginning **Dear Sir** or **Dear Madam**, you should end it with **Yours faithfully**.

2 ✗ Dear Mum and Dad, ... Yours, Erich
✓ **Dear Mum and Dad, ... Love, Erich**

Yours is often used at the end of letters to friends but NOT to parents and close relatives.

yourself ✗ I hope you are both enjoying yourselfs.
✓ **I hope you are both enjoying yourselves.**

Yourself is singular.
Yourselves is plural.

Checklist of misspellings

Error	Correction
accomodation	accommodation
adress	address
arguement	argument
begining	beginning
comittee	committee
dinning room	dining room
disapear	disappear
disapointed	disappointed
embarass	embarrass
fortunatly	fortunately
garantee	guarantee
habitant	inhabitant
immediatly	immediately
independance	independence
independant	independent
medecine	medicine
nowaday	nowadays
old-fashion	old-fashioned
outskirt	outskirts
pronounciation	pronunciation
recieve	receive
responsability	responsibility
seperate	separate
therefor	therefore
truely	truly
unfortunatly	unfortunately
unpolite	impolite
untill	until
wonderfull	wonderful

Glossary

active See PASSIVE

adjective a word which describes a noun or pronoun: 'He bought himself a <u>new</u> tie.' 'The university is fairly <u>new</u>.' 'She's quite <u>tall</u>.'

adverb a word which describes or adds to the meaning of a verb ('drink it <u>slowly</u>'), adjective ('<u>extremely</u> cold'), another adverb ('<u>very</u> quickly') or sentence ('<u>Unfortunately</u> there was nowhere to sit.')

affirmative (also **positive**) See NEGATIVE

article 'a/an' or 'the'

attributive An attributive adjective is one that is placed before the noun it describes: 'a <u>green</u> raincoat'. 'a <u>serious</u> disease'. 'a <u>large brown</u> envelope'. A predicative adjective is one that is used after a verb such as 'be/seem/appear/look/become' etc.: 'We were <u>afraid</u> of missing the plane.' 'Her father looks very <u>ill</u>.' Many (but not all) adjectives can be used both attributively and predicatively.

auxiliary See MAIN VERB

clause a group of words containing a subject and a verb. which either forms a sentence by itself ('I'm going out tonight.') or forms part of a sentence ('if it doesn't rain').
See also MAIN CLAUSE, SUBORDINATE CLAUSE

colloquial See INFORMAL

common noun See PROPER NOUN

comparative the form of an adjective or adverb that is used to express a greater or smaller degree. Most comparatives end in '-er' or are formed with 'more' or 'less': 'Her work is <u>better</u> than it used to be.' 'The problem was <u>more difficult</u> than I thought.' 'John always speaks <u>more politely</u> than his brother.'

compound A compound word is one that is made up of two or more parts: 'boyfriend'. 'fingertip'. 'six-foot'. 'second-hand'. 'mother-in-law'. 'cassette recorder'. 'training college'.

conditional 1 a clause beginning with a word such as 'if' or 'unless'. or a sentence containing such a clause 2 a form of the verb made with 'would/should' and the infinitive (WITHOUT 'to'): 'I <u>would like</u> to see that film again.' '<u>Would</u> you <u>like</u> a cup of tea?'

conjunction a word like 'and/but/since/when/if/although' which joins words, phrases. or clauses together. or shows how they are related to each other: 'He was a very good boy <u>and</u> obeyed his parents all the time.' '<u>Although</u> I was frightened. I couldn't scream.'

context 1 the word or words which come immediately before and/or after a word or phrase 2 the situation in which language is used

contraction a short form used in everyday conversation. informal letters. etc.: 'isn't'. 'he'll'. 'they've' (compare: 'is not'. 'he will'. 'they have').

countable A countable noun is a noun which has both singular and plural forms: 'tree – trees'. 'apple – apples'. 'man – men'. The singular form may follow 'a/an': '<u>a</u> tree'. '<u>an</u> apple'. '<u>a</u> man'.

derogatory expressing an unfavourable quality, attitude or opinion

determiner a word like 'a/an/my/this/some/every' that limits the meaning of a noun or noun phrase: '<u>an</u> apple'. '<u>my</u> house'. '<u>every</u> member of staff'.

direct object See OBJECT

direct speech speech that is written down in the exact words of the original speaker. without changing tenses. pronouns. adverbs. etc. Compare: "My parents were killed in a road accident." (direct speech); She said that her parents had been killed in a road accident. (reported speech). Direct speech is usually shown by inverted commas.
See also REPORTED SPEECH

double negative the use of two negative words when only one is required.

emphasis the special force that is sometimes given to a word or phrase to draw it to the listener's or reader's attention: 'I <u>do</u> hope your mother gets better soon.' 'She's <u>really</u> enjoying her stay in London.' 'They <u>themselves</u> have never been to Italy.'

fixed phrase two or more words which are always used together and which cannot be changed in any way: 'on the contrary' (not 'on <u>a</u> contrary'. 'on the contrar<u>ies</u>'. etc.)

formal Formal language is the type of language that is used in official reports. public speeches. business letters. etc.
See also INFORMAL

full infinitive See INFINITIVE

future There are several ways of talking about the future in English. One of these is often called the 'future tense'. This is formed with 'will/shall' and the infinitive (WITHOUT 'to'): 'will send'. 'shall go'. etc.
See also PROGRESSIVE

identifying relative clause See RELATIVE CLAUSE

indirect object See OBJECT

indirect question An indirect question is the form

that is used to report a question that has been asked previously. Compare: "What's the time?" (direct question); She asked me what the time was. (indirect question)

infinitive the form of a verb that is shown in a dictionary. There are two types of infinitive, the 'full infinitive' shown in this book as 'to-v' ('to come', 'to take', 'to send') and the 'bare infinitive' ('come', 'take', 'send').

informal Informal or colloquial language is the language that is used in everyday conversation, for example between friends or members of a family. Compare: 'I regret to inform you that your application for a position with our company has been unsuccessful.' (formal); 'I'm afraid you didn't get the job.' (informal)

See also FORMAL

intensify Worlds like 'very/extremely/absolutely' are used to make adjectives stronger. These words are known as 'intensifiers' because they are used to 'intensify' (= make stronger).

intransitive An intransitive verb is a verb that is used without an object: 'The man suddenly disappeared.'

irregular not following the usual pattern or rules. For example, the past tense of an irregular verb does NOT end in '-ed' ('went', 'took', 'gave'). Similarly, the plural form of an irregular noun does NOT end in '-s' ('children', 'mice', 'criteria')

main clause (also **independent clause**) a group of words containing a subject and verb, which can form a sentence: 'I'm going out tonight, if it doesn't rain.'

See also SUBORDINATE CLAUSE

main verb a verb like 'speak/take/go' which can be used as the only verb in a sentence: 'She speaks German and Russian.' 'He took her to the cinema.' 'They went on holiday in April.' A main verb is often used with an auxiliary verb such as 'be/do/have' in order to form a tense, question, passive form, etc.: 'My husband is learning English.' 'Do you speak French?' 'The car was stolen during the night.'

modify (also **qualify**) A word is often used with one or more other words which provide additional information about it or limit its meaning. In such cases the word is said to be 'modified'. For example, in the sentence 'Japanese cars are quite cheap', the noun 'cars' is modified by the adjective 'Japanese' and the adjective 'cheap' is modified by the adverb 'quite'.

negative A verb is negative when it is used with a word like 'not/never/rarely' etc.: 'She never answers my questions.' A clause or sentence containing a negative verb is also negative. Compare: 'He wanted to go to bed.' (affirmative verb/sentence); 'He didn't want to go to bed.' (negative verb/sentence)

non-identifying relative clause See RELATIVE CLAUSE

noun a word used to name a person, animal, place, thing, etc. which can be used with an article or a determiner: 'Each visitor received a small gift.'

noun phrase a group of words which is used like a noun or pronoun: 'Each visitor received a small gift.'

object the word or group of words affected by the action of the verb, usually placed immediately after the verb. There are two types of object. A 'direct object' is affected directly by the verb: 'She opened the door.' 'she wrote a long letter.' A sentence which has a direct object can also have an 'indirect object' (= an object that is affected indirectly by the verb): 'She wrote me a long letter.' 'They have sent him an invitation.'

participle See PAST PARTICIPLE, PRESENT PARTICIPLE

passive When the subject of a sentence performs the action expressed by the verb, the verb is said to be 'active': 'the government spends a lot of money on cancer research.' However, when the subject does not perform the action expressed by the verb but is affected by it, the verb is said to be 'passive': 'A lot of money is spent on cancer research.' We use the passive when we are interested in knowing what is done, not who or what is doing it. The passive is also used when we do not know who or what has performed the action: 'My watch has been stolen.'

past participle the verb form that is used to make the present perfect and past perfect: 'kicked', 'gone', 'fallen'. Some past participles are also used as adjectives: 'a frightened cat', 'a folded newspaper'.

past perfect the form of the verb that is made with 'had' and the past participle: 'After she had picked the flowers, she got back into the car.' 'If I'd known your address, I would've come to see you.'

See also PROGRESSIVE

past tense The past tense of a regular verb is the same as the past participle ('-ed'): 'cooked', 'thanked', 'opened'. The past tense of an irregular verb is formed in many different ways: 'went', 'took', 'saw', 'thought', 'found', 'left', 'spoke'.

See also PROGRESSIVE

perfect conditional the form of the verb that is made with 'would/should have' and the past participle: 'would have opened', 'should have sent'.

See also PROGRESSIVE

phrase a group of words which may be used like a noun ('many people'), a verb ('has been working'), an adjective ('very interesting'), or an adverb ('in the summer').

plural the form of a word that is used when talking about two or more people, things, etc.

See also SINGULAR

plural noun a noun that is always used with a plural verb: 'trousers', 'scissors', 'police', 'goods'.

possessive the form of a word which expresses ownership or connection: 'Have you met my wife?' 'It wasn't the driver's fault.' 'She said that the book wasn't hers.' The possessive is also used in time expressions: 'She'll be back in two days' time.'

predeterminer a word like 'such/half/quite/both/ all' that can be used before 'a/an' or 'the': 'David is such a good boy.' 'All the other children are very naughty.'

predicative See ATTRIBUTIVE

preparatory subject Instead of using a clause or infinitive structure as the subject of a sentence, it is often better to begin the sentence with 'it' and put the clause or infinitive structure towards the end of the sentence: 'It is impossible to see in the dark.' 'It's a pity that she couldn't come.' In these cases 'it' is known as a preparatory subject. 'There' is sometimes used in a similar way to introduce a new piece of information: 'There is a bottle of milk in the fridge.'

preparatory object Instead of using a clause or infinitive structure as the object of a sentence, it is often better to use 'it' as a preparatory object and put the clause or infinitive structure towards the end of the sentence: 'he found it impossible to leave the office before six o'clock.' 'They made it clear that he was not welcome.'

preposition a word such as 'in/over/of/through/at/ for' which is used before a noun, pronoun, etc. to show its connection with a previous word: 'I spoke to the man sitting behind me.' He was born in a town just outside Paris.' 'We were afraid of missing the plane.'

present participle the '-ing' form of a verb: 'coming', 'speaking'.

present perfect the present perfect tense is made with 'have/has' and the past participle: 'I've seen the new Mercedes but I haven't seen the new Datsun.' 'Have you seen it?'

See also PROGRESSIVE

present progressive (also **present continuous**) The present progressive tense is made with 'be' and the present participle: 'I'm waiting for a taxi.' 'Are you waiting for a taxi too?'

present simple Unlike the present progressive tense, the present simple is made WITHOUT 'be': 'I like fish but I don't like meat.' 'Do you like meat?'

progressive (also **continuous**) a form of the verb made with 'be' and the present participle: 'It was raining this morning.' (past progressive); 'Are you coming with us tonight?' (present progressive); 'I've been waiting here for an hour.' (present perfect progressive); 'Where had you been living before you moved to London?' (past perfect progressive); 'At six o'clock I shall be waiting for you outside the station.' (future progressive)

See also SIMPLE

pronoun a word like 'he/her/mine/themselves' that is used in place of a noun or noun phrase: 'Ann spoke very softly and nobody could hear her.' ('her' is the pronoun for 'Ann'); 'The little girl fell over and hurt herself.' ('herself' is the pronoun for 'the little girl')

proper noun the name of a particular person, place, or thing: 'Mary', 'Oxford', 'Daily Telegraph'. A proper noun always begins with a capital letter. All other nouns are common nouns: 'letter', 'table', 'cassette recorder', 'state'.

qualify See MODIFY

reflexive pronoun A reflexive pronoun is used when talking about the subject doing something to himself or herself: 'Henry has hurt himself.' 'I found myself a seat and sat down.'

reflexive verb A reflexive verb is a verb that is used with a reflexive pronoun: 'We all enjoyed ourselves.' 'You mustn't blame yourself for the accident.'

relative clause a descriptive clause usually beginning with 'that/who/whom/whose' or 'which'. There are two types of relative clause, 'identifying' and 'non-identifying'. An identifying relative clause answers the question 'which?' It identifies or defines the preceding noun: 'The man who was carrying a torch showed us to our seats.' (Which man? The man carrying the torch.) A non-identifying relative clause does not identify or define the preceding noun but merely adds further information: 'The man, who was carrying a torch, showed us to our seats.'

relative pronoun 'that/who/whom/whose' or 'which', used to introduce a relative clause
See also RELATIVE CLAUSE

reported speech (also **indirect speech**) someone's words reported indirectly, with changes of tense, pronouns, adverbs, etc.
See also DIRECT SPEECH

reporting verb a verb like 'say/answer/ask' which is used when reporting what someone has said, asked, etc.: 'She said that she needed more time.' ' "I can't afford a new car," he replied.'

simple These are simple verb forms: 'Yesterday it rained all day.' (past simple); 'What time does the postman come?' (present simple); 'I've sent your sister an invitation.' (present perfect simple)
See also PROGRESSIVE

singular the form of a word that is used to refer to one person, thing, etc. Compare: 'This pen was made in Japan.' (singular); 'These pens were made in Japan.' (plural)

subject the word or group of words in a sentence about which something is said. In a statement, the subject usually appears at the beginning of the sentence and is followed by the verb: 'Parents should spend more time looking after their children.' 'The way he dresses is rather unusual.' 'Fighting crime keeps the police very busy.'

subordinate clause (also **dependent clause**) a clause that cannot be used by itself as a sentence but depends grammatically on a main clause: 'If the sun is too hot perhaps you would like to sit in the shade.' (subordinate clause + main clause). A subordinate clause often begins with a word like 'if/when/although/since/that' etc.
See also MAIN CLAUSE

suffix A group of letters added to the end of a word to change its use or meaning: 'friendly.' 'delightful.' 'kindness'.

superlative the form of an adjective or adverb that is used to express the greatest or smallest degree. Most superlative forms end in '-est' or are formed with 'most' or 'least': 'She's the prettiest baby I've ever seen.' 'We all agreed that the first of the three questions was the most difficult.'

to-v See INFINITIVE

transitive A transitive verb is a verb that is used with an object: 'She opened the drawer and took out a knife.'

uncountable An uncountable noun is a noun which has no plural form and which is not usually preceded by 'a/an': 'accommodation'. 'research'. 'furniture'. 'information'. 'luggage', 'advice'.

verb a word expressing an action or state: 'I visited her in London.' 'He knows a lot about engineering.'

v-ing the '-ing' form of a verb, often used like a noun: 'I enjoy speaking foreign language.' 'Please forgive me for interrupting you.'

vowel a speech sound made when the breath escapes freely, without being blocked or restricted in the mouth or throat, such as /ɪ:/ as in 'key'/kɪ:/, or /a:/ as in 'car'/ka:/. The letters of the alphabet which stand for these sounds ('a'. 'e'. 'i'. 'o'. 'u') are known as 'vowels'.

wh- 'When/where/why/how/who/whom/whose/ what/which/whether' are commonly known as 'wh- words'. A clause beginning with one of these words is a 'wh- clause': 'I didn't know what to do.' 'She told me where he was.'